Praise for

Practical Wisdom

"An important new book."   —*The Wall Street Journal*

"As the authors see it, practical wisdom roughly amounts to being a mensch—
that is, having honor and integrity, but also rising above workaday ephemera
to recognize and enact wise decisions for the greater good. . . . They have
valid, thoughtful points to make."   —*The New York Times*

"Schwartz and Sharpe write with a clear simplicity that resonates with their
own suggestions that our institutions (government included) could fix these
problems by simply giving people the room to be wise and to create a wise
society."   —*The Providence Journal of Books*

"Schwartz and Sharpe explore our increasing distrust of and disenchantment
with our institutions—governmental, medical, legal. . . . This highly
recommended and important book offers an antidote to the mistrust that
plagues the morale both in the workplace and beyond."   —*Publishers Weekly*

"As surprising as it is convincing, this thoughtful work will long stay with
readers."   —*Booklist*

"When Barry Schwartz presented this book's core idea to the TED audience,
he earned one of the longest, most heartfelt standing ovations in TED's
history. With so much of modern life being ground down by endless, soulless
bureaucratic process, his call for a new wisdom centered on human values
struck a powerful chord. I'm thrilled to see that talk turn into this irresistible
book, one that every politician, CEO, parent, and citizen in America should
read."   —Chris Anderson, curator of the TED conferences

"*Practical Wisdom* reminded me that we all have the capacity for wisdom, no
matter what our age or stature in life. And more important, it taught me that
wisdom is the ultimate tool for us to flourish in this age of complication and
clutter."   —Chip Conley, founder of Joie de Vivre Hospitality,
and author of *Peak: How Great Companies Get Their Mojo from Maslow*

"Invaluable . . . indeed, everyone could benefit from reading it."   —*Choice*

"Barry Schwartz and Kenneth Sharpe have crafted a call for practical wisdom in modern governance, a call that is at once humane and savvy. . . . Readers will follow the stories, agape. The fetish for simple rules in a complex megademocracy is not just intemperate; it is out of control. *Practical Wisdom* is full of uplifting lessons, and restores our sense of proportion about what matters. The Aristotelian mean has never been put to so timely a use."
                                        —J. D. Trout, professor of philosophy and psychology,
                                        Loyola University Chicago and author of
                                        The Empathy Gap

"According to Barry Schwartz and Kenneth Sharpe . . . rules and incentives can't ensure that our institutions and businesses reflect human values such as empathy and fairness. . . . *Practical Wisdom* is rich with actual case studies illustrating how it has been applied in real-world situations. . . . *Practical Wisdom* offers an intriguing analysis of a concept that could transform societies by transforming how we think."   —Scientific American Book Club

ALSO BY BARRY SCHWARTZ

Behaviorism, Science, and Human Nature (with Hugh Lacey; 1982)

The Battle for Human Nature:
Science, Morality and Modern Life (1986)

The Costs of Living: How Market Freedom
Erodes the Best Things in Life (1994)

The Paradox of Choice: Why More Is Less (2004)

ALSO BY KENNETH SHARPE

Peasant Politics: Struggle in a Dominican Village (1977)

Transnational Corporations versus the State:
The Political Economy of the Mexican Automobile Industry
(with Douglas Bennett; 1985)

Confronting Revolution: Security Through Diplomacy in
Central America (with Morris Blachman and William LeoGrande; 1986)

Drug War Politics: The Price of Denial
(with Eva Bertram, Morris Blachman, and Peter Andreas; 1996)

Practical Wisdom

THE RIGHT WAY TO DO THE RIGHT THING

Barry Schwartz

and Kenneth Sharpe

RIVERHEAD BOOKS
New York

RIVERHEAD BOOKS
Published by the Penguin Group
Penguin Group (USA) Inc.
375 Hudson Street, New York, New York 10014, USA
Penguin Group (Canada), 90 Eglinton Avenue East, Suite 700, Toronto, Ontario M4P 2Y3, Canada
(a division of Pearson Penguin Canada Inc.)
Penguin Books Ltd., 80 Strand, London WC2R 0RL, England
Penguin Group Ireland, 25 St. Stephen's Green, Dublin 2, Ireland (a division of Penguin Books Ltd.)
Penguin Group (Australia), 250 Camberwell Road, Camberwell, Victoria 3124, Australia
(a division of Pearson Australia Group Pty. Ltd.)
Penguin Books India Pvt. Ltd., 11 Community Centre, Panchsheel Park, New Delhi—110 017, India
Penguin Group (NZ), 67 Apollo Drive, Rosedale, Auckland 0632, New Zealand
(a division of Pearson New Zealand Ltd.)
Penguin Books (South Africa) (Pty.) Ltd., 24 Sturdee Avenue, Rosebank, Johannesburg 2196,
South Africa

Penguin Books Ltd., Registered Offices: 80 Strand, London WC2R 0RL, England

While the author has made every effort to provide accurate telephone numbers and Internet addresses at
the time of publication, neither the publisher nor the author assumes any responsibility for errors, or for
changes that occur after publication. Further, the publisher does not have any control over and does not
assume any responsibility for author or third-party websites or their content.

First Riverhead hardcover edition: December 2010
First Riverhead trade paperback edition: November 2011
Riverhead trade paperback ISBN: 978-1-59448-543-5

The Library of Congress has catalogued the Riverhead hardcover edition as follows:

Schwartz, Barry, date.
  Practical wisdom : the right way to do the right thing / Barry Schwartz and Kenneth Sharpe.
  p. cm.
  ISBN 978-1-59448-783-5
  1. Wisdom.   2. Knowledge.   I. Sharpe, Kenneth.   II. Title.
BF431.S358 2010   2010029239
170'.44-dc22

PRINTED IN THE UNITED STATES OF AMERICA

10 9 8 7 6 5 4 3 2

To Myrna Schwartz and Madeleine Thomson,

with love and gratitude

CONTENTS

PART I

What Wisdom Is and Why We Need It

1. Introduction: The Need for Wisdom   3

2. What Wisdom Is: The Janitor and the Judge   13

3. Balancing Acts: Why Wisdom Is Practical   27

PART II

The Machinery of Wisdom

4. Born to Be Wise   51

5. Thinking with Feeling: The Value of Empathy   69

6. Learning from Experience: The Machinery of Wisdom   81

PART III

The War on Wisdom

7. Ruling Out Wisdom: When Judges Stop Judging
   and Doctors Stop Prescribing   113

8. Eroding the Empathy to Be Wise   129

9. Right by Rote: Overstandardization and
   the Rise of the Canny Outlaw   155

10. The War on Will   177

11. Demoralizing Institutions   197

PART IV

Sources of Hope

12. System Changers   233

13. Wisdom and Happiness   274

    Acknowledgments   289

    Notes   291

    Index   317

PART I

What Wisdom Is and Why We Need It

1.

Introduction:
The Need for Wisdom

We Americans are growing increasingly disenchanted with the institutions on which we depend. We can't trust them. They disappoint us. They fail to give us what we need. This is true of schools that are not serving our kids as well as we think they should. It is true of doctors who seem too busy to give us the attention and unhurried care we crave. It's true of banks that mismanage our assets, and of bond-rating agencies that fail to provide an accurate assessment of the risk of possible investments. It's true of a legal system that seems more interested in expedience than in justice. It's true of a workplace in which we fulfill quotas and hit targets and manage systems but wind up feeling disconnected from the animating forces that drew us to our careers in the first place.

If it were only patients, clients, and students who were dissatisfied, it would be easy to affix the blame on the doctors, lawyers, and teachers for not caring or for lacking the expertise to help. But the disenchantment we experience as recipients of services is often matched by the dissatisfaction of those who provide them. Most doctors want to practice medicine as it should be practiced. But they feel helpless faced with the challenge of balancing the needs and desires of patients with the practical demands of hassling with insurance companies, earning enough to pay malpractice premiums, and squeezing patients into seven-minute visits—all while keeping up with the latest developments in their fields. Most teachers want to teach kids the basics and at the same time excite them with the prospects of educating themselves. But teachers feel helpless faced with the challenge of reconciling these goals with mandates to meet targets on standardized tests, to adopt specific teaching techniques, and to keep up with the ever-increasing paper-work. No one is satisfied—not the professionals and not their clients.

So how are we to make things better? Generally we reach for one of two tools. The first tool is a set of rules and administrative oversight mechanisms that tell people what to do and monitor their performance to make sure they are doing it. The second tool is a set of incentives that encourage good performance by rewarding people for it. The assumption behind carefully constructed rules and procedures, with close over-sight, is that even if people *do* want to do the right thing, they need to be told what that is. And the assumption underlying incentives is that people will not be motivated to do the right thing unless they have an incentive to do so. Rules and incentives. Sticks and carrots. What else is there?

There is no doubt that better rules and smarter incentives have an important role to play in improving the way our institutions perform. If you're trying to improve the quality of medical care while simultane-ously reducing its costs, it's crazy to reward doctors for doing *more* pro-cedures. And if you want to prevent banks from taking foolish risks with other people's money, it's crazy to let them speculate in whatever way they want, using enormous leverage, confident in the knowledge that if disaster strikes, the government will bail them out.

But rules and incentives are not enough. They leave out something essential. This book is about what that "something" is. It is what classical philosopher Aristotle called *practical wisdom*. (His word was *phronesis*). Without this missing ingredient, neither rules (no matter how detailed and well monitored) nor incentives (no matter how clever) will be enough to solve the problems we face.

The term *practical wisdom* sounds like an oxymoron to modern ears. We tend to think of "wisdom" as the opposite of "practical." Wisdom is about abstract, ethereal matters like "the way" or "the good" or "the truth" or "the path." And we tend to think that wisdom is something for sages, gurus, rabbis, and scholars—for white-bearded wizards like Harry Potter's mentor, Dumbledore. Aristotle's teacher, Plato, shared this view that wisdom was theoretical and abstract, and the gift of only a few. But Aristotle disagreed. He thought that our fundamental social practices constantly demanded choices—like when to be loyal to a friend, or how to be fair, or how to confront risk, or when and how to be angry—and that making the right choices demanded wisdom. To take the example of anger, the central question for Aristotle was not whether anger was good or bad, or the abstract question about what the nature of the "good" in fact was. It was the particular and concrete issue of what to do in a *particular* circumstance: who to be angry at, for how long, in what way, and for what purpose. The wisdom to answer such questions and to act rightly was distinctly practical, not theoretical. It depended on our ability to *perceive* the situation, to have the appropriate *feelings* or desires about it, to *deliberate* about what was appropriate in these circumstances, and to *act*.

Aristotle distilled the idea of practical wisdom in his classic book, *Nicomachean Ethics*. Ethics, said Aristotle, was not mainly about establishing moral rules and following them. It was about performing a particular social practice well—being a good friend or parent or doctor or soldier or citizen or statesman—and that meant figuring out the right way to do the right thing in a particular circumstance, with a particular person, at a particular time. This is what took practical wisdom. Aristotle's *Ethics* was not an abstract discourse on the human good or on "right" behavior. Its subject was what we needed to learn in order to succeed at our practices and to flourish as human beings. We needed to learn certain character traits like loyalty, self-control, courage, fairness, generosity, gentleness, friendliness, and truthfulness—a list that today would also include perseverance, integrity, open-mindedness, thoroughness, and kindness. Aristotle called these traits "excellences" (*arete*)—often translated as "virtues." But the master excellence—the virtue at the heart of his *Ethics*—was practical wisdom. None of these other traits could be exercised well without it.

Why "wisdom"? Why "practical"? Why not just a good set of rules to follow? Most experienced practitioners know that rules only take them so far. Rules can't tell practitioners how to do the constant interpretation and balancing that is part of their everyday work. Consider the doctor who has been well educated in the rules of how to practice medicine but is constantly called on to make more complicated decisions. How should such a doctor balance respect for the autonomy of her patients when it comes to making decisions with the knowledge that sometimes the patient is not the best judge of what is needed? How should the doctor balance empathetic involvement with each patient with the detachment needed to make sound judgments? How should the doctor balance the desire to spend enough time with each patient to be thorough, compassionate, and understanding with the need to see enough patients in a day to keep the office solvent? How should the doctor balance the desire to tell patients the truth, no matter how difficult, with the desire to be kind?

Doctors—and teachers attempting to teach *and* inspire, or lawyers attempting to provide proper counsel *and* serve justice—are not puzzling over a choice between the "right" thing and the "wrong" thing. The common quandaries they face are choices among right things that clash, or between better and best, or sometimes between bad and worse. A good doctor needs to be honest with her patients, *and* kind to her patients, *and* to give them the hope they need to endure difficult treatments. But in diagnosing or treating a patient, these aims can be at odds, and the doctor must decide whether to be honest or kind, or more likely how to balance honesty and kindness in a way that is appropriate for the patient in front of her.

These sorts of quandaries don't have pat, one-size-fits-all answers. Good rules might be useful as guides as we try to manage these multiple aims, but they will never be subtle enough and nuanced enough to apply in every situation. Aristotle recognized that balancing acts like these beg for wisdom, and that abstract or ethereal wisdom would not do. Wisdom has to be practical, because the issues we face are embedded in our everyday work. They are not hypotheticals being raised in college ethics courses. They are quandaries that any practitioner must resolve in order to do her work well. Practical wisdom is not musing about how someone else in a hypothetical situation ought to act. It's about "What am I to do?"—right here and right now, with this person. A practically wise person doesn't merely speculate about what's proper; she does it.

Acting wisely demands that we be guided by the proper aims or goals of a particular activity. Aristotle's word for the purpose or aim of a practice was *telos*. The telos of teaching is to educate students; the telos of doctoring is to promote health and relieve suffering; the telos of lawyering is to pursue justice. Every profession—from banking to social work—has a telos, and those who excel are those who are able to locate and pursue it. So a good practitioner is motivated to aim at the telos of her practice. But it takes wisdom—practical wisdom—to translate the very general aims of a practice into concrete action.

People who are practically wise understand the telos of being a friend or a parent or a doctor and are motivated to pursue this aim. A wise practitioner wants to do the right thing not because of some monetary reward or punishment but because it is what being a good teacher or a good doctor demands. But aiming at the right thing is not sufficient. That's why we say that the road to hell is paved with good intentions. Translating our aims into action demands expertise. Answering the question "What should I do?" almost always depends on the particulars of the situation. Friends, doctors, parents, and teachers all need to perceive what others are thinking and feeling. They need to imagine the consequences of what they do. They need to figure out what's possible and not just what's ideal. Practical wisdom is akin to the kind of skill that a craftsman needs to build a boat or a house, or that a jazz musician needs to improvise. Except that practical wisdom is not a technical or artistic skill. It is a moral skill—a skill that enables us to discern how to treat people in our everyday social activities.

So practical wisdom combines will with skill. Skill without will—without the desire to achieve the proper aims of an activity—can lead to ruthless manipulation of others, to serve one's own interests, not theirs. And will without skill can lead to ineffectual fumbling around—the sort of thing we see in people who "mean well" but leave situations in worse shape than they found them.

How, then, are we to learn to be practically wise? There is no recipe, formula, or set of techniques. Skills are learned through experience, and so is the commitment to the aims of a practice. That's why we associate wisdom with experience. But not just any experience will do. Some experiences nurture and teach practical wisdom; others corrode it. And it is here that Aristotle focuses our attention on something critically important: character and practical wisdom must be cultivated by the major institutions in which we practice. Aristotle wrote his book on ethics not simply to underline the importance of practical wisdom to a good life and a good society, but also to urge the citizens and statesmen of the Athenian city-state to build institutions that encouraged citizens to learn to be practically wise. Faced with today's "wisdom deficit"—

the lack of the wisdom we need to succeed in our daily life and work— he would urge us to examine whether our institutions are discouraging the wisdom of practitioners and, if so, what can be done to make up the deficit.

Aristotle would have had a hard time imagining the complexity and breadth of our contemporary institutions, but he would have understood the central problem that informs this book. The rules and incentives that modern institutions rely on in pursuit of efficiency, accountability, profit, and good performance can't substitute for practical wisdom. Nor will they encourage it or nurture it. In fact, they often corrode it.

Working for incentives is not the same as working to achieve the telos of an activity. A (good) doctor aims at recommending the right kind of treatment and has the know-how to tailor the treatment to this particular patient with this particular history and in these particular life circumstances. If we simply fix the problem of incentivizing doctors to do too much (rewarding them with a fee for any service) by paying doctors bonuses for doing less, they may end up doing too little. Worse, they may learn to make their decisions because of the incentives. We want doctors with the will and skill to do the right amount, and do it *because it's the right amount*. This goal can be achieved only if doctors embrace the proper aims of medicine and know how to pursue them. Incentives, even smart ones, will do little to help us reach this goal, and often, we'll see, they may move the goal farther away. Even with bankers, we want them to do the right thing because it's the right thing— because it serves the interests of the depositors who have trusted them with their money and borrowers who have trusted them to provide sound mortgages and loans. Our confidence in the banks depends on our trust in the bankers. We wouldn't fault bankers for being "greedy" if we thought the only point of banking was to make money. If we thought that, we'd call them "successful."

Rules cannot substitute for practical wisdom any more than incentives can. We need rules to guide and govern the behavior of people who are not wise: one reason we suffered the recent financial crisis was that weak and loosely enforced rules and regulations allowed bankers to run amok with shrewd moneymaking schemes like derivatives. But tighter rules and regulations, however necessary, are pale substitutes for wisdom. Aristotle might say that we need rules to protect us from disaster. But at the same time, rules without wisdom are blind and at best guarantee mediocrity—forcing wise practitioners to become outlaws, rule-breakers pursuing a kind of guerrilla war to achieve excellence.

———

This book is about the urgency of making ourselves more practically wise and about the importance of institutional change if we are to learn how to do that. We can borrow some fundamental insights from Aristotle. But we'll need to do much more if we are going to understand the modern relevance of practical wisdom and the challenges faced by those who want to practice wisely.

We need to understand, in a modern context, what practical wisdom is, why we need it, and what it requires.

We need to examine, with help from insights from modern psychology, why practical wisdom is not the privileged preserve of wizards and sages. It is accessible to all of us. We are "born to be wise." And that capacity can be nurtured.

We need to see how the current reliance on strict rules and regulations and clever incentives to improve practices like medicine, education, and law risks undermining the very wisdom of practitioners that is needed to make these practices better. Well-meaning reformers are often engaged in a kind of unintended stealth war on wisdom.

We absolutely must understand that the corrosion of wisdom is not inevitable. It can be resisted. There are legions of "canny outlaws" who struggle to find ways to exercise wisdom within organizations that actively discourage it. And there are growing ranks of system changers who have been able to reform the way institutions are run—how practi-

tioners are trained and how they practice—in ways that nurture and
sustain wisdom rather than destroy it.

And finally, again relying on research in psychology, we need to
appreciate that cultivating wisdom is not only good for society but
is, as Aristotle thought, a key to our own happiness. Wisdom isn't just
something we "ought" to have. It's something we want to have to
flourish.

———

Our central aim in writing a book about practical wisdom is to update
the very old and often forgotten "excellence" of practical wisdom—to
see why Aristotle thought of it as the master virtue that allows individuals and society to thrive. Currently, it is little mentioned in the
academy, rarely mentioned in books about happiness or living well, and
never mentioned in the public debate about how to heal and reform our
major health care, educational, legal, and financial institutions. We
want to make practical wisdom a part of our public discourse because
it plays an essential part in making our modern practices and our own
lives work well.

All too often, the diagnosis of the problems in the institutions that
serve us is that people don't really care about their work; they are
blamed for just caring about making money, or gaining status, or amass-
ing more power. And if greed, gain, and glory are all that motivate
people, then it seems as if we have only two choices to induce them to
do better: (a) design rules that will compel and enforce better performance; and (b) create incentives that will bribe people to do better work.
It's no accident, then, that our main focus in fixing the recent financial
crisis has been more regulation, to prevent bad behavior, and better-
crafted incentives, to get bankers and brokers to act more in the public
interest. It's no accident, then, that we think we can get better teaching
by requiring teachers to follow scripted curricula tied to standardized
tests and by punishing or rewarding them for their students' perfor-

mance. It's no accident that we think we can get better and cheaper medical care by rewarding doctors for successful patient outcomes rather than medical procedures.

Rules and incentives are an inevitable and necessary part of our social and political life—the banking crisis would have been far less serious had Depression-era regulations not been removed and had existing regulations been enforced. For all the importance of rules and incentives, however, a debate that focuses only on the proper mix of these two mechanisms leaves out an important ingredient. The kind of work that most practitioners want to do, and that those they serve also want them to do, demands practical wisdom. Rules and incentives may improve the behavior of those who don't care, though they won't make them wiser. But in focusing on the people who don't care—the targets of our rules and incentives—we miss those who do care. We miss those who want to do the right things but lack the practical wisdom to do them well. Rules and incentives won't teach these people the moral skill and will they need. Even worse, rules can kill skill and incentives can kill will.

Aristotle called people who were practically wise *phronemoi*. Our grandparents would have called such a person a mensch. This book is about what practical wisdom is and why we need it. It's about how we develop it and what threatens it. It's about how we can nurture and reclaim it and, in the process, reclaim the institutions that are now in so much trouble. And it's about how practical wisdom is a key to happiness.

2.

What Wisdom Is:
The Janitor and the Judge

THE WISE CUSTODIAN

Luke (we don't know his last name) works as a custodian in a major
teaching hospital. In an interview with social scientists interested in
studying how people structure their work, Luke reported an incident
in which he cleaned a comatose young patient's room—twice. He had
already done it once, but the patient's father, who had been keeping a
vigil for months, hadn't seen Luke do it and had snapped at him. So
Luke did it again. Graciously. Why? Here is how he explained it:

> Luke: I kind of knew the situation about his son. His son had been here
> for a long time and . . . from what I hear, his son had got into a fight and
> he was paralyzed. That's why he got there, and he was in a coma and he
> wasn't coming out of the coma . . . and I heard how he got that way. He
> had got into a fight with a black guy and the black guy really, well, you
> know, because he was here. Well . . . I went and cleaned his room. His
> father would stay here every day, all day, but he smoked cigarettes. So,

he had went out to smoke a cigarette and after I cleaned the room, he came back up to the room. I ran into him in the hall, and he just freaked out . . . telling me I didn't do it. I didn't clean the room and all this stuff. And at first, I got on the defensive, and I was going to argue with him. But I don't know. Something caught me and I said, "I'm sorry. I'll go clean the room."

Interviewer: And you cleaned it again?

Luke: Yeah, I cleaned it so that he could see me clean it . . . I can understand how he could be. It was like six months that his son was here. He'd be a little frustrated, and so I cleaned it again. But I wasn't angry with him. I guess I could understand.

At first glance, the need for wisdom is not built into Luke's work as a custodian. Indeed, look at his job description:

> Operate carpet shampooing and upholstery cleaning equipment
> Operate mechanical cleaning and scrubbing equipment
> Strip and wax floor surfaces
> Maintain entrance area by performing such duties as sweeping, salting, and shoveling
> Clean grounds and area by performing such duties as picking up paper or trash
> Unplug commodes, urinals, and sink drains without dismantling the fixture
> Wet mop floors and stairways
> Operate vacuum cleaning equipment
> Clean and wax furniture, cases, fixtures, and furnishings
> Clean mirrors, interior side of exterior glass, and both sides of interior glass

Clean toilet rooms and fixtures

Stock restroom supplies

Dust venetian blinds while standing on floor or stool

Clean patient bedside equipment

Make beds and change linen

Collect and transport waste materials to central location

Wet mop small areas of floor or stairs to clean up such items as
    spilled liquid or food

Replace burned-out incandescent lightbulbs

Move and arrange furniture and furnishings

Collect and transport soiled linen to central location

Luke's job description says nothing about responsibility or care for patients. He has a long list of duties, but not a single item on it even mentions another human being. From this description, Luke could be working in a shoe factory or a mortuary instead of a hospital.

If Luke were doing *this* job, it would have been reasonable for him to have simply explained to the father that he'd already cleaned the room, and perhaps to have brought in his supervisor to mediate if the father remained angry. Luke might have ignored the man and just gone about his business. He might have gotten angry himself.

But Luke was doing a different job. That's what a team of research psychologists found when they conducted in-depth interviews with Luke and other hospital custodians about their jobs at a major midwestern academic hospital. The researchers had asked the custodians to talk about their jobs, and the custodians began to tell them stories about what they did. Luke's stories told them that his "official" duties were only one part of his *real* job, and that another, central, part of his job was to make the patients and their families feel comfortable, to cheer them up when they were down, to encourage them and divert them from their pain, to give them a willing ear if they felt like talking. Luke aimed to do something different from mere custodial work.

What Luke aimed at would have grabbed Aristotle's attention. Aristotle laid great stress on the importance of the aims—the telos—of practices like medical care. The aims of the practice—promoting health, curing illness, relieving suffering—need to be embodied in the institution where that practice takes place. Hospitals need to make promoting health their primary aim; it's the soul of the organization. The practitioners—the hospital staff—need to understand that aim and be encouraged to make it their aim too. To make wise choices at work, these practitioners need to aim at caring for the patients; they need to be motivated by this aim, as Luke was. Aristotle would have talked about the importance of practitioners desiring the right thing if they were to do their work well. Aiming at the right thing doesn't tell them exactly how to do it—that takes practical skill, not just will. But knowing what to aim at frames and guides their choices—it enables them to choose wisely.

The amazing thing the researchers discovered about Luke and many of his coworkers was that they understood and internalized these aims in spite of their official job description, not because of it. The job they were actually doing was one they had crafted for themselves in light of the aims of medical care. Mike, another custodian, told the researchers how he stopped mopping the hallway floor because Mr. Jones, recovering from major surgery, was out of his bed getting a little much-needed exercise by walking slowly up and down the hall. Charlayne told them about how she ignored her supervisor's admonitions and refrained from vacuuming the visitors' lounge while some family members, who were there all day, every day, happened to be napping. These custodians crafted their jobs with the central purpose of the hospital in mind. They were not generic custodians; they were *hospital* custodians. They saw themselves as playing an important role in an institution whose aim was to see to the care and welfare of patients. So when Luke was confronted by the angry father and he had to decide what to do, he could not look it up in his official job description, because the rules that defined his job said nothing about situations like this. What guided him was the aim of the job he had crafted.

JUDGMENT DAY

"Michael's case appeared routine," explained Judge Lois Forer. When he was brought before the Criminal Division of Philadelphia's Court of Common Pleas, he was "a typical offender: young, black, and male, a high-school dropout without a job. . . . And the trial itself was, in the busy life of a judge, a run-of-the-mill event." The year before Michael had held up a taxi driver while brandishing a gun. He took $50. Michael was caught and tried. "There was no doubt that Michael was guilty," said Forer. She needed to mete out punishment. She turned to the state's sentencing guidelines. They recommended a minimum sentence of twenty-four months. The law seemed clear. Until Forer looked at the particular circumstances. The gun that Michael brandished, Forer explained, was a toy gun. Further, this was his first offense:

> Although he had dropped out of school to marry his pregnant girl-friend, Michael later obtained a high school equivalency diploma. He had been steadily employed, earning enough to send his daughter to parochial school—a considerable sacrifice for him and his wife. Shortly before the holdup, Michael had lost his job. Despondent because he could not support his family, he went out on a Saturday night, had more than a few drinks, and then robbed the taxi.

Judge Forer thought that the twenty-four-month sentence was disproportionate. But the sentencing guidelines allow a judge to deviate from the prescribed sentence if she writes an opinion explaining the reasons. "I decided to deviate from the guidelines," she explained, sentencing Michael to eleven and a half months in the county jail and permitting him to work outside the prison during the day to support his family:

> I also imposed a sentence of two years probation following his imprisonment conditioned upon repayment of the $50. My rationale for the lesser penalty, outlined in my lengthy opinion, was that this was a first offense, no one was harmed, Michael acted under the pressures of unemployment and need, and he seemed truly contrite. He had never committed a violent act and posed no danger to the public. A sentence of close to a year seemed adequate to convince Michael of the seriousness of his crime.

Luke's choice of how to confront the angry father and Forer's choice of the appropriate punishment for Michael couldn't seem more different. Forer's work as a judge demands that she interpret general rules in particular circumstances. She needs to know when and how to make an exception. She needs to know how to craft a punishment to fit a person and the circumstances. Wisdom is at the heart of what she does, if it is to be done well. It's what we need, and what we expect, in judges—the ability to exercise judgment. And judicial wisdom is profoundly practical. Forer could not do her work well without it. And neither could Luke.

Forer was committed to finding a just punishment for Michael, but there were competing aims—all legitimate ones—that she had to sort out and balance. It was right that Michael receive a punishment that fit the crime and that the community be protected from any danger he might pose. But it was also right that Michael be rehabilitated so that he would not commit another offense upon release. And it was important that Michael's sentence do minimal harm to his wife and children, and to his chances of being reintegrated into the community. For Lois Forer, judging was a balancing act. She had to balance retribution, deterrence, and rehabilitation. She had to balance justice and mercy.

And when the angry father confronted him, Luke also had to sort out conflicting aims. There were other legitimate things he might have chosen to do. Be honest: tell the father he had cleaned the room already. Be courageous: stand up to the father's anger and refuse the unfair demand to clean the room again. But Luke had to determine how to balance these competing aims in this circumstance.

Aristotle knew that figuring out what to do in situations like the ones faced by Luke and Judge Forer demanded more than just knowledge of "the facts." It demanded more than knowledge of the law and the rules and the job description. It demanded more than knowing how to deduce the right thing to do from a set of abstract principles about truth or justice or freedom or goodness. There was no general rule or principle to which Forer or Luke could turn to balance or choose among several good aims that were in conflict. To do this kind of balancing and choosing, Luke and Forer needed wisdom. They needed practical moral skill.

Aristotle emphasized two capacities that were particularly important for such practical skill—the ability to *deliberate* about such choices and the ability to *perceive* what was morally relevant in a particular circumstance. Good deliberation and discernment were at the heart of practical wisdom. Forer articulates how she deliberated about Michael's case. A good judge needs to do this all the time in publicly defending her decisions, and in Michael's case the law demanded that she explain why she was deviating from the recommended sentence.

Luke's deliberation took place in radically different circumstances— in a situation in which we largely expect neither wisdom nor nuanced accountability—but it is equally important, if not more important, to consider both how he deliberated and how he talked about his decision. He figured out that the confrontation with the father was not one that should be framed in terms of honesty and integrity, nor as a defense of Luke's rights. Although Luke was tempted to react to the father's demands as an issue of injustice, he quickly saw that something else was at stake—helping to comfort and heal the sick and injured. So Luke framed the issue as one of how to care for and sustain the relationship of *this* father and *this* son at *this* particular trying moment in their lives. Justice and fairness could wait for another day.

And Luke's deliberation went further. He also had to figure out what courses of action were possible in this situation. Should he calmly explain to the father that he recognized the father's pain and understood? Should he offer to sit down and discuss the situation? Luke chose not to make an issue of it, not to fuel the father's anger. He decided that the best and most practical way to handle the situation was to clean the room again and to let the father think he'd accomplished something for his son. Luke had the skill to respond generously and with good grace.

When we think about deliberative skills, the first image that often comes to mind is a process in which we lay out the options, weigh the pros and cons, and then pick what seems best. All of us have deliberated this way. Courses in business and management schools often teach this method as the model of good decision making. This kind of decision making can be particularly useful when we are faced with new or tough problems and have the time to ponder them. But Luke's behavior makes us think about other kinds of deliberative skills.

Luke did not lay out conflicting aims or weigh the pros and cons of all the options. What was important for Luke was how to frame the situation. The unreasonableness of the request and the father's anger may have tempted Luke to frame the situation as one about honesty, rights, or justice, but instead he framed it in light of the job as he had crafted it, the way he saw the purpose of being a hospital custodian. And

Luke's ability to do this was enabled by a capacity he had for good story-telling. Luke could tell himself, and the interviewer, a narrative about this patient who "had got into a fight" and about an upset father who had been visiting him, caring for him, for months. This story, and the frame it provided, enabled Luke to discern what to do. Luke wasn't laying out options. And he wasn't simply deducing what to do from some general principle of proper behavior (like "be kind to patients' families"). The story Luke told explained how the father came to be yelling at Luke to clean the room again, why the anger made sense, and why it was forgivable. And *this* story helped Luke figure out his role in the evolving narrative. Our ability to frame situations well and tell good stories is critical to practical moral skill. So, too, is the ability to use analogies and metaphors to draw on our past experiences. Luke knew what to do not because he had done exactly the same thing before, but because he could draw on previous experiences that were something like the current situation. He knew what the consequences had been of actions he had taken in these past cases. He wasn't just repeating what he'd always done; he was crafting something new from what had or had not worked in the past.

This may seem like making a lot of Luke's instant decision, but Judge Forer used the same deliberative skills. To interpret the law in Michael's case she needed more than the facts, more than the legal guidelines, and more than the ability to make logical deductions. She needed to create an accurate narrative that made sense of Michael's actions and his intentions in light of his character and circumstances—his stable family and work history, the job crisis and the depression he was going through, the nature of the crime and choice of weapon, the harm done—all this to judge the seriousness of his crime and the severity of his punishment. She understood Michael by drawing on her past experience, by interpreting the similarities and differences he shared with other criminals she had judged.

Aristotle tells us that "in matters concerning action and questions of what is beneficial, the agent must consider on each different occasion what the situation demands, just as in medicine and in navigation." Figuring out what is appropriate in a particular situation rests on *moral perception*. "A man of practical wisdom," argued Aristotle, must "take cognizance of particulars." Particular facts are the "starting points" for our knowledge of "the goal of action" and, to deliberate and choose well, "one must have perception of particular facts." Every day in court, Judge Forer had to sort through a deluge of information about the lives of the defendants and the nature of their misdeeds. To determine motives, to parcel out responsibility, to understand how this crime was different from or similar to others, to determine the future danger to the community—these tasks demanded an ability to pick what was significant out of a lot of background noise. These tasks demanded an ability to see the nuance—the gray—of a particular situation, and not simply the black-and-white of the legal and the illegal.

Luke, too, was faced daily with patients who were upset, confused, disoriented, troubled; who were experiencing multiple and contradictory emotions. When he was confronted with choices about how to care for such people, just like judges, doctors, lawyers, therapists, or teachers, Luke had to sort through a welter of information and figure out which things were the most important to deal with in the moment. A critical part of the context that Luke had to perceive was what the father was thinking and feeling. If Luke had been unable to discern this, he wouldn't have had a clue about what the problem was, what the options were, or what the consequences of his response to the father might be. Luke had to imagine how arguing with the father would affect the man's feelings of anger and frustration, and his ability to remain hopeful and to maintain his vigil day after day. Moral imagination—the ability to see how various options will play themselves out and the ability to evaluate them—is thus critical to perception. It represents, philosopher John Dewey explained, "the capacity to concretely perceive what is before us in light of what could be."

Not surprisingly, then, empathy—the capacity to imagine what someone else is thinking and feeling—is critical for the perception that practical wisdom demands. Such empathy involves both cognitive skill—the ability to perceive the situation as it is perceived by another—and emotional skill—the capacity to understand what another person is feeling. Luke had to put himself in the shoes of the father even though he knew the father was wrong. Luke could not have provided the narrative he did without this capacity for getting himself into the heart of the father. And the same was true of Judge Forer. To find the right sentence, she needed the empathy to put herself in Michael's shoes and to imagine the likely consequences of letting Michael work outside of prison during the day. She asked herself: Was this an irrational crime? Was there wanton cruelty? Is this a hostile person? Can this person control himself?

Emotion is critical to moral perception in another way. It is a signaling device. The emotion of the father—"he just freaked out"—signaled to Luke that something was wrong. With that kind of anger, the signal was not subtle, but often it is. Reading the facial expressions, the body language, the tone of voice of another alerts us that something is wrong and that we need to make choices about how to respond. Our own feelings of anger, guilt, compassion, or shame signal us to reflect, to pay special attention to what is happening. This may sound obvious, but all too often the rules and incentives that govern our lives are all about removing emotion from our decision making—about not trusting the signal we're sending ourselves. Luke recognized his own frustration and rising anger as well as the father's, and was alerted to consider whether this confrontation was about Luke or about the father and his situation.

There is a long history of suspicion that emotion is the enemy of good reasoning and sound judgment, and rightly so. Emotions can often control us instead of the reverse. "The devil made me do it." Emotions can prejudice us toward people we love, and against those we don't. Emotions can be unstable and therefore unreliable as guides. Emotions are sometimes too particular: we can feel so passionately about something that happened to us, or about this wronged patient or that ill-fed child, that our judgment is clouded about "what is just" or "what is fair" in general. And emotions almost got the better of Luke. For a moment, he felt angry at the injustice of the father's demand. But emotion also served Luke well. He felt compassion for the father: "It was like six months that his son was here. He'd be a little frustrated, and so I cleaned it again. But I wasn't angry with him." So emotion was critical in guiding Luke to do the right thing. Luke's emotions were not random—unstable and uneducated. He was compassionate about the right things and angry about the right things. And he had the self-control—the emotion-regulating skills—to choose rightly. Emotions properly trained and modulated, Aristotle told his readers, are essential to being practically wise:

> We can experience fear, confidence, desire, anger, pity, and generally any kind of pleasure and pain either too much or too little, and in either case not properly. But to experience all this at the right time, toward the right objects, toward the right people, for the right reason, and in the right manner—that is the median and the best course, the course that is a mark of virtue.

Sizing up the situation, figuring what's relevant in *this* particular case and *these* particular circumstances, imagining what someone else is thinking and feeling, recognizing the options and imagining the consequences—all these skills are part of being perceptive. It is this perception that enables us to recognize the uniqueness of a particular situation. Such perception is "a process of loving conversation between rules and concrete responses, general conceptions and unique cases, in which the general articulates the particular and is in turn further articulated by it."

Practical wisdom demands more than the skill to be perceptive about others. It also demands the capacity to perceive oneself—to assess what our own motives are, to admit our failures, to figure out what has worked or not and why. We get a glimpse of the importance of such self-reflection in Luke. "At first, I got on the defensive, and I was going to argue with him. But I don't know. Something caught me and I said, 'I'm sorry. I'll go clean the room.'" Such self-reflection is not always so easy when, like Luke, we feel we've been wronged. And it's also difficult when we've been wrong—thoughtless, careless, too self-interested. Being able to criticize our own certainties is often a painful struggle, demanding some courage as we try to stand back and impartially judge ourselves and our own responsibility. For Luke to be a good hospital custodian, and Forer a good judge, they needed the ability to recognize their mistakes so they could do better next time.

Luke and Judge Forer help us understand some of the key characteristics of practical wisdom. To summarize:

1. A wise person knows the proper aims of the activity she is engaged in. She wants to do the right thing to achieve these aims—wants to meet the needs of the people she is serving.
2. A wise person knows how to improvise, balancing conflicting aims and interpreting rules and principles in light of the particularities of each context.
3. A wise person is perceptive, knows how to read a social context, and knows how to move beyond the black-and-white of rules and see the gray in a situation.
4. A wise person knows how to take on the perspective of another—to see the situation as the other person does and thus to understand how the other person feels. This perspective-taking is what enables a wise person to feel empathy for others and to make decisions that serve the client's (student's, patient's, friend's) needs.

5. A wise person knows how to make emotion an ally of reason, to rely on emotion to signal what a situation calls for, and to inform judgment without distorting it. He can feel, intuit, or "just know" what the right thing to do is, enabling him to act quickly when timing matters. His emotions and intuitions are well educated.

6. A wise person is an experienced person. Practical wisdom is a craft and craftsmen are trained by having the right experiences. People learn how to be brave, said Aristotle, by doing brave things. So, too, with honesty, justice, loyalty, caring, listening, and counseling.

3.

Balancing Acts:
Why Wisdom Is Practical

Our lives are structured by rules: administrative and bureaucratic rules that tell us how to relate and act in the complex organizations that dominate our modern world, moral rules that tell us how to behave ethically, rules legislated by governments, and the criminal and civil codes that mete out punishment for law breaking. We couldn't live without these rules. This reliance on law and rules instead of the judgment of men and women has deep roots. In designing the constitution of the early American republic, the founders knew they could not depend on the goodness or wisdom of men. "But what is government itself," asked James Madison in Federalist No. 51 (1788), "but the greatest of all reflections on human nature? If men were angels, no government would be necessary." That is why John Adams argued for "a government of laws, and not of men" in the Massachusetts Constitution of 1780. With well-crafted laws—and constitutional checks and balances—we would be less dependent on our public officials being statesmen or on our citizens being virtuous or wise. A system of "wise" laws would minimize the need for "wise men." The ideal legal system, mused Supreme

Court Justice Benjamin Cardozo, "would be a code at once so flexible and so minute, as to supply in advance for every conceivable situation the just and fitting rule."

There is only one problem: substituting rules for wisdom does not work. However important moral rules and laws are, the ideal, Cardozo concluded, is impossible: "life is too complex to bring the attainment of this ideal within the compass of human powers." With law came the need for judges, and judgment. And so, too, with all the moral rules we turn to for guidance. We all need to be judges.

That's what Aristotle figured out in fourth-century B.C. Athens, watching the carpenters, shoemakers, blacksmiths, and boat pilots. Their work was not governed by systematically applying rules or following rigid procedures. The materials they worked with were too irregular, and each task posed new problems. Aristotle thought the choices craftsmen made in acting on the material world provided clues to the kind of know-how citizens needed to make moral choices in the social world. Aristotle was particularly fascinated with how the masons on the Isle of Lesbos used rulers. A normal, straight-edged ruler was of little use to the masons who were carving round columns from slabs of stone and needed to measure the circumference of the columns. Unless you bent the ruler. Which is exactly what the masons did. They fashioned a flexible ruler out of lead, a forerunner of today's tape measure. For Aristotle, knowing how to bend the rule to fit the circumstance was exactly what practical wisdom was all about.

The English common law system, upon which our legal system is based, built in this kind of flexibility. It rejected the old Saxon code that held that intention and circumstance did not matter. Whether a man deliberately shot an arrow and hit another man, or intended to shoot a deer but hit another man, or the arrow ricocheted off a rock and hit a man, if the harm was the same, then the crime was the same and the penalty was the same. English common law, and later the American legal system, changed this and said that liability in criminal cases generally required proof of blameworthiness. Intent and motives matter. So do circumstances. That's what Judge Forer was doing, and that's why we need such judges. Our common sense supports such common law. Even a child who breaks the family china knows that her intentions ("It slipped," "I thought it was the unbreakable kind," "I hate this food," "I was aiming for Johnny's head") will matter—and *should* matter—to the parental judge. What this child knows is something that we all know: however important laws and rules are for telling us what to aim at, they always need interpretation when they are applied.

Sometimes, we bend rules to *avoid* doing what's right. We sometimes talk about lawyers as masters of this skill. But the masons of Lesbos didn't bend the rule to cheat or deceive. They bent the rule to do what was right, and to do it well. And that was Aristotle's point: to do our work and lead our lives well, we have to know when and how to bend the rule.

BALANCING ACTS

Anybody who has raised a child, sustained a friendship or marriage, supervised others in the workplace, or worked to serve others knows the limits of rules and principles. We can't live without them, but not a day goes by when we don't have to bend one, or make an exception, or balance them when they conflict. We're always solving the ethical puzzles or quandaries that are embedded in our practices because most of our choices involve interpreting rules, or balancing clashing principles or aims, or choosing between better and worse. We're always trying to find the right balance. Aristotle called this balance the "mean." The mean was not the arithmetic average; it was the right balance in a particular circumstance. And it was computed not by adding and dividing, but by deploying the flexible rule used by the masons of Lesbos.

Some of our everyday balancing acts are so ordinary that we don't even think about them as choices, let alone ethical choices. When a friend asks us "How do I look?" we need to balance honesty and kindness, and know how to be honest and kind. When we reveal the confidences of a friend because we are worried about his well-being, we're balancing loyalty and care. Care for our child demands we correct his mistakes—how else will he learn? But *all* of his mistakes, *all* the time? Do we try to protect him from making mistakes that will harm him? Of course. But we also need to avoid being overprotective. The child needs the freedom to fall if he is to learn to be responsible and stand on his own. As commonplace as these balancing acts are, doing them well is essential. We're always performing balancing acts. We're always interpreting principles, aims, and rules in the light of a specific context. We're constantly called upon to exercise practical wisdom in our most fundamental human decisions, and we trust ourselves—and others—to do so. There is no reason this shouldn't apply in broader contexts.

WHO DECIDES? BALANCING ASKING AND TELLING

At the heart of any code of professional ethics is the injunction to put the client's interests first. It's a good principle: serving a patient or a student or a client is the primary duty of a professional. But what does following this principle mean in practice?

When young lawyer William Simon took on the case of Mrs. Jones, the housekeeper of a senior partner, he wanted to work assiduously on her behalf. Mrs. Jones was a home owner, a churchgoer, and, at sixty-five, a well-respected member of a lower-middle-class black community outside Boston. Her car had been hit in the rear—a minor traffic accident. Mrs. Jones stopped to identify herself, but the other driver, a white woman, fled the scene, called the police, and reported Mrs. Jones as the one who fled. Without investigating, the police called in Mrs. Jones. "They reprimanded her like a child," says Simon, "addressing her—a sixty-five-year-old woman—by her first name, while referring to the much younger complainant as 'Mrs. Strelski.'" Mrs. Strelski eventually withdrew her complaint, but the police insisted on prosecuting Mrs. Jones for leaving the scene of the accident.

Simon wanted to prove Mrs. Jones innocent and also protest the indignity and injustice she had suffered. He planned to expose the racism of the police "through devastating cross-examination." But he had no court experience. He turned to a lawyer friend who was an expert in traffic cases.

They met in a corner of the courtroom, just before the trial. Dismissal on racism charges? His friend rolled his eyes. The judge and the police were repeat players in this process who shared many common interests. If Mrs. Jones lost—unlikely, but possible, said his friend—she would lose her driver's license, be fined, and perhaps even face a jail term of up to six months. Mrs. Jones would also have to experience the anxiety of a trial and of having to testify.

Simon's friend negotiated a deal with the prosecutor. Mrs. Jones would enter a plea of nolo contendere (the defendant neither admits nor disputes the charge). She would get six months' probation, but because this was a first offense, her criminal record could be sealed after a year. Simon was bothered. "The plea bargain would deprive her of any sense of vindication. Mrs. Jones struck me as a person who prized her dignity, deeply resented her recent abuse, and would attach importance to vindication." He presented the plea bargain to Mrs. Jones and her minister, who was there to support her and serve as a character witness. They talked for about ten minutes and ultimately turned to Simon for his advice: "You're the expert. That's what we come to lawyers for."

I insisted that, because the decision was hers, I couldn't tell her what to do. I then spelled out the pros and cons. . . . However, I mentioned the cons last, and the final thing I said was, "If you took their offer, there probably wouldn't be any bad practical consequences, but it wouldn't be total justice." Up to that point, Mrs. Jones and her minister seemed ambivalent, but that last phrase seemed to have a dramatic effect on them. In unison, they said, "We want justice."

"No deal," Simon told his friend. "She wants justice."

"Let me talk to her," said his friend. His friend took Mrs. Jones and her minister through the same considerations, but he concluded with a discussion of the disadvantages of going to trial and described the possible consequences of going to jail more fully. And he did not include his thoughts on "total justice." When he was done, Mrs. Jones changed her mind and decided to accept the plea bargain.

In the end, Mrs. Jones got what she said she wanted. But did Simon act successfully on his client's behalf? Simon is now an experienced lawyer and a distinguished professor of law, and his own judgment is: no. Neither he nor his friend was able to exercise the practical wisdom needed to solve a central problem in any legal case like this—figuring out what it means to genuinely work on a client's behalf.

From a classroom perspective, determining a client's interests would seem to be relatively straightforward if we simply follow a fundamental principle of modern ethics: every individual should be free to choose what's best for herself. Respect for persons means respect for them as rational beings capable of determining their own interests. Lack of such respect smacks of paternalism or, worse, manipulation. Codes of professional ethics talk about this as the principle of client or patient "autonomy." Lawyers serve clients by being their advocates, by working on their behalf, and when it comes to the fundamental choices of what to advocate, that choice is the client's. So to help Mrs. Jones, Simon first needed to help Mrs. Jones determine whether what she had done was illegal. When they had determined it wasn't, he then needed to lay out what her legal options were now that she was falsely accused. Then it was up to Mrs. Jones to decide what to do. Simon and his colleague laid out the same options to Mrs. Jones so she could decide "for herself." Yet she decided in two different ways. Why?

A slight change in intonation, and in the way the options were ordered, changed the way Mrs. Jones understood the issues, making the danger of going to jail a bit less and then a bit more salient; making "justice" a bit more and then a bit less salient. Could Simon have come up with a neutral way to frame the issues so that Mrs. Jones *really* could have decided for herself? There are better and worse frames, frames that are more or less manipulative, frames that are well intentioned and ill intentioned. But any way of explaining options to a client will always involve some kind of framing, and any frame will tilt the client in one direction or another. There is no neutral. Leaving the choice to Mrs. Jones after listing the options and the consequences created only the illusion of autonomy. So the ubiquity of framing rules out the simple solution, "Let the client decide."

Good lawyers know that the solution to this problem is not simply finding ways to frame options more neutrally or insisting on more client autonomy. Rather, respecting a client's right and responsibility to choose means providing a client with guidance in making that choice. That guidance demands more than laying out the options and detailing the risks and benefits of each. Mrs. Jones was unclear about what she wanted and about the risks she was willing to incur. She was anxious about going to trial and wanted to avoid being punished for a crime she did not commit. That made the plea bargain attractive. However, she was being falsely accused and she did want justice. That tilted her toward fighting for her innocence in court. Simon knew that it was not up to him to balance these aims for her. But he didn't know how to give her what she needed—the good counsel that would allow her to sort out what was best.

To provide good advice, Simon needed a lot of practical knowledge about the specifics of the situation—of *this* particular judge and court, *these* police officers, the local biases of race and class, the mechanics of how deals are made. It was a good thing he brought along a colleague whom he trusted. But Simon also needed other kinds of practical knowledge and skills. He needed to understand Mrs. Jones and not just depend on stereotypes about "oppressed people" and what they want. He did have the good intuition his colleague lacked that Mrs. Jones would likely be concerned about justice. Mrs. Jones *was* concerned about justice and so was her minister. But she needed help deliberating: weighing this concern against the other considerations in her life. To offer wise counsel, Simon needed to help Mrs. Jones perceive her situation and imagine alternatives. To do that he needed the know-how to listen and the skill to ask the kinds of questions that would help her reflect on her situation. He needed the empathy to understand what she was thinking and feeling. Developing that empathy required that Simon get to know Mrs. Jones. This kind of knowledge doesn't come in the five minutes before a hearing begins. Simon did not have this wisdom to counsel, and neither did his friend. So they went through the motions of letting Mrs. Jones choose for herself.

Like Mrs. Jones, many clients may have objectives that are hazy or in conflict. Or a client might be impetuous. He may, says Anthony Kronman, professor and former dean at Yale Law School, be "in the grip of some domineering passion like anger or erotic love," having "made a quick decision to change his life in an important way, for example, by dissolving a long-standing partnership or rewriting his will for a lover's benefit." Or the client may not be clear about the long-term consequences of one or another course of action. Or the short-term and long-term consequences may themselves be in conflict. The desire of one party in a divorce case to get even may make it impossible to create the future relationship needed to share the upbringing of the children in coming years. Kronman argues that lawyers who think of themselves as zealous advocates aiming only to get what clients say they want forget the other half of lawyering: being good counselors. In fact, he says, to be a really good advocate you need the wisdom to be a good counselor because that's the only way to actually work on a client's behalf.

It is not just lawyers who need the wisdom to counsel. Such wisdom is needed by almost anyone who works on another's behalf. Take the hairdressers whom Mike Rose studied in his book *The Mind at Work*. Rose found that they were constantly serving clients who came in with a picture clipped from a beauty magazine and told the stylist, "This is the look I want—cut my hair like this." A stylist could just do the cut and take the money and tell the customer that she got exactly what she wanted. But the good stylist knows that what a customer thinks she wants is often not what she really wants. The "look" in that picture will frequently not be the "look" on this particular customer. Rose found that most of the stylists he studied wanted to do a good job, and those who succeeded knew that the job was not just perfectly executing the cut they had been asked for. It's a challenge, explained one stylist, because you "don't assume you know what they want, because *they* may not know what they want."

The hairdressers' technical expertise and their experience styling hair gave them some of the knowledge they needed. They knew how the face and bone structure and the condition of the hair—its density, texture, and wave pattern—would change the look in the client's favorite picture. They also knew, or quickly found out, some basic things about their client, like how she managed her hair between visits—or didn't. But the good hairdressers could not just let the client choose for herself. And neither could they simply tell the client what was best and do it. These hairdressers had the skill to help the clients figure out what they really wanted. They knew how to listen to the client, hear what the client was thinking and feeling. They knew how to ask questions to help the client decide if what she wanted was more "sassy" or more "demure." The conversations were a delicate interplay of talking and listening, of subtle interpretations—almost an improvised dance by which each steered the other in the right direction. Being a good hair stylist demands the wisdom to be a good counselor.

However much we want to avoid manipulating others, however much we want to help or serve others by respecting their knowledge about what's best for themselves, it's never as simple as just letting them choose. It's the human condition to have hazy or conflicting goals, or to be in the grip of some domineering passion, or to be unclear about the consequences of our actions. We see this not only in our work but in our everyday personal lives as well: being a good parent or a good friend constantly involves helping those we care for discern what acting on their own behalf really means—and figuring out what we can do to help. We can say, "Do your own thing," or "It's your choice," or "I'll help you do whatever you want." Or we can say, "If I were you, I would do this," or "Father knows best," or "Over my dead body." But most of the time it's going to take practical wisdom and not some moral rule to actually help them work things out.

BALANCING HONESTY WITH CARE AND KINDNESS

Dr. Jerome Lowenstein, a physician at New York University Medical Center, had been caring for Mr. N., a still-practicing Hungarian-born lawyer in his seventies, for about ten years. But now antibiotics were not helping Mr. N.'s persistent cough and fever. Dr. Lowenstein ordered a CT scan that revealed masses in the patient's lungs that turned out to be malignant. The condition was not curable. Dr. Lowenstein explained all this to Mrs. N. She told him bluntly: "You can't tell [Mr. N.] that he has cancer." Dr. Lowenstein argued, but she insisted "that under no circumstances was I to tell her husband the diagnosis."

"I tried to convince her," explained Dr. Lowenstein, "that it was important for me to maintain an honest relationship with Mr. N." and that if the deception became apparent as the disease progressed, it "would then be difficult for me to care for him." Mrs. N. did not budge. Her husband had experienced bouts of depression throughout his life, and she was worried that news of the cancer would just do him in. She assured Dr. Lowenstein that if he just told Mr. N. that the procedures he had in mind were "necessary for further treatment," her husband would comply.

Since the time of Hippocrates and the oath he created for doctors, a foundational principle of medicine has been "First, do no harm." Historically, doctors were taught that their obligation was to use their expertise to decide what best helped and least harmed a patient. The obligation to act in such a way came to be known in medical ethics as the principle of beneficence. But this does not address how much doctors should tell patients about their condition. Should doctors tell patients the truth?

Until recently, there was widespread concern in the medical profession about the harm that could be done by telling the truth to patients with grave illnesses. Under such conditions truth telling could be sacrificed. But in the last decades of the twentieth century, most doctors— Dr. Lowenstein among them—became strong advocates for telling patients the truth about their condition and life chances. And for good reason. Patients could be harmed by not knowing—they would not know to settle affairs, say good-bye, make choices about how to be cared for, or make end-of-life decisions. Dishonesty also undermined the fundamental relationship of trust between the doctor and the patient upon which good health care depended.

Decisions like this are never simple, says Dr. Lowenstein. They "cannot be made according to a uniform rule or universal principle." We "cannot and should not return to the time, not very long ago, when patients were told very little and were expected to listen to the advice of a physician 'who knew best.'" But he also knew that a "measure of paternalism" was sometimes essential to do his work well. "'Truth' and 'facts' are not discrete, defined entities like so many colored marbles, to be handed to the patient to accept or reject." For some patients, he realized, "it may be more appropriate to use the truth judiciously."

Dr. Lowenstein agonized. He consulted other physicians. He talked to his wife. He talked to Mr. N.'s daughter. He talked to a psychiatrist who had treated Mr. N. for depression some years earlier. Finally, Dr. Lowenstein decided to honor Mrs. N.'s request. Mr. N. accepted the diagnosis of "complicated pneumonia." He lived a decent life for most of the next eighteen months. Then he died quietly and comfortably.

To do his work properly, Dr. Lowenstein needed the wisdom to know how to bend the truth in the pursuit of care. But it's not just dramatic, life-or-death cases that demand practical wisdom. Any time any doctor talks to any patient about a diagnosis, a prognosis, or a treatment, she must decide how much to tell, when to tell it, and how to tell it. She needs to figure out how much the patient is capable of understanding and how to tell the truth without destroying the hope and determination so important even to palliative care. These choices are part of the everyday fabric of good medical care. Determining how to balance truth and care, honesty and kindness, is part of the fabric of our everyday lives too, as our friend Miriam reminded us.

Miriam's mother, now deceased, was ninety years old, with Alzheimer's disease. She was living in a nearby nursing home. A few years earlier, Miriam's mother had lost her husband after more than sixty years of marriage. When her husband died, she grieved, but then seemed to bounce back, surprisingly quickly considering that she and her husband had been virtually inseparable. The reason for her resilience became clear when she told Miriam that her husband hadn't died. He was away, or he was sick, or he had left her for another woman (the story changed from day to day, even moment to moment). On occasions when Miriam arrived at the nursing home for a visit, her mother might say that she had "just missed Daddy. He was here, but then he left."

Miriam is an inveterate truth teller. She tells the truth because it's the "right thing to do" and because it's disrespectful to lie. So in each visit she slowly and carefully reminded her mother of her husband's death, vividly describing the funeral and pointing out the family members who had attended. This produced nothing but agitation in her mother. "But Mom, why would I lie to you, especially about something like this? You know I never lie."

"Honey, I know you're not lying. You're just very badly mistaken."

With the encouragement of the nursing staff, our friend swallowed hard and started to improvise, playing along, not on every occasion, but most times. Each visit, she had to determine, at that moment, what narrative her mother was living, and then participate in that narrative in an appropriate way. It wasn't easy. Each visit brought its own surprises. But her mother was much happier.

BALANCING EMPATHY WITH DETACHMENT

Empathy is a character trait that we value in ourselves and in our friends, colleagues, and the professionals who serve us. We saw that the know-how to be empathetic is central to practical wisdom: unless we can understand how others think and feel, it's difficult to know the right thing to do. But empathy has its dark side: too much understanding and sensitivity, too much seeing things from the other's perspective, can cloud judgment and paralyze choice. Edmund Pellegrino, a scholar and chairman of the President's Council on Bioethics from 2001 to 2009, explains it like this: "If a physician identifies too closely as co-sufferer with the patient, she loses the objectivity essential to the most precise assessment of what is wrong, of what can be done, and of what should be done to meet those needs. Excessive co-suffering also impedes and may even paralyze the physician into a state of inaction."

Consider Brad, a young literature professor with a love of running who developed bone cancer in a knee. The doctor who treated him came to know him quite well and to like him. Brad was one of his favorite patients, and the doctor was particularly eager to spare him discomfort.

Normally cancer in the knee would require amputation, but a drug had recently become available that could shrink tumors enough that surgical excision rather than amputation became possible. The problem with the drug was that it was extremely toxic. It had very unpleasant and debilitating side effects, some of which were serious enough that they required constant monitoring. So Brad was wiped out—too weak to get out of bed and too nauseated to eat.

At the end of the third round of the drug, Brad developed a fever. His doctor examined him but could find no source of infection. Later that day, Brad went into septic shock. The source, it turned out, was an abscess in his left buttock. His doctor explained why he missed it: in examining Brad, his "favorite patient," he had spared the weak, listless man the ordeal of turning him over so that he could check for bedsores. The doctor had lots of empathy, but not enough detachment.

The ability to balance empathy and detachment is an ability to balance seeming opposites. On one side is "feeling with" and "understanding from the inside." On the other side is "coolness" and "objectivity." But the ability to balance such opposites is central to practical wisdom.

Professor Anthony Kronman at Yale offered a perfect metaphor for this balance. He compared the capacity to see things from two different perspectives at the same time to wearing bifocal lenses. One lens sees the situation and choices up close, from the inside, through the eyes and the heart of another; the other lens sees things at a distance, through the perspective of a reasonable person, or of the law, or of medicine, or of the other parties involved. "Anyone who has worn bifocal lenses," Kronman says, "knows that it takes time to learn to shift smoothly between perspectives and to combine them in a single field of vision. The same is true of deliberation. It is difficult to be compassionate, and often just as difficult to be detached, but what is most difficult of all is to be both at once. Compassion and detachment pull in opposite directions and we are not always able to combine them, nor is everyone equally good at doing so." Doing any practice well demands learning how to balance empathy and detachment in the particular interactions we are having. The ability to balance these two opposites is at the heart of practical wisdom.

WISDOM AS MORAL JAZZ

How do wildland firefighters make decisions in life-threatening situations when, for instance, a fire explodes and threatens to engulf the crew? They are confronted with endless variables, the most intense, high-stakes atmosphere imaginable, and the need to make instant decisions. Psychologist Karl Weick found that traditionally, successful firefighters kept four simple survival guidelines in mind:

1. Build a backfire if you have time.
2. Get to the top of the ridge where the fuel is thinner, where there are stretches of rock and shale, and where winds usually fluctuate.
3. Turn into the fire and try to work through it by piecing together burned-out stretches.
4. Do not allow the fire to pick the spot where it hits you, because it will hit you where it is burning fiercest and fastest.

But starting in the mid-1950s, this short list of survival rules was gradually replaced by much longer and more detailed ones. The current lists, which came to exceed forty-eight items, were designed to specify in greater detail what to do to survive in each particular circumstance (e.g., fires at the urban-wildland interface).

Weick reports that teaching the firefighters these detailed lists was a factor in decreasing the survival rates. The original short list was a general guide. The firefighters could easily remember it, but they knew it needed to be interpreted, modified, and embellished based on circumstance. And they knew that experience would teach them how to do the modifying and embellishing. As a result, they were open to being taught by experience. The very shortness of the list gave the firefighters tacit permission—even encouragement—to improvise in the face of unexpected events. Weick found that the longer the checklists for the wildland firefighters became, the more improvisation was shut down. Rules are aids, allies, guides, and checks. But too much reliance on rules can squeeze out the judgment that is necessary to do our work well. When general principles morph into detailed instructions, formulas, unbending commands—wisdom substitutes—the important nuances of context are squeezed out. Better to minimize the number of rules, give up trying to cover every particular circumstance, and instead do more training to encourage skill at practical reasoning and intuition. Weick likens the skills of an experienced firefighter to the improvisational skills of a good jazz musician.

Jazz saxophonist Stan Getz said that jazz is "like a language. You learn the alphabet, which are the scales. You learn sentences, which are the chords. And then you talk extemporaneously with the horn." Good improvisation is not making something out of nothing, but making something out of previous experience, practice, and knowledge. So jazz improvisation, writes Weick, "materializes around a simple melody, formula, or theme that provides the pretext for real-time composing. Some of that composing is built from pre-composed phrases that become meaningful retrospectively as embellishments of that melody. And some comes from elaboration of the embellishments themselves."

Custodians like Luke, judges like Lois Forer, doctors like Jerome Lowenstein, daughters like Miriam made themselves wise with practice, like jazz musicians and firefighters. The more they learned how to perceive the relevant details of their situations and the more they built their skills at improvisation, the easier it became to improvise—to combine old skills and knowledge in new ways to deal with the unexpected.

Practical wisdom is a kind of moral jazz. It sometimes depends on rules and principles—like the notes on the page and the basic melodies in jazz. But rules by themselves can't do the job. Moral improvisation is the interpretative tune we play around these notes and melodies, in order to do the right thing.

BALANCING RULES TALK AND WISDOM TALK: BRINGING ARISTOTLE BACK

The world we face is too complex and varied to be handled by rules, and wise people understand this. Yet there is a strange and troubling disconnect between the way we make our moral decisions and the way we talk about them.

From ethics textbooks to professional association codes to our everyday life, any discussion of moral choices is dominated by Rules Talk. If we're asked to explain why we decided to tell the painful, unvarnished truth to a friend, we might say, "Honesty is the best policy." But if we're asked why we decided to shade the truth we might say, "If you can't say anything nice, don't say anything at all." It's clearly not a rule that is telling us what to do. Both maxims are good rules of thumb, but we don't talk about why we picked one and not the other in any particular case. "Better safe than sorry." But "He who hesitates is lost." "A penny saved is a penny earned." But "Don't be penny wise and pound foolish." When we hear the maxim, we nod. End of story. It's as if stating the rule is sufficient to explain why we did what we did.

The same is true of professional ethics texts and codes: they are built around following rules and principles. We take refuge in this Rules Talk. This silence about practical wisdom is diverting and disempowering. It keeps us from understanding what we are really doing. It blocks us from asking what we, as individuals or as a society, need to do to nurture the capacity for wise judgment. And even more worrisome, it blinds us to forces that stultify this capacity.

In a way it's not surprising that Ethics Talk is Rules Talk and not Wisdom Talk. Practical wisdom seems to be a slippery thing. It lives in a gray world, not a black-and-white one. It is context dependent. You can just hand someone a set of rules to follow, but wisdom must be nurtured by experience. And when people who are unwise are given the discretion to "use their judgment," the results can be disastrous. The emotions that signal and motivate Luke and Judge Forer are potentially fickle, biased, and "irrational." The imagination so important to practical wisdom seems always to be in motion, never settled. Empathy seems dangerous because too much understanding of another's situation could cloud our judgment. The capacity to frame? Frames bias and distort. They are the tools advertisers and politicians use to manipulate us. Storytelling? We tell our kids to stop telling stories because we see stories as a kind of self-justifying framing of events that relieves them of responsibility. Given these well-founded fears, it's not surprising that Rules Talk seems like an insurance policy against disaster.

But rules are never enough. We blind ourselves by locking our public conversation into Rules Talk. Rules Talk needs to be supplemented with Wisdom Talk. Aristotle can give us a road map. Open Aristotle's classic *Nicomachean Ethics*, and you'll be hard-pressed to find *any* discussion of moral rules and principles. Aristotle's main concern was with creating people of good character, particularly practical wisdom. *Ethics* was about knowing the proper thing to aim at in any practice, wanting to aim at it, having the skill to figure out how to achieve it in a particular context, and then doing it. Aristotle is an anchor for us because he urges us to temper Rules Talk with Wisdom Talk.

Rules Talk asks: What are the universal principles that should guide our moral choices? Wisdom Talk asks: What are the

proper aims of this activity? Do they conflict in this circumstance? How should they be interpreted or balanced?

Rules Talk tends to be about absolutes. Wisdom Talk is context
talk—talk about nuance.

Rules Talk sidelines, or even labels as dangerous, moral imagination and emotion. Wisdom Talk puts them at the center because they allow us to see and understand what needs to be seen
and understood.

Rules Talk ends with determining the right principle or rule to
follow. Wisdom Talk ends with determining whether to follow it and how to follow it.

Rules Talk marginalizes the importance of character traits like
courage, patience, determination, self-control, and kindness.
Wisdom Talk puts them at the center.

Rules Talk urges us to consult a text or a code. Wisdom Talk
urges us to learn from others who are practically wise.

Rules Talk is taught by teachers in the classroom. Wisdom Talk
is taught by mentors and coaches who are practicing alongside us.

PART II

The Machinery
of Wisdom

The Machinery of Wisdom

Aristotle has guided much of our exploration of practical wisdom. But a lot has changed since the fourth century B.C. Aristotle couldn't have imagined the world we live in. Our world is much more complex and contradictory than his was—and the need for practical wisdom is even greater. Such practical wisdom requires nuanced thinking, flexibility, creativity, and empathetic engagement with others.

Are most of us capable of developing and exercising it? There is evidence from psychology that human beings are born with the capacity to be wise. The raw materials are there, waiting to be developed. But this capacity must be cultivated by the right kind of experience.

4.

Born to Be Wise

Aristotle understood that ethical choices are rarely black-and-white. It is the same thing that Judge Forer and Dr. Lowenstein understood—that whether and how to follow rules depends on an appreciation of context. This is why Aristotle thought that ethics could never be a "science"—that ethical decisions could never be derived from a set of clear-cut rules and principles. That, he said, is why practical wisdom was needed.

But perhaps, in our times, it is too much to ask of people that they develop practical wisdom. And it is too much to ask that they trust the practical wisdom of others. Is wisdom the sort of characteristic we find in gifted sages but not in ordinary mortals? If so, perhaps the sages should use their wisdom to hand down rules for the rest of us to follow. Aristotle didn't think that practical wisdom was the special province of sages. He had faith that ordinary citizens could learn to judge wisely in practical matters. Was he right?

Modern psychological research has taught us a good deal about the components of moral skill—perceptiveness, nuanced thinking, appreciation of context, the ability to integrate intellect with emotion and to experience empathy—and how they work. It has taught us that developing these skills is within the grasp of each of us. Indeed, it has taught us that people are "born to be wise."

Not "hardwired." Not "plug-and-play." But born to be wise in the sense that each of us has the capacity to develop moral skill of just the kind that wise judgment requires. We are born to be wise in a way that is similar to the way we are born to master language. We don't come into the world equipped with "English," but we *do* come into the world equipped to *learn* English, or Japanese, or any other language, with relative ease. Similarly, we are predisposed to organize the world into categories that appreciate subtlety and nuance. We are predisposed to be sensitive to context. We are predisposed to think with our hearts and feel with our heads. And we are predisposed to understand the needs and feelings of others. In effect, yes, Aristotle was right.

However, in the case of language, minimal experience is all it takes to turn a predisposition into full-blown mastery; the language of your culture sprouts like a weed. Developing the ability to make wise judgments is more fragile. It requires cultivation. A practically wise person needs to be able to perceive the complexities of context, to see the gray and the nuance, to appreciate both similarity and difference. It turns out that we are born with the capacity to do these things. The psychological tools for wise judgment come naturally to us. But it isn't easy to be wise; the tools must be nurtured by experience.

ORGANIZING EXPERIENCE: FUZZY, GRAY, AND DYNAMIC CATEGORIES

There is a rule for computing the area of a rectangle: length times height. No problem. When should that rule be applied? Again, no problem. It should be applied to all rectangles, and we can specify exactly what makes a geometric form a rectangle: four sides, joined by right angles. When we encounter a geometric shape, it either is or is not a rectangle. If it is, we apply the rule. If it isn't, another approach is required. We can say, more technically, that the definition of a rectangle includes necessary and sufficient features so that we can always know whether a geometric shape belongs to the class or not. Not only that, but every rectangle is as much a rectangle as any other.

Now consider the sentencing rule for armed robbery, or the principle of telling the truth to patients. The central concepts or categories in these rules and principles—"armed" robbery, "truth," and "lie"—are not like rectangles. Whatever these words mean, they do not mean the same thing in every situation. They should not always be applied in the same way. And the same is true for the categories underlying all moral rules and principles—concepts like respect, harm, contracts, kindness, fair wages or living wages, patience, loyalty, and so on. All these categories are "fuzzy" because the issues they involve are fuzzy. So the moral rules that depend on these concepts—tell the truth to your patients, be honest and kind with your friends—can never be like the rule for computing the area of a rectangle because it's not clear what the moral rectangle is. Instead of a clear, unambiguous, yes-or-no relationship between the core categories in a rule and the circumstances in which we consider using it, we find a "more-or-less" relationship, a *graded* relationship. Michael's case is an armed robbery in certain ways but not in others. Not telling the patient he has cancer unless he asks directly is a lie of one kind but not of another kind.

Distinguishing among different kinds of robberies or lies is critical for making wise choices, but how can we do it if these concepts and issues are so fuzzy? It might seem at first that this fuzziness is a problem characteristic of abstract or moral categories. If only the categories were more concrete or tangible, like "fruit"—or "birds"—we could be clear about what was in the category or what wasn't. But these categories are not as concrete or tangible as they first appear, and the same mental capacity we have for dealing with these everyday categories enables us to deal with moral categories too.

Fuzziness is a feature of most of the categories we use. "Fruit," for example, is less like "rectangle" than we might think. Though biologists might be able to provide a rectangle-like definition of fruit (the seed-carrying part of a plant), that's not the one that most of us carry around in our heads. Instead, we think of fruits as edible parts of plants, usually juicy, and often sweet. Not only that, but some fruits are "fruitier"—more typical—than others. If we asked you what comes to mind as an example of fruit, you'd probably say an apple or a pear or an orange. These are typical fruits. You certainly wouldn't say kumquat or persimmon or pomegranate. The category "fruit" has a set of core examples, or core features. No one of these features "defines" fruit, but the more critical features an example has, the better an example of fruit it is. Some fruits are great examples; other fruits are less good examples. And there are some non-fruits (avocados, for example) that are "almost fruits." We often call these core examples "prototypes," and the capacity we have to use prototypes is very important in allowing us to appreciate the nuance and complexity in everything from fruits to lies.

We now know quite a bit about our extraordinary capacity to categorize our fuzzy world. A century ago, the philosopher Ludwig Wittgenstein made the important argument that most of our everyday categories are like "fruit" and "truth" and decidedly not like "rectangle." These everyday categories have come to be called "natural categories," to distinguish them from more formal, precisely defined categories like "rectangle." More than thirty years ago, psychologist Eleanor Rosch started subjecting such natural categories to psychological research. Over the years, much has been learned about the structure of natural categories. We know now that the mind has a tremendous capacity to deal with categories like these, a capacity that can serve us well in enabling the kind of perception and judgment that practical wisdom demands.

Some of what we know is this:

1. When people are asked to list examples of things like fruit or furniture or games, there is broad agreement about the pro- totypical examples, but much less agreement about more pe- ripheral examples (e.g., everyone names apples, most people name bananas, many people name raspberries, and few peo- ple name persimmons).

2. When people are given a list of fruits (or furniture or games) and asked to rate how good each is as an example of the cat- egory, again there is agreement. Apples get high scores and kumquats get low ones.

3. When people are asked to push a button as fast as possible to indicate whether sentences like "An apple is a fruit" are true or false, they respond much faster when the example is a good one, like "apple," than when it is a bad one.

Findings like these show that the structure of these natural categories is very different from that of formal categories like "rectangle." They have "graded" membership—that is, there are degrees of "fruitiness." They also have fuzzy boundaries. At the boundaries, people might dis- agree about whether something is a fruit or a lie. But our capacity to make distinctions by degree, to know whether something falls in one category or another, is essential for us in organizing our world and mak- ing choices. Also, both the structure of a category and its boundaries can change. Kiwis were once a very bad example of a fruit; as they have become more common in American groceries and restaurants, they have become a pretty good one.

A celebrated example of the importance of such natural categories is Wittgenstein's discussion of a "game." If asked to define "game," you

might start with an example—say, tag. Tag is usually played by children, has rules, is engaged in for fun, has multiple players, is competitive, and is engaged in during periods of leisure. This is a good start on
a definition. But what about the Olympic Games? They are dead serious and the players are adults. What about solitaire or video games,
played alone? What about professional sports? The problem here isn't
that you started with the wrong example. No matter what example you
started with, there would be lots of "games" that did not share all the
relevant features of your start-off example. But the category "game"
allows us to organize and understand a complex set of activities in a way
that no definition would allow.

There is great variety to the organization of natural categories.
Sometimes they are organized by physical features, sometimes by function, and sometimes, even, by a causal theory that lurks beneath the
instances. Consider: You spill cranberry juice on a white tablecloth. Your
friend suggests that you pour salt on it. "It works with wine," she says.
Or you can't get your lawn mower to start. You go into the house, turn
on the ball game, and chill out for a while. Why? Because sometimes
you can't get your car started because you've flooded your engine with
gas, and if you wait a little bit for some of the gas to evaporate, your
engine will start. In each of these cases, you are putting very different
things (wine and cranberry juice; cars and lawn mowers) into the same
category. And your reason for doing so is that you have a hunch about
causality. Whatever it is, chemically, that allows salt to get red wine out
of a tablecloth may also work with dark-colored juice. And perhaps all
internal combustion engines can be flooded, and when that happens,
letting gas evaporate will solve the problem. You're using analogical
thinking to connect red wine and juice—lawn mowers and cars—into
common classes. For purposes of stain removal, wine and cranberry
juice are part of the same category. If salt works, you may try to broaden
the category ("Does it have to be something made from fruit, or will salt
also get out grease stains?"). If it doesn't work, you'll narrow the category,

or broaden it in a different direction ("Maybe it's because of the alcohol. Will it work with beer?"). And putting wine and cranberry juice into a common class for *this* purpose doesn't mean you'll treat them as interchangeable for other purposes. You won't ask a six-year-old if he wants apple juice, cranberry juice, or wine with his dinner, nor will you make coq au vin with cranberry juice.

We also categorize items based on their history. Imagine encountering a piece of fruit that seems to be a lemon. It has the right shape, the right smell, the right color, and the right texture. "It's a lemon," you think. But then we paint it with red nail polish, we coat it with ammonia, and we squash it flat. Is it still a lemon? Of course it is. It's just a lemon that has been abused. But note that it is no longer similar in any obvious ways to other members of the category. What makes it a lemon is a narrative we construct about how it started and how it came to be the way it is now. Or consider a fake $20 bill that you have just seen come off your friend's color laser printer. It's a perfect replica, to your eyes, of a real $20. It looks right, it feels right, it even smells right. So is it a $20 bill? Of course not. It's a fake $20 bill.

In addition to being fuzzy and gray, categories change as our experience changes. If we encounter lots of modern chairs, we may change the prototype, or add these chairs to our set of examples, or extract from them important features that many modern chairs share, adding them to our feature list and thus revising our category of chair. And perhaps more significant, we can create categories pretty much on the fly. "Things to do on a rainy Sunday," "foods to eat on a diet," "ways to amuse a four-year-old who is sick in bed with the flu," "things to carry out of your house in case of a fire"—these are all "categories" that may not exist until the relevant circumstances arise. But when those circumstances do arise, we have little trouble creating such categories. This nimbleness and creativity in our conceptual organization is just like the improvisation of the jazz musician. The sax player has the notes on the page, and probably has some ideas about what his next solo will be like, but then the piano player's solo changes everything, creating new possibilities. The sax solo gets formed in the moment—the jazz musician's version of the set of things to take out of the house in case of a fire.

Without nimble, graded categories like these, Judge Forer would have been forced to adhere to sentencing guidelines in Michael's case. Does a toy gun make a robbery "armed"? It probably never occurred to Judge Forer to ask this question until Michael's case came before her. Is withholding part of the truth a lie? Without an appreciation of the fuzziness of truth and lie, Dr. Lowenstein would have had no choice but to tell his elderly patient he had cancer.

THE ILLUSORY SIMPLICITY OF "SIMILARITY"

Whatever way a category is organized, when we encounter a new thing and ask ourselves what category it belongs to, what we have to determine is whether or not it is similar enough to the core to belong in the category. This is true of fruit, games, and furniture, and it is true of honesty, fairness, and respect.

Judgment of similarity seems straightforward, but it isn't. All objects are similar in many, many ways. Take a plum and a lawn mower. They are both found on earth, they both weigh less than a ton, they can both be dropped, they both cost less than $1,000, they are both bigger than a grape. And obviously, they are also different in many, many ways. Whether they are similar or different in ways that matter depends on why we are making a judgment and on what else is around for these two items to be compared with.

Most of the time, in real life, it will be pretty obvious what the "ways that matter" are, as anyone who has tried to cut grass with a plum discovers. But this depends on our knowledge and experience in the world and on the context and the purpose of our categorization.

Think about the desire of a third-grade teacher to treat his students "fairly." Does this mean treat every child *exactly* the same? Even if you think that's what it means, you still have to determine what "same" means. Does it mean use exactly the same words? The same tone of voice? No, it presumably means treat all children the same in the ways that matter. But what are the ways that matter? Or suppose you think that fair treatment means not treating every child the same, but treating like cases alike. Again, since all "cases" are alike in some respects and different in some respects, treating like cases alike means "alike in the ways that matter." But how do we figure out which ways "matter"? Differences in levels of attainment in the classroom will matter for some purposes but not others (e.g., all kids should be expected to be respectful, but they should not all be given the same lists of spelling words). Our capacity to recognize similarity *and* difference helps us to figure out which ways matter. If our minds weren't organized in this way, wise judgments would not be possible.

Consider "truth" and "lies." Dr. Lowenstein tells a lie. But for him to decide whether and how to tell a lie, and what kind, he first needs to recognize what counts as the "truth" and what counts as a "lie" and how to categorize what he is doing. His capacity to recognize a prototypical lie and to see the similarities and differences among different kinds of lies is critical. What counts as a "lie" or the "truth"?

"I have a million papers to grade."

"The average life expectancy with your condition is two years, but statistics don't tell us anything about individual cases."

"You look great in that dress!"

"You did a fine job on that assignment."

"Two objects dropped from the same height will hit the ground at the same time."

"I did not have sex with that woman."

Which of the six statements above are lies?

The first statement is an exaggeration. The speaker's intent is to communicate that she has a lot of work to do. Is an exaggeration a lie?

The second statement is a distortion. Statistics *can* tell us something about individual cases. If the average life expectancy of someone with your condition were fifteen years, you'd have good reason to walk out of the office feeling a lot better than if it were fifteen months. What the doctor was trying to do with his comment was communicate two things: first, averages do not *determine* your fate, because there is variability; second, don't give up. Was this distortion a lie?

The third statement, made even when you think your friend doesn't look so good in her dress, is a lie in that it is contrary to what you actually believe and is intended to deceive. But it isn't intended to harm; it's intended to aid and comfort. Is a "white lie" like this still a lie? Does a moral rule about always telling the truth extend to white lies?

The fourth statement is incomplete: what the teacher really thinks is "You did a fine job on that assignment (for you, a pretty mediocre student who has been struggling all semester)." Does withholding part of the truth count as a lie?

And what about gravity? Is oversimplification a lie? Are we supposed to tell fourth-graders the whole complicated story of what determines how objects fall to the ground? If oversimplification is a lie, then every teacher, at every level, spends most of every day lying through his teeth.

Finally, in the sixth statement, we come to a bona fide, prototypical lie (though even here, it depends on how you define "sex"). Someone who has transgressed is trying to deceive—not for the sake of others, but to protect his status and reputation. But what should be clear is that not all "lies" are created equal, and if we tried to create a rigorous definition of "lie" (as rigorous as the definition of a rectangle, specifying necessary and sufficient conditions), its lack of nuance and context sensitivity would make it close to useless when we're trying to judge the moral status of what others do, or when we're trying to figure out what to do ourselves. What we need is not a black-and-white definition of "lie," but a natural category, with some clear examples at the heart of our understanding, with less clear examples at the periphery, and with fuzzy boundaries between lies, incomplete truths, exaggerations, oversimplifications, kind distortions, jokes, and plain old mistakes. "Lie" as a natural category serves us well. "Lie" as a precise category does not.

Our capacity to categorize ordinary objects and activities ("fruit" and "games") into categories that reflect an appreciation of nuance, and can change as a function of our experience and our purposes, is just the kind of capacity we need to categorize morally significant concepts like "fair" and "lie." Our ability to categorize like this gives us the potential to be practically wise. It enables wise judgment. But it's no guarantee. The actual shape and content of specific categories get filled out by experience, and people with the wrong kind of experience may end up with categories—and decisions—that are profoundly unwise.

FRAMING AND BEING FRAMED

Psychologists sometimes use the word *frame* to acknowledge the importance of context to the categories we use and the judgments we make. "Frame" is a wonderful metaphor because it emphasizes our capacity to take the chaos of the social world around us and organize it in an understandable way. In framing the scene, we are setting the picture off from its surroundings, excluding what is on the outside and defining what is inside as special and worthy of attention. Frames tell us what is important and help us establish what should be compared with what. The capacity we have to frame enables us to do one of the most important things that practical wisdom demands—discern what is relevant about a particular context or event in regard to the decision we face. Learning to frame well helps make us wise.

Recent research underscores the big impact frames have on the judgments we make and the actions we take. For example, in one series of studies, participants played a version of the famous "prisoners' dilemma" game. The prisoners' dilemma game is structured so that the two players do better if both cooperate than if both defect, but each does best if the other player cooperates and they defect. When the game is played, the players are anonymous, and even if they are allowed to communicate, there is no way for them to enforce agreements to cooperate. The game is of great interest to social scientists because it seems to embody many situations in life in which cooperation would make everyone better off, but choosing to cooperate makes you vulnerable to exploitation by a defector. For example, in the arms race between the United States and the Soviet Union, both nations would have been better off "cooperating" and disarming than "defecting" and continuing to spend billions on weapons that merely kept them even with each other. The problem was that if either nation disarmed (cooperated) unilaterally, it would be vulnerable to exploitation and domination by its defecting adversary.

In the study, all participants played the same game, but for some, it was framed as the "Wall Street Game," whereas for others, it was framed as the "Community Game." What a difference a "frame" makes. Participants were much more likely to defect during the "Wall Street Game" than during the "Community Game." A similar study was labeled the "Business Transaction Study" for some and the "Social Exchange Study" for others. More cooperation occurred in the second case than in the first. The "Social Exchange" frame, the researchers suggest, induced a motivation for the players to do what was right; the "Business Transaction" frame induced the motivation to get as much money from playing the game as they could.

"Framing" has gotten a bad name. In a marketing context, it is characterized as an effort to manipulate us into buying things we don't need. In a political context, it is labeled as "spin" and characterized as an effort to slant or distort the truth in the direction of our favored position. And evidence that we depend on the frame, or context of comparison, for making judgments is sometimes regarded as a defect of human reason. We should be able to see and evaluate things as they "really" are, unbiased by the way they are packaged. But in fact, it is our capacity to frame that enables all our judgments, and it is nearly impossible to make judgments that do not depend on frames. Consider: Are eagles large? Are cabins small? The answer to these questions seems obvious. But why? Because we are implicitly comparing eagles with other birds and cabins with other dwellings. But suppose we compared them with each other? Now the eagle would be small and the cabin would be large. When we make the snap judgment that eagles are large, we don't consciously appreciate that we're comparing eagles with other birds and not with buildings. But it is only our capacity to do this automatic framing that enables us to make sensible judgments at all.

Framing is pervasive, inevitable, and often automatic. There is no "neutral," frame-free way to evaluate anything. Consider this example. College students were asked whether they would support a multimillion-dollar airline safety measure that would save the lives of 150 people who would be at risk. Is 150 lives a lot or a little? Well, compared with what? Other students were asked whether they would support a safety measure that would save 98 percent of the 150 lives at risk. These students were *more* favorable toward it than the students who were told it would save 150 lives. Obviously, saving 150 lives is better than saving 98 percent of 150 lives, but a measure that saves 98 percent of the lives at risk seems clearly cost-effective. The 98 percent figure provides the students with a frame, a context of comparison, that 150 lives by itself does not. Are we supposed to compare the 150 lives saved with the number of people who would be saved by eliminating famine and childhood diarrhea in the developing world? Or with the number of people saved by requiring

circuit breakers in bathroom electrical fixtures? Whether the money
spent on airline safety is seen as a wise decision or not will depend on the
context of comparison. When people are told that an airline safety measure will save 98 percent of 150 lives, a frame is created in which the only
comparison that needs to be made is between 150 lives and 98 percent of
150 lives.

Thus our task when we make decisions is not to avoid being influenced by frames, but to choose the *right* frames—frames that help us to
evaluate all that is relevant. And judging what is the right frame will
depend on the purposes of our evaluation and impending decision. A
striking example of the framing problem was described by Michael
Pollan, Berkeley professor and bestselling author, in an article that asks us
to consider the "true" cost of a pound of beef. We know what we pay for
it in the market, but is that a broad-enough frame for assessing its cost?
Pollan details the other costs—what economists call "externalities"—
that are not reflected in the market price. The taxes we pay subsidize the
corn that cattle are fed, making it artificially cheaper for farmers than
feeding cattle grass. Another hidden price is the cost to our health: corn-
fed beef is fattier than grass-fed beef and the *kind* of fat is worse for
human health. Another hidden price is the dependence on petrochemicals that go into the fertilizers to grow the corn. If the "cost" of beef were
framed with the aim of evaluating the cost to our overall well-being, it
would have to include the tax subsidies and the costs of cardiovascular
disease—treatment, mortality and morbidity, workdays lost, and de-
creases in quality of life. And it would have to include some fraction of
the cost—in money and in lives—of a foreign policy that is partly driven
by the need for reliable access to petrochemicals. The supermarket price
puts all these other considerations outside its narrow frame. Pollan's
frame turns our grocery shopping into a matter of public health and geo-
politics. There is no neutral frame. Both frames are making us sensitive
to the context of our choices, but each aims at making us aware (or un-
aware) of different things. Both frames affect our judgment.

Our predisposition to put frames around the things we are considering helps us to appreciate the importance of context to decisions. The predisposition to impose frames, like our ability to categorize, enables wise decisions, but it is no guarantee of them. Whether we frame wisely or not will depend on the experiences we have. There will be occasions when we frame too broadly, or too narrowly, or otherwise inappropriately, and we will learn by experience the error of our ways. If we get feedback about our mistakes, and are attentive to it, our framing will grow more perspicacious. So, too, will our ability to choose frames that enable the people we serve to make wise decisions. Think about the different results that lawyer William Simon and his friend had in traffic court when they framed Mrs. Jones's options for her. The order and emphasis with which Simon presented the options to Mrs. Jones framed the problem as a justice problem. His friend, with more experience in traffic court, took the same "facts" and reframed the problem as "avoiding jail." If Mrs. Jones ought to be deciding for herself, wouldn't it be better if neither lawyer influenced her with the frame used? Wouldn't it be better if they presented the facts to her in a neutral way? That would maximize her autonomy and let her truly decide what best served her interests. But as we've said, there is no neutral. No matter what they said, their tone of voice, their body language, the order in which they put the facts and how they emphasized them would have framed the issue for her. What Simon and his colleague could have done if they were wiser counselors was to enable Mrs. Jones to frame the situation better by helping her reflect more calmly about her interests and beliefs and about the consequences of each option given the particulars of her life.

We might wish to see things "as they *really* are," but there is no way that things "really are," at least not in the complex and chaotic social world we inhabit. Neither Mrs. Jones, nor her lawyers, nor the judge, nor the prosecutor could make the choices they faced without a way to frame the context. It is our capacity to frame that at least provides the possibility of choosing wisely.

FRAMING WITH NARRATIVES

Stephen Covey, a management expert, was riding the New York subways on a quiet Sunday morning:

> Then, suddenly, a man and his children entered the subway car. The children were so loud and rambunctious that instantly the whole climate changed.
>
> The man sat down next to me and closed his eyes, apparently oblivious to the situation. The children were yelling back and forth, throwing things, even grabbing people's papers. It was very disturbing. And yet, the man sitting next to me did nothing.
>
> It was difficult not to feel irritated. . . . So finally, . . . I turned to him and said, "Sir, your children are really disturbing a lot of people. I wonder if you couldn't control them a little more?"
>
> The man lifted his gaze . . . and said softly, "Oh, you're right. I guess I should do something about it. We just came from the hospital where their mother died about an hour ago. I don't know what to think, and I guess they don't know how to handle it either."
>
> Suddenly, I *saw* things differently, and because I saw differently, I *thought* differently, I *felt* differently, I *behaved* differently. My irritation vanished. I didn't have to worry about controlling my attitude or my behavior; my heart was filled with the man's pain. Feelings of sympathy and compassion flowed freely. . . . Everything changed in an instant.

Covey initially acted on the basis of a story he told himself about the man on the subway: these children are running and screaming out of control because their father is irresponsible, uncaring, or oblivious. This was a reasonable story, a perfectly plausible frame. The father did not argue or reason with Covey. In fact, he seemed to accept that Covey was right. He apologized—by telling another story. The new story created a totally different context for Covey. He saw and evaluated the father and the children in a wholly different way. He had a different explanation. As a result, he empathized. Had he known this other story, he would have acted differently to begin with.

"We tell ourselves stories in order to live," said novelist and essayist Joan Didion. What she meant was that we understand our own lives as stories, as narratives, with narrative "arcs." Where we are in our own life story provides the context within which we evaluate relationships and experiences and make decisions. Job offers, illnesses, disagreements with friends or family—each of these will mean something different to us at different points in our lives. We can't understand ourselves as frozen in time. Self-understanding is a narrative construction.

Covey's story shows that the same is true of our understanding of others. Luke's response to the angry father depended on the story Luke told himself about how the father got to where he was. And Lois Forer's decision about how to sentence Michael depended on her story about him. Even judging whether the squashed, foul-smelling red thing in front of us is a lemon depends on the story we tell ourselves about how it came to be that way.

CONCLUSION

Natural categories, frames, and narratives: these are the tools we use to organize and interpret the world. We do it naturally. We do it effortlessly. And these tools are incredibly useful. They enable us to perceive the particularities of context that practical wisdom demands. The world is gray. Natural categories enable us to see gray. Judgments are almost always relative. Frames help us see relations. And isolated events or episodes occur in the context of ongoing lives being lived. Narratives enable us to appreciate lives as lived and make sense of the episode before us.

We learn how to categorize and frame—and recategorize and reframe—through our own experiences and by being around mentors who provide models and correct our mistakes. A young teacher, for example, might begin with the highly principled but rigid idea that fairness is treating all students the same. A young doctor may begin with a highly principled but rigid idea that honesty means telling patients the unvarnished truth as you best understand it, nothing held back. Then the teacher and the doctor both get "mugged" by experience. Given the context and what they are aiming at—the education of their students, the health of their patients—they discover that it just doesn't make sense to treat all students alike and that the unvarnished truth can be incredibly hurtful. They begin to develop more nuanced categories. Their experience treating students differently and "varnishing" the truth gives them a family of examples of fairness and honesty. These examples differentiate and enrich their categories. Wisdom is not automatic. It must be nurtured by experience. But experience has excellent raw materials to work with.

5.

Thinking with Feeling: The Value of Empathy

With all their ethics men would never have been anything but monsters if nature had not given them pity in support of reason. . . . It carries us without reflection to the aid of those whom we see suffer; in the state of nature, it takes the place of laws, morals, and virtue, with the advantage that no one is tempted to disobey its gentle voice. . . . Although it may behoove Socrates and minds of his stamp to acquire virtue through reason, the human race would have perished long ago if its preservation had depended only on the reasonings of its members.

—JEAN-JACQUES ROUSSEAU, 1754

Stephen Covey's encounter with the bereaved father on the subway has another important lesson. The father's narrative didn't just get Covey to *think* differently; it got him to *feel* differently. Indeed, it may be because Covey felt differently that he came to think differently.

The aim of good and fair rules is to encourage us to approach situations neutrally—to treat everyone the same, or to treat like cases alike. Thus, Rules Talk induces us to be wary of emotion. Emotion is so particular—so "in the moment"—that it endangers our ability to judge and decide impartially. Much medical training is designed to teach doctors to approach their patients' problems "objectively," with the cool eye of reason, and not to give in uncritically to the desperate wishes of people who are afraid and in pain. And lawyers are taught to help their clients see past their anger of the moment to what will actually serve their best interests.

This stance toward emotion is a kind of "official story." But our actual experiences tell us a different story. There is good reason to be careful of emotion, but a wise person depends on it. The father's story to Covey didn't substitute reason for emotion. It substituted one emotion for another, and this changed the way Covey felt and thought about the episode. In the last few decades, psychological research has taught us a good deal about how reason and emotion can be allies. It has provided some science to back up our everyday intuitions. We have learned about how emotion enables us to experience empathy. We have learned about how emotion contributes to our moral judgments. And we have learned about how emotion spurs us to act. Without thoughtful emotion, there would be no wise judgment or wise action.

EMPATHY: MAKING REASON AND EMOTION ALLIES

People we have already met in this book have demonstrated our need for empathy if we are to act wisely toward others. It was empathy that allowed Judge Forer to inhabit the frustration that moved Michael to use a toy gun to hold up a cabdriver and to understand the effect that jail time (versus probation) would have on him. Of course, Forer could have been mistaken; just because judgments are informed by empathy does not guarantee that they are correct. But without empathy, Forer's judgment could never have been made at all. Making choices about a friend, client, plaintiff, defendant, patient, or student demands knowing something about what this person thinks and feels, what motivates her, how she is likely to act or react. That means putting ourselves in that person's place.

Most of us think about empathy as a "feeling" or an "emotion." It is.

To be empathetic is to be able to feel what the other person is feeling. But empathy is more than just a feeling. In order to be able to feel what another person is feeling, you need to be able to see the world as that other person sees it. This ability to take the perspective of another demands perception and imagination. Empathy thus reflects the integration of thinking and feeling. It was the new "cognitive" frame—the new understanding—that the father's story created for Stephen Covey that enabled Covey to feel differently. He felt differently because he thought differently. And he thought differently because he felt differently. Forging the kind of alliance between reason and emotion that produces empathy is always a work in progress, but it is an achievement worth striving for.

Psychologists Martin Hoffman and Nancy Eisenberg have each written about the development of empathy in children. Seeing it manifested, imperfectly, in young children, gives a sense of just what an achievement real empathy is. For example, two-year-old Judy will feel badly when she sees two-year-old Becky crying, and she'll try to provide aid and comfort to Becky. What will she do? She'll take Becky's hand and walk her over to *Judy's* mother. You can almost see the wheels turning in Judy's little mind. "Becky is sad. When I'm sad, my mommy gives me a hug and makes me feel better. Maybe that's what Becky needs—a hug from *my* mommy." And developmental psychologist Alison Gopnik writes about how she burst into tears one day when she came home from work (the life of a not-yet-tenured college professor can be pretty stressful), and her two-year-old rushed to her aid—with a box of Band-Aids. As kids develop, their ability to take another person's perspective grows more sophisticated, and they can act more effectively to relieve the suffering of others. "What does she need?" is a very different question from "What would *I* need if I were in her position?" Genuine empathy requires that we not confuse the two questions and that we be able to answer the first one.

Development of genuine empathetic understanding is not automatic.

It depends on experience. But we seem to be predisposed to profit from the experience if we have it. Research on how empathy can be encouraged—or discouraged—in children gives us some clues to what the right kind of experience is. Parents can punish an older sibling for bullying her sister, but if they aim to nurture empathy they should accompany the punishment with a question like "How do you think your sister felt when you took her toy?" Questions like this encourage children to reflect on what they are thinking *and* what they are feeling, and also on what others are thinking and feeling. Children with responsive caregivers like this develop more empathy than children whose caregivers are strict disciplinarians who just lay down rules—even if the rules are good and humane ones. The best route to raising empathetic, morally sensitive children is to be a parent who explains, and who gives kids opportunities to make decisions themselves. Empathy can also be increased in school, but not by didactic education. Classrooms that emphasize community and foster concern for others increase empathy in children.

There is, as yet, no final and complete story about how empathy develops in children. But what *is* known about the importance of the right kind of experience in nurturing empathy in children provides important lessons if we are interested in nurturing empathy in adults. Adults, too, need the right kind of experience, and disciplined rule-following doesn't provide it.

EMOTION AND MORAL EVALUATION

Julie and Mark are a sister and a brother. They are traveling together in France on a summer vacation from college. One night they are staying alone in a cabin on the beach. They decide that it would be interesting and fun if they tried making love. At the very least it would be a new experience for both of them. Julie was already taking birth control pills, but Mark uses a condom too, just to be safe. They both enjoy making love, but they decide not to do it again. They keep that night as a special secret, which makes them feel even closer to each other. What do you think about it? Was it okay for them to make love?

When psychologist Jonathan Haidt asked this question to the people he surveyed, most people were appalled, and perhaps even disgusted. Of course it isn't okay for a brother and a sister to make love. The question is why—why did Haidt's respondents feel so strongly that what Julie and Mark did was wrong?

Haidt has suggested that the way most people tend to think about judgments like this is that the judgments begin with the intellect. Reason enables people to decide whether a given action was good or bad—right or wrong. Emotions kick in only after the evaluation is done. After all, how can a person feel disgust or contempt without first judging that an action was disgusting or contemptible? If judgments began with the intellect, then Haidt's respondents would have first searched for a relevant moral principle: "Close relatives should never have sexual relations" or "Incest is harmful and should always be avoided." And the proper emotion would have been the result of the moral evaluation. It is because incest is wrong that people will react to Mark and Julie with emotions like disgust, anger, horror, or contempt. First the rational evaluation, then the emotion. Emotion, in this model, is not so much an ally of reason as a spectator. Its proper place is not to interfere with the moral choice making.

But what Haidt found is that many moral evaluations are not made this way. There are times when rapid intuition bypasses reasoning altogether. What happens in these cases is that an evaluation just appears, instantly, along with the emotion—anger, outrage, disgust, regret, remorse, shame, guilt, or some other moral emotion. People may still be able to provide reasons to justify their evaluation, but the reasoning process, says Haidt, *follows* the evaluation rather than causing it. Haidt tells us that confronted by the story of incest, respondents feel a quick flash of revulsion and know intuitively that something is wrong. Then, if called upon to justify this belief, they act "like a lawyer, trying to build a case, rather than a judge, searching for the truth." They may not have any trouble making the case, but their arguments are post hoc.

And sometimes that may be a good thing. According to Haidt, moral intuitions are fast, nonconscious, and automatic. People have conscious access to the results of this automatic process, but not to the process itself (in the same way that people have access to the results of their color vision processes ["That's a red shirt"] without access to how color vision actually works). In contrast, the reasons provided to justify intuitions are slow, conscious, and volitional. This does not mean that reason and intuition don't speak with each other or can't work with each other. Haidt points out that people use reasons to win others over to their side. When people communicate their judgments to others, they don't just say things like "My gut tells me that incest is wrong." Why should I care what your gut tells you? Instead, people offer their reasons. And these reasons may provide frames for evaluation that help shape the intuitions of others.

The fact that people seem to have such moral intuitions and make fast, automatic judgments does not mean they always judge wisely. Intuitions may be self-serving. They may be distorting, like prejudiced racial stereotypes. But without the intuitive capacity that emotions help enable, the practical wisdom we need for daily judgments would simply be impossible. Luke could not have responded as quickly as he did to the angry father if he had had to go through a complex process of deliberation. Sometimes deliberation allows people to step back from the rapid flow of events and check or manage their intuitions, but frequently it is emotion that's in the driver's seat.

GETTING US TO ACT:
EMOTION AND MOTIVATION

Thinking needs feeling as an ally for another, critical reason. Practical wisdom is not simply knowing the right thing to do but actually being motivated to do it. And often it is emotion that propels us to act. This was evident when Luke confronted the angry father in the hospital. It was Luke's empathetic skills that enabled him to understand the father's perspective, but it was his compassion for the father and his son that got him to clean the room again. Emotion is, in this way, also a moral signal. It alerts us that something demands our attention, that something has gone wrong, that action is required.

We read an article in the newspaper about a famine that is starving three million children in sub-Saharan Africa. We shake our heads and turn the page. Then we see a TV documentary that explores the life of one such child and his family. Our check is in the mail. Why is it that a matter-of-fact account of the suffering of many spurs little while a vivid account of the suffering of one immediately gets us to do something? Psychologist Paul Slovic suggests that we are driven in situations like this by our emotional reactions to suffering. An explicitly identified single individual, with a face, a name, and a life story, elicits far more empathy and compassion than a number, no matter how big the number. And it is our empathy and compassion—our emotions—that compel us to act. In many studies, Slovic and his collaborators have shown that people are more willing to volunteer time, or contribute money, when they read, for example, a detailed account of a single flood victim than when they read a less vivid account of hundreds or thousands who have lost their homes. It seems logical that if one victim is worth a $5 contribution, then five hundred victims are worth a contribution that is many times larger. But instead, such accounts elicit smaller contributions, or no contributions at all.

The compassion aroused by seeing a single suffering victim is what gets us moving. Of course, we *could* be built so that the thought of three million arouses even more compassion. But we aren't. It's not that reason and thinking are unimportant. It's that the kind of reasoning that simply focuses on facts and figures does not trigger the moral emotions that motivate us to do something. And since practical wisdom is about action as well as judgment, we couldn't be practically wise without the emotion that impels us to act.

Large-scale suffering can be grasped intellectually but is close to unfathomable emotionally. Writer Annie Dillard captures the problem facetiously: "There are 1,198,500,000 people alive now in China. To get a feel for what that means, simply take yourself—in all your singularity, complexity, and love—and multiply by 1,198,500,000. See. Nothing to it." Dillard describes a conversation with her seven-year-old daughter about 138,000 people who drowned in Bangladesh in 1991. At dinner, she mentions to her daughter how hard it is to imagine 138,000 people drowning. "No, it's easy," says her daughter. "Lots and lots of dots in blue water."

But in fact, dots don't do the trick. Christopher Hsee and Yuval Rottenstreich did a study in which donations to "Save the Panda" were solicited. The study participants were told that a team of zoologists had found a number of pandas (one or four) in a remote part of Asia and they were soliciting donations for a rescue effort. The number of pandas at risk was represented either by big dots (one or four) on a board or by photos of a panda (one or four) on a board. People offered larger donations to save pictured pandas than dot-represented pandas. Dots may represent numbers, but they don't evoke emotion, and thus they are not very effective at triggering action.

In describing our lack of emotional response to numbers, Slovic observes that writers and artists have long recognized the power of narrative to bring feelings and meaning to tragedy. He quotes novelist Barbara Kingsolver:

> Confronted with knowledge of dozens of apparently random disasters each day, what can a human heart do but slam its doors? No mortal can grieve that much. We didn't evolve to cope with tragedy on a global scale. Our defense is to pretend there's no thread of event that connects us, and that those lives are somehow not precious and real like our own. It's a practical strategy . . . but the loss of empathy is also a loss of humanity, and that's no small tradeoff.
>
> Art is the antidote that can call us back from the edge of numbness, restoring the ability to feel for another.

Art, or personal contact—with a distraught father keeping vigil in a hospital, a despairing young man worrying about how to provide for his family as he enters a taxicab, a wife who is desperately concerned about how her husband will respond to a bleak medical report—as long as we keep ourselves open to feeling for the people we face every day.

Slovic's argument about the importance of emotion to action is supported by the research of neurologist Antonio Damasio. Damasio studies the psychological consequences of various kinds of brain injury. He presented a group of brain-injured patients with the kinds of standard, scripted moral dilemmas often presented in ethics texts—whether it's right to lie or steal or cheat or take another's life in a particular set of circumstances. He found that the patients' responses were indistinguishable from the responses of normal people. They had no trouble reasoning about right and wrong. That is, they had normal moral competence.

But something crucial was missing. When these patients were shown photos that arouse strong emotion in people with intact brains (nudity, mutilation, people dying), they *knew* that what they were seeing was exciting or horrible. But they *felt* nothing. Damasio found that this kind of brain injury leaves basic memory, intelligence, and the capacity for rational thinking intact but disconnects these cognitive processes from emotion. It severs the capacity for reason and emotion to be allies. People with what seems to be normal moral competence lack the circuitry that allows this knowledge to be bathed with emotion so that it guides action.

Damasio found that patients like this are virtually incapable of making any decisions and taking any actions at all. Elliot, one of Damasio's early patients, seemed totally normal on personality and intelligence tests. But he couldn't follow a schedule and even had a hard time motivating himself to get dressed in the morning. Damasio never observed a tinge of emotion in Elliot—"no sadness, no impatience, no frustration with my incessant and repetitive questioning." "The machinery for his decision making," said Damasio, "was so flawed that he could no longer be an effective social being. In spite of being confronted with the disastrous results of his decisions, he did not learn from his mistakes." The emotions, argued Damasio, act as "practical action programs that work to solve a problem, often before we're conscious of it. These processes are at work continually, in pilots, leaders of (military) expeditions, parents, all of us."

The reason that the disconnection of thinking from feeling is so debilitating, Damasio thinks, is that in the ordinary course of development, the situations that induce us to act also produce emotions, and over time these emotions serve as action triggers. In the brain-injured people Damasio studied, with the emotional trigger disconnected from the rational "bullets," no shots got fired.

In Damasio's patients, it was brain damage that disconnected emotion and inhibited empathy, moral action, and often any action at all. But it is not just brain damage that can have this effect. Social psychologists J. M. Darley and C. D. Batson did a study of students at a theological seminary who were told they would have to give a brief lecture on the parable of the Good Samaritan who stops on the road to help a robbery victim after both a priest and a Levite have passed the man by. The lecture was to occur in another building, and some of the seminarians were told they were late and had to hurry. As they rushed off, they passed a man slumped in an alleyway with his head down and his eyes closed. Only 10 percent stopped to help. Other seminarians were told that they had some time before the lecture. Now, 63 percent stopped to help. Nobody would argue that the first group of seminarian-Samaritans did not have the disposition or the capacity to help. But they had other dispositions as well—fear of embarrassment at being late, perhaps. Being put in a situation of great time pressure discouraged the disposition to help, perhaps by reducing the attention they paid to the man slumped on the ground, and thus reducing the empathetic concern he would otherwise have aroused.

CONCLUSION

Having the emotional capacity for experiencing empathy doesn't mean we'll use it. People can be put in institutional settings—like the one that created time pressure for the seminarians—that can discourage emotions like empathy and encourage other emotions like fear, embarrassment, and anxiety about pleasing superiors. If the routines of work systematically discourage people from experiencing and using an emotion like empathy—and encourage countervailing emotions instead—there is a danger that our capacity for practical wisdom will be undermined. People won't develop the disposition or the moral skill to perceive the thoughts and feelings of others. This will prevent them from discerning what needs to be done and drain them of the motivation to do it.

It does not have to be this way. Rules Talk has set reason and emotion apart in ways that discourage us from imagining how the heart can be educated by the mind. But research on *emotional intelligence* (a term coined by psychologists Peter Salovey and John D. Mayer and popularized by writer Daniel Goleman) suggests that this can be done. People can learn to be emotionally intelligent. They can learn to be perceptive: to detect the emotions of others, or themselves, in a word, a tone of voice, a glance. They can learn to harness their emotions, as Luke did, in the service of their goals and responsibilities. They can learn to appreciate the subtle differences among emotions—between being happy and being overjoyed, between anger at unfairness and anger at selfishness. And they can learn to regulate emotions—both in themselves and in others—to rein in their anger if they think they're overreacting, or to stimulate it if they think they're not outraged enough. They don't learn these things by following rules or rigid scripts. The alliance between reason and emotion that makes practical wisdom possible develops as we try to discern what is going on in others, or in ourselves, sometimes get it wrong, and then have our judgments refined by our experience. We need experiences that encourage us to do this.

6.

Learning from Experience: The Machinery of Wisdom

Luke, Judge Forer, Stephen Covey, and most of the other wise actors we've discussed thus far were responsive to the particulars of the situations they encountered. They asked: "How are this person and this situation before me like others I have faced? How are they different? And what matters here: the similarity to previous cases or the differences?" As we said when we discussed natural categories, everything is alike *and* everything is different. Because we can find similarities and differences in any two situations, identifying whether it's the similarity or the difference that's important, and also *which* similarity or difference is important, is crucial if we're going to figure out the right thing to do. How do we do it? How do we recognize what is crucial in the barrage of information we face? Obviously, we learn from experience, but the latest research on how the mind and brain work has taught us a lot about *how* we learn and *what* exactly we learn. This understanding, in turn, helps us explain our ability to make wise decisions.

In recent years cognitive scientists—both cognitive psychologists and neuroscientists—have focused a lot of study on how and what people learn from experience. These scientists have not studied wisdom but rather more basic psychological processes. In this chapter we will take what they *have* studied and apply it to wisdom. Our aim is to make a plausible, though speculative, case that human beings have just the cognitive and neural machinery they need to be practically wise.

PATTERN RECOGNITION: UNSEEN AND OMNIPRESENT

The world we inhabit is incredibly complex. There are always millions of things going on at once. The father of psychology, William James, called it a "blooming, buzzing, confusion." But it doesn't seem that way to us. We make order out of the chaos by coming to recognize patterns. We all engage in pattern recognition every day, usually without realizing we're doing it. When you're driving, and you see a sign up ahead, you don't ask yourself, "What shape is it?" and answer "Um, octagon!" You don't ask, "What color is it?" and answer "Red!" You simply recognize that it's a stop sign. When you're in an elevator, with Muzak playing in the background, you don't ask yourself what song is on, and answer "Beatles song 'Yellow Submarine.'" You simply recognize the pattern. This is how most of our perceptual processes work: mechanisms for pattern recognition are operating all the time while our conscious mind is doing other things. These mechanisms deliver answers ("stop sign," "Beatles song") to questions we don't even know we're asking. We have conscious access to answers they provide, but not to the processes by which we arrive at those answers.

Moreover, though we come into the world with the machinery that enables us eventually to perform instant and automatic recognition of a stop sign, we certainly aren't born with the "stop sign" template lodged in our brains. What counts as a pattern worth recognizing depends on our experience. Thus, for instance, while *we* might see smoke and fire, feel heat, hear a roar and sirens and people screaming in a chaotic scene that seems anything but patterned, an experienced firefighter sees "electrical fire" or "grease fire" or "controlled and contained fire" or "fire that needs more firefighters on the scene."

Malcolm Gladwell, in his book *Blink*, provides several vivid examples of such rapid, automatic pattern recognition in action. There is the case of psychologist Paul Ekman, who after a career spent studying the facial expression of emotion, can now "read people's minds" at a glance. And there is the case of psychologist John Gottman, who for thirty years has been studying married couples, looking for predictors of marital success and failure. Gottman's experience has his "marital discord detectors" so well tuned that he can spot a marriage in trouble after watching a couple talk for just a few minutes, even about a relatively unimportant subject.

There is a lot going on in a face from moment to moment, just as there is a lot going on when a married couple interacts. But after years of studying videotapes of the facial expression of emotions, Ekman has learned to look at features of facial expression that are the product of involuntary muscle movements that can't be faked—the same thing poker players look for ("tells") when they try to read their opponents. And after years of careful study of videotapes of couples interacting, Gottman has learned to look for telltale expressions of contempt. At this point, neither Ekman nor Gottman needs a videotape, multiple viewings, and careful analysis to come to the right conclusions. They can do it on the fly. They see lying, anger, fear, and contempt. What they are recognizing are patterns, and after years of experience, the patterns just jump out at them.

All these examples of pattern recognition have important things in common. They are rapid. They are automatic (probably the only way Ekman could avoid doing his "mind reading" is by closing his eyes). And they are the product of substantial experience—of expertise. They involve the same sort of pattern recognition that enables us to perceive stop signs and Beatles songs, only the situations these experts are perceiving are more complex. This is how perception works.

It may also be how moral perception works—of whether the situation and people we face require honesty or kindness, courage or caution, loyalty or abandonment, empathy or detachment. Like Ekman, wise people are also mind readers. And heart readers too.

When we recognize a pattern, some part of our mental apparatus detects that we've encountered it, or something like it, before (to "recognize" is to "re-cognize"). The teacher recognizes that this child needs a mix of kindness and sternness just like that girl from two years ago. At the same time, we recognize that this pattern is not *identical* to the one we encountered before. The lawyer recognizes that *this* client needs to be told how to proceed with the divorce and child-custody negotiations, unlike the client he saw yesterday morning, who needed to make the decision for herself. We use templates that come from experience, and we use those templates to tell us how the present is like, and unlike, the past.

Though it seems natural to the point of being mundane, the ability to recognize similarity and do it quickly is really quite extraordinary. No two students and no two clients are exactly alike. Even stop signs differ from one another (some have dents in them, some have faded or chipped paint, some catch the light through the trees in an unusual way). Each experience we have is in some respects unique, if for no other reason than *we've* likely changed since the last time. At the same time, each experience we have is in some ways like past experiences. As Greek philosopher Heraclitus put it, "Just as the river where I step is not the same, and is, so I am as I am not." All things are alike and different. The task we face is to be sensitive to both similarity and difference, and to appreciate when what matters most is similarity and when what matters most is difference.

Imagine an oncologist trying to figure out how best to give a patient bad news. The patient is a young lawyer who is usually energetic, upbeat, and eager to take on the next new challenge. The doctor has had experience with patients like this and has found it best to be direct. But this patient is not like many of the doctor's previous patients in that he has no significant other and his family lives across the country. Perhaps, like most people, he'll need support when he hears the news. But support isn't at hand. Alike and different. Perhaps, with this patient, being direct is not such a good idea.

No knowledge would be possible without an appreciation of how the case before us is like past cases. But wise decisions would not be possible without an appreciation that the present case is not *exactly* like past cases. That's what Aristotle meant when he said that practical wisdom as opposed to a universal rule was necessary because of the priority of the particular. A wise person knows how to do the right thing, in the right way, with *this* person, in *this* situation. To be wise, we need cognitive and perceptual machinery that picks up on similarities without being blind to differences.

PATTERNS AND RULES

When we recognize patterns, our ability to see similarities and differences often exceeds our ability to describe them in words. "She looks just like her sister," we say. But of course we don't really mean "just like." We can tell the two sisters apart. Nonetheless we may be hard-pressed to say exactly how they look alike and what makes them look different. Similarly, we can see, from facial expression or body language, that our friend is angry, without being able to specify exactly what the tip-off is. The fact that many of the patterns we recognize are not easily captured in language has important implications when it comes to thinking about moral rules as guides to conduct. Rules are linguistic entities: "Tell the truth," "Help people in need," "Be loyal to your friends and family." If we rely on rules to tell us what to do, then we shut ourselves off from information and understanding we may have that cannot be put into words. And doing that may deprive us of the opportunity to make far more nuanced judgments than any rules would allow.

Even worse, reliance on rules or, more generally, on aspects of a situation that we can describe with words may distort our judgment. Psychologists Jonathan Schooler and Timothy Wilson did a study in which college students were asked to rate the quality of a number of different strawberry jams. Their judgments lined up very well with the judgments of experts. But another group of students was given the same task, except that they had to enumerate the reasons for their taste ratings—they had to justify their ratings in words. The correlation between the student judgments and the expert judgments vanished. The reason for this, Schooler and Wilson suggest, is that the features of a taste experience that are most important to us may not be easy to verbalize, and the features that are easy to verbalize may not be that important. In cases like this, when you ask people to give their reasons, you induce them to pay attention to the wrong things—perhaps, in this instance, scrutinizing jam labels to figure out what makes one jam "good" and another "bad." Wilson and several colleagues found similar results when college romantic couples were asked about the quality of their relationship and its likely future trajectory. Those who were asked to give reasons for their current assessments were less accurate in predicting the status of the relationship six months later than those not asked to give reasons. When words are your tools for evaluation, then you try to cram everything you are experiencing into a verbal format. When words, in the form of rules, are your tools for moral evaluation and decision making, then you limit your consideration to aspects of the situation that the rule speaks to. If all you have is a hammer, everything is a nail. Words are good—even essential—for many of the challenges we face in our lives. But they are not always friends of pattern recognition. And they are not always friends of wisdom.

Neuropsychologist Elkhonon Goldberg has written about the power and importance of pattern recognition in *The Wisdom Paradox*. Goldberg's focus is on how the brain and mental function change as we age. The straight news isn't good: brain cells die, memory gets worse, mental operations become slower and more effortful, we tire out more quickly. It seems as though the story of our mental life is a saga of slow and inexorable decline, starting in our early twenties. But no. Goldberg argues that even though our raw materials have ever-diminishing capacity, our experience in the world is making us ever better at recognizing patterns. The mature mind and brain can make good decisions with much less effort than the inexperienced mind and brain. The result, Goldberg suggests, is that we do more with less. A rich ability to recognize patterns, shaped by experience, makes us wiser. We may have more trouble recalling the names of our neighbors' kids, but we'll have less trouble figuring out how to talk to our neighbors about them.

In thinking about how his own mental processes have changed over time, Goldberg says:

Something rather intriguing has happened in my mind that did not happen in the past. Frequently, when I am faced with what would appear from the outside to be a challenging problem, the grinding mental computation is somehow circumvented, rendered, as if by magic, unnecessary. The solution comes effortlessly, seamlessly, seemingly by itself. What I have lost with age in my capacity for hard mental work, I seem to have gained in my capacity for instantaneous, almost unfairly easy insight.

What's going on as the mind and brain grow wiser? What does experience do to enable us to detect patterns and do it quickly? How can we simultaneously appreciate that the present is like the past, and also different from the past? Recent developments in cognitive science may begin to give us answers to these questions.

COGNITIVE NETWORKS
AND PATTERN RECOGNITION

The way you learn good judgment, Will Rogers reminded us, is experience. And most of that experience is bad judgment. Developing practical wisdom through practice usually means learning through trial and error. Researchers in cognitive science argue that this is exactly how we learn to recognize patterns. Through trial and error we develop cognitive networks that allow us to detect similarities and differences across a range of situations. Each time we get feedback from our successes and failures, we increase the capacity of the cognitive network to guide us in new situations.

Philosopher and cognitive scientist Paul Churchland provides an example of how cognitive networks might develop and work when he asks us to imagine the ways that an engineer might develop a perception device—say, a sonar device that would allow a submarine to detect an explosive mine and distinguish it from a rock. The engineer could "tell" the device exactly what to look for. She could figure out all the features that mines share that rocks do not and build into the mine detector sensitivities to those key features. But this is not easy: mine designers thwart efforts at detection by building rocklike features into their mines. Mines, like rocks, will vary in shape, density, and sound-transmitting properties. In other words, the category *mine* does not have clear-cut, defining features, at least not features that would be of use to a sonar system. *Mine* is like the natural categories we discussed before: we know what it is when it blows up, but precisely defining it is problematic.

What then? Instead of telling the sonar system what to look for, the engineer could let it learn. She could present it with a wide variety of mines and rocks, have it guess which is which, and give it feedback about whether it's right or not. The engineer—the teacher—will obviously know what's a mine and what's a rock, since she's setting up the training procedure, but she might not know the best, most reliable way to tell them apart. She could, however, use a trial-and-error method to help the mine detector learn what a teacher can't directly teach.

This trial-and-error method could be engineered by equipping the student mine detector with a large number of sensors, each designed to pick up one or another property of objects in its vicinity. The various detectors would be interconnected so that when one of them is activated or triggered by the presence of features in its environment, it could communicate that activation to the other detectors. At the start of its training, the sonar system's detectors might be completely interconnected in an undifferentiated way—that is, everything would be connected to everything else. But each time the sonar system was presented with an object—an input—and two (or more) sensors happened to be triggered simultaneously or nearly simultaneously, the connection between them would be strengthened. At the same time, the connections between those sensors and others that were not triggered at the same time would be weakened. Then the sonar system would guess: rock or mine. If it guessed right, the connections between activated sensors would be strengthened still more. If it guessed wrong, those connections would be weakened. Over time, the architecture of the connections would change. Its ability to distinguish the relevant similarities and differences between rocks and mines would be quite bad at first. But as some connections between sensors got stronger and others got weaker, its performance would keep getting better. Eventually, the system would outperform its designers. Indeed, the system would do better than it would have done if at the start its designers had built into it the list of features to look for. Why? Because in order to build the detector so that it's ready to distinguish mines from rocks right off the shelf, the designer would need to know about all the features that enable one to distinguish mines from rocks. She may have some good ideas about this, but they are likely to be incomplete. If, instead, the designer decides to let the sonar system learn how to be a good mine detector, she doesn't have to know what to teach it in advance. The designer needs to be able to tell the detector what's a mine and what's a rock, but not how a sonar system might be able to tell them apart. Given enough experience, with this kind of feedback the network of detectors will be tuned to match the object types it will be encountering in its world. If it could talk, it might well not be able to explain how it was making its decisions. The answer to the question "Is this a mine?" would reside in the entire pattern of activation of the network of sensors that the training regimen had tuned.

There are several impressive examples in varied domains in which networks like the mine detector actually have been created and trained, by trial and error, with results that match or exceed the judgments of experts. There is evidence that members of the U.S. military serving in Iraq learn to recognize IEDs (improvised explosive devices) in exactly the way Churchland's hypothetical mine detector "learns" to recognize mines—often they can tell whether something is an IED without being able to say how they know. In other arenas, computer networks have done as good a job at "judging" the medium-term financial prospects of companies as have auditors. They have predicted the plays football teams are about to run as well as opposing coaches can predict. They have anticipated the future wholesale price of crude oil as well as commodities traders do. They have judged whether shadows on X-rays are tumors as accurately as radiologists do.

A computer network has even been designed to make judgments about ethically appropriate sales strategies and tactics in an e-commerce setting. There were no ethical rules built into the computer program. But with experience and feedback, the program learned that withholding information, misrepresenting what products can do, and hiding costs from customers were all unethical. It also learned what counted as examples of withholding information, misrepresenting products, and hiding costs. It learned these ethical principles by being exposed to examples, making judgments, and getting feedback about those judgments. Having learned, for example, that it is unethical to withhold information about the limited battery life of a laptop computer, the program would judge as unethical the withholding of information about the annual operating costs of an energy-inefficient washing machine.

In general, trained networks like these behave as if they are following a set of rules they have been given by their designers. But, in fact, there are no rules in the networks. The rules are embodied in the connections among the elements. Particularly interesting and well-studied examples of networks acting as if they are following rules come from efforts to teach computers the grammar of languages like English—to show that they can understand and produce word strings that are consistent with the rules of grammar without ever being given those rules as input. The computers can be taught to behave as if they know the way to make the present tense of a verb into the past tense (by adding "ed" to the end of the verb) without ever being given that particular piece of information. These programs behave as if they are following grammatical rules, but the rules are not in any way represented in the programs.

In each of these cases, researchers supplied the raw materials (inputs) to teach the computer networks. In no case was a network told what to look for or what to do. The networks learned something that the teacher didn't, and perhaps couldn't, program directly. For cognitive scientists, the demonstration that computer programs learn to recognize patterns as people do, when given the kinds of experiences that people have, is prima facie evidence that the human mind works in similar fashion. The computer programs, aside from solving practical problems, are taken as simulations of the human mind at work. We share this view. And these are just the kinds of mental operations we need if trial-and-error experience is to turn us into wise decision makers.

THE ARCHITECTURE AND OPERATION OF COGNITIVE NETWORKS

To help understand how they work, it may be useful to examine the nature of cognitive networks in a little more detail. The pioneering work on network theories of mental processes has been done by psychologists James McClelland and David Rumelhart, and over the years they have been joined by many others. There are different specific theories of how networks operate that all belong to the same general family, and the family has come to be called connectionism or parallel distributed processing (PDP).

Such theories envision the mind as a vast array of millions of interconnected elements. A very simple schematic network is depicted in Figure 6.1. At the bottom are individual elements ("input units") that are responsive to particular inputs from the environment (sights, sounds, odors, and so on). The outputs from these units are multiply connected to another, intermediate set of units ("hidden units") in the middle of the figure. And these units, in turn, are multiply connected to a set of units ("output units") that produce speech, facial expressions, and body movements. When one input element is stimulated, it sends stimulation to other elements via the many interconnections of input units to intermediate units. But the strength of connections among elements is dynamic. Connections are strengthened when individual elements are stimulated together; otherwise they may weaken. Connection strength is also affected by feedback from the environment following an output (if, for example, you mispronounce a word, or misidentify a rock as a mine, and are corrected). Cognitive network theories hypothesize that the process of going from a naive child to an experienced, pattern-recognizing adult is a process by which the vast set of connections is tuned by this kind of experience. And most of the tuning is done by changing the pattern and strength of connections in the intermediate units. This is where the pattern that is to be recognized resides. It is the tuned network that produces rapid pattern recognition.

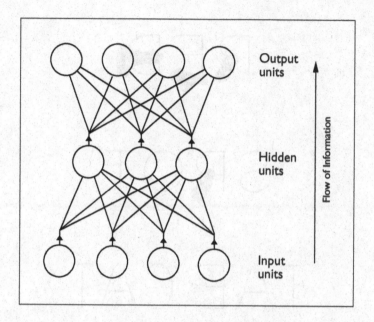

FIGURE 6.1 *A Schematic Connectionist Network.* Information excites input units, which are connected to hidden units and, through them, to output units that yield the perception of patterns, speech, or actions. Experience strengthens some connections among units, and weakens others. This network is quite simple, with only a handful of units at each level. The presumption is that in actual human minds and brains, there are hundreds of thousands of such units.

Why rapid? That's because the elements of networks can operate in parallel, that is, all at once. You don't have to wait for one element to send information to the second, which will then send the information to the third, and so on. As each element begins to get activated, it starts sending signals to other units. These, in turn, can begin to send signals back as they start to get activated. In the end, each unit essentially influences, and is influenced by, many others. Also, elements are redundantly distributed throughout the network; it's not as though there is a single element on the lookout for red, and one on the lookout for C-sharp. This is why theories like this are called parallel distributed processing theories.

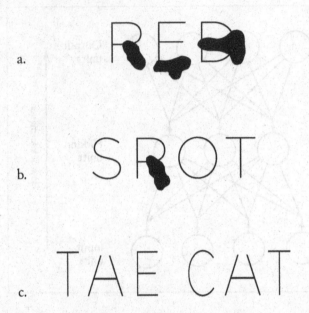

a.

b.

c.

FIGURE 6.2 *Networks as Parallel and Context Sensitive.* In 6.2a, the network figures out that the obscured word is "red" by processing all three letters in parallel. In 6.2b, with only one letter obscured, the network uses the context (S, O, and T) to determine that the obscured letter must be a P. In 6.2c, the network uses context to interpret the same stimulus as an H or an A, simultaneously sensitive to the physical identity of those patterns and their different, context-driven interpretations.

To get a sense of what *parallel* means, look at Figure 6.2a. There are three letters there, each obscured by an ink blot. What are the letters— R or P, E or F, D or B? Looked at in isolation, the identity of each letter is ambiguous. Yet, you have no trouble interpreting the string as R-E-D. But how do you do it? It's not as if you say to yourself, "Well, there's an R and a D, so the middle letter must be E" (which is the way you might handle the example in Figure 6.2b, where only one letter is ambiguous).

The only thing that eliminates the ambiguity is the entire pattern of stimulation. Your network is simultaneously processing the three letters and coming up with the most likely—indeed the only plausible—answer.

Importantly, the overall functioning of the network does not depend on an "executive" sitting in a corner office, telling individual units what to do. Nothing tells the "reading" network to get ready to go because it may be needed. Activation comes from the environment, not from a commander in chief.

Finally, elements in a network are usually part of more than just a single, well-tuned pattern. A specific feature of the environment may activate an element. But which part of the network that activation affects may depend on what else is being activated. For example, consider the middle letter in Figure 6.2c. Is it an H or an A? The answer is, it depends. In the word on the left (THE) it's an H, but in the word on the right (CAT), it's an A. Of course, physically it's the same set of markings on a page, and the elements activated by those markings will be the same either way. Indeed, the network will enable you to see the similarity between the H and the A, even as you treat the two markings as different letters (after all, only certain kinds of H's and A's look similar). But those elements will be connected both to the parts of the network that enable you to read THE and to the parts of the network that enable you to read CAT. The context in which those marks on the page appear will affect which parts of the network are activated, and thus how those marks on the page are interpreted.

Indeed, in general, the architecture of networks can contain patterns of interconnection that work to pull apart similar things (like the A in CAT and the H in THE). Think about how similar a shade of red can be to a shade of orange. You can see them as similar, but at the same time you have a category *red* and a different category *orange*. The prototypes that exemplify *red* and *orange* are, let us say, significantly more different from each other than are the particular red and orange you're looking at. The existence of these categories enables you to enhance the difference you perceive between this particular red and orange, by assimilating each to its prototype.

To choose a more complex example, the visual information you get from seeing a well-dressed, apparently affluent man handing money to a very shabbily dressed man will be quite similar, whether it's "man giving money to a beggar" or "man giving money to a mugger," but having these distinct categories for beggar and mugger enables you to enhance the perceptual differences between these two scenes. Networks can be created that at one level of organization pretty directly reflect perceptual similarity while, at a different level of organization, they respond to conceptual or categorical dissimilarity. To use terminology we have used before, the categories you have can provide frames that influence the way in which you interpret, or even see, the outputs of the network. And these categories or frames may themselves reflect the operation of a network at a higher level of remove from the details of the visual world you are perceiving.

Research on cognitive networks is not typically based on experiments with real people in natural settings to determine if this is the way their minds actually recognize patterns. What researchers do instead, for the most part, is design computer programs that are structured as cognitive networks. Researchers then give these programs "experiences" (inputs) of the kinds that people have, and see if the programs behave (i.e., produce outputs) in the way people do in analogous, laboratory settings. The computer program, then, represents a kind of theory of how people perform the same tasks.

These computer networks are explicitly designed to conform to what we currently know about the brain and nervous system. What we've been calling "elements" in networks are more or less like individual neurons or small groups of neurons. We know that the nervous system contains millions and millions of neurons, each of them with myriad connections to other neurons. And we know that experience changes both the strength and the architecture of connections (new connections get formed; old, useless connections get pruned). Most important, a key fact about the nervous system is that neurons are "dumb." They "know" only one thing: fire faster (get more activated) when your inputs cross a certain threshold. They are on or they are off, but they have no "idea" what's turning them on or off. The intelligence that these dumb neurons produce is the product of their organized interconnections. And so it is with cognitive networks: elements are dumb; patterns of activation of those dumb elements are smart.

These computer programs are vastly simplified: instead of having millions of components, they may have dozens, or perhaps hundreds. And instead of being exposed to the vast array of objects and events people encounter in daily life, they are exposed to just a limited subset. The critical thing about these simulated networks is that they start out with a bunch of dumb elements that are interconnected but know nothing about the domain to which they are about to be exposed (like neurons). Then researchers train the networks, to see if they can turn dumb elements into a smart system.

You can think of networks as analogous to the systems that websites like Netflix use to make recommendations to you. You might type in the name of a movie—say, *The Godfather.* Information about that movie will come up on your screen, but Netflix will also be ready to recommend other movies. Which others? That depends. Partly, it may depend on what other Netflix customers who chose and liked *The Godfather* also chose and liked (and Netflix knows whether customers liked *The Godfather* because it asks them). In part it may depend on your own past pattern of inquiries and movie rentals. If you're a gangster movie buff, you might get a list of other gangster movies. But if your own past history suggests that you're an Al Pacino fan, you may get a list of Pacino movies, and not just any Pacino movies, but the ones other customers with tastes like yours have liked. And if you're in the midst of a project to see all the Academy Award winners, you might get still a third list of recommendations. You don't have to tell Netflix a lot about your taste in movies. It already has a pretty good idea, based on your past choices and on the expressed reactions of others who choose the same movies you do. Each time you interact with Netflix, the program it uses to provide you with recommendations is updated. Indeed, each time anyone interacts with Netflix, the recommendation program is updated. Connections between movies get formed, and the strengths of those connections get modified, based upon the accumulated experience of Netflix users. It is as if you are all part of one gigantic network—a network that appreciates that no site visitor is completely unique, but *also* appreciates that no site visitor is exactly like any other. The recommendation system used by Netflix doesn't know anything about movies. It is built to detect patterns of preferences among users, and it gets smarter (the connections among its elements get better tuned) as it gets feedback from past recommendations and learns from its mistakes. From the perspective of modern cognitive science, the pattern recognition capacities of human beings get smarter in much the same way.

FROM COGNITIVE NETWORKS TO MORAL NETWORKS

This quick tour through modern cognitive science was meant to give you a sense of what cognitive networks are and how they operate to recognize patterns. But distinguishing mines from rocks, diagnosing the financial health of companies, and predicting football plays seem pretty far removed from the kinds of patterns wise practitioners must be able to recognize in the people they serve.

Can we plausibly extend this model of cognitive networks to explain the moral pattern recognition we do? We don't know.

Researchers have not yet tried to model pattern recognition specifically connected to wisdom or moral judgment. Research on cognitive networks has aimed to model things like visual pattern recognition, memory, the production and comprehension of language, and the playing of strategic games like backgammon, bridge, and chess. The closest actual example of pattern recognition relevant to some of the moral skills we have discussed was an effort to teach a computer program to recognize the facial expressions of emotion—exactly the kind of perception we would need in order to know when and how to be empathetic. The network started out with connections among elements determined at random. Then it was trained by exposing it to 160 photos—twenty expressing each of eight different emotions (astonishment, delight, pleasure, relaxation, sleepiness, boredom, misery, and anger). It learned to classify many (but not all) of the emotions correctly. Then it was given a set of new faces to classify, and it performed almost as well on these faces as on the ones it was trained with. Interestingly, the types of emotions the computer program had trouble with (sleepiness, boredom, and misery) are the same ones that real human beings have trouble classifying accurately.

Though no one has explicitly tried to study what philosophers Paul Churchland and Owen Flanagan have called "moral networks," moral networks seem to have all the properties we've been ascribing to cognitive networks—and to wisdom. "There is a straightforward analogy," Flanagan says, "between the way a submarine sonar device that needs to learn to distinguish rocks from mines might acquire the competence to do so and the way a human might acquire moral sensitivities and sensibilities." Flanagan argues, for example, that children's moral networks are tuned through experience and feedback:

Children learn to recognize certain prototypical kinds of social situations, and they learn to produce or avoid the behaviors prototypically required or prohibited in each. Children come to *see* certain distributions of goodies as a *fair* or *unfair* distribution. They learn to recognize that a found object may be someone's property. . . . They learn to

discriminate *unprovoked cruelty*, and to demand and expect punishment
for the transgressor and comfort for the victim. They learn to recognize
a *breach of promise*, and to howl in protest. They learn to recognize these
and a hundred other typical social/moral situations, and the ways in
which . . . society generally reacts to those situations and expects them
to react.

Consider, Flanagan goes on, how children learn to tell the truth.
One thing that is clear is that we do not teach children that they should
tell the truth whenever they know it—nor do we want to. Rather, children need to learn what truth telling is (why jokes and fairy tales,
though "untrue," aren't lies), which situations call for truth telling, and
how to tell the truth. Beyond this, children need to learn which situations call for straightforward truth telling ("Did you throw that ball
through Ms. Baker's window?" asks Dad), which call for tact ("Do you
want more of these yummy lima beans?" asks Aunt Betty), which call
for white lies ("Doesn't Grandma look young in those capri pants?"
asks Mom), and which call for outright misinformation ("Where do you
live?" asks the menacing-looking stranger). How the developing child
will respond to a particular situation depends on which network(s) the
situation activates. Kids will make mistakes, much to the chagrin and
embarrassment of their parents. There will also be ambiguity, and thus
room for disagreement, about what kind of situation this particular
situation is.

Nonetheless, with time and experience, and feedback, the child will
build up a network of pattern recognizers that will come to work more
and more like the adult's.

In confronting a new situation, the child will identify a pattern and
recognize what is relevantly similar to or different from past patterns,
and there will be patterns of past actions (precedents, if you will) that
will suggest what choice is appropriate now. Years ago, when Aunt
Betty asked if you wanted any more of those yummy lima beans, you

avoided the white lie ("yes") and said instead, "I saw dessert in the oven and I simply must save room." This works. No lie. No hurt feelings. Laughter all around. And a second helping of dessert. Now, when your friend comes into the room and wants to know how she looks in her dress, instead of saying "Great!" (a white lie) or "Honestly, not so good" (hurtful), you quickly respond, "You know, I was really hoping you'd wear your lovely blue silk dress tonight. You look *so* good in that." No rule about lying tells you what to do. You don't go through a complicated decision-making procedure in your mind. You may not even remember the lima bean incident. But the pattern is established for perceiving that the question about the dress is similar in some important respects to the question about the lima beans, and it evokes a response in you of reframing the question so that you can say something positive.

If a network of patterns is built up with experience and feedback, it's not surprising that our moral networks are tuned by the moral communities we live in. They are the source of feedback for mistakes. We are all moral pupils, even as adults. We learn to be wise doctors by doctoring, wise teachers by teaching, and so on. Members of a moral community, says Paul Churchland, must learn how to evaluate their own conduct and the conduct of others: "Moral learning is driven by social experience, often a long and painful social experience."

What the moral pupil is learning, says Churchland, is "the structure of social space and how best to navigate one's way through it." In anticipation of the arguments in this book, Churchland tells us that what the pupil is learning is "practical wisdom: the wise administration of her practical affairs in a complex social environment. . . . This is of fundamental importance for the character and quality of any individual's life, and not everyone succeeds equally in mastering the relevant intricacies."

Notice the implications of this perspective. A moral network is tuned up by the relevant community (parents, teachers, friends). If the community is out of tune, the network will be badly tuned too. Thus, you can't make better teachers, doctors, and lawyers by simply telling them how to care for students, patients, and clients. They have to watch you doing it the right way, and you have to be correcting their mistakes, and tuning their networks, as they learn. We will see, in the chapters to come, that our communities of doctors, lawyers, teachers, and other professionals are badly out of tune. But we will also see that they, and their networks, can be retuned.

PATTERN RECOGNITION, MORAL NETWORKS, AND MORAL SKILL

The kind of pattern recognition modeled by moral networks helps us understand a lot about the limits of moral rules and procedures, the importance of practical wisdom, and the actual capacity we have for exercising such wisdom.

First, it explains the capacity a practically wise person has to solve the problem of context that befuddles rules. Answers to questions about which rule is relevant, which rule to pick when rules are in conflict, when to make an exception to a rule, and how actually to apply a rule all depend on the particular context, and there is no rule to tell us exactly how context matters. Moral networks help handle the problem of context. The current situation (e.g., the particular student, client, or patient in front of us) will have elements in common with past situations, which is what enables us to profit from past experience. But at the same time, it will have novel elements, which is what will enable us to say or do something that we have never said or done before. This simultaneous responsiveness to both similarity and difference is what enables us to respond with suppleness and creativity to the situation before us. It's what enables moral improvisation.

It might seem plausible to imagine that the best way to develop moral sensitivity, suppleness, and perceptiveness in people is to combine good moral rules with relevant experience. The rules provide the anchors—the scaffolding—that get the network going, and then experience adds the nuance that encourages wise improvisation. Later, we'll explore an innovative medical training program that does exactly this.

But rules must be used with care. There is reason to believe that too much reliance on rules can actually be counterproductive. A rule can "entrench" particular patterns of activation in a network, making the network extremely difficult to change, so that even if a person subsequently has a wide range of experience, including experience that throws the rule into question, the experience will not result in subtle and sensitive changes to the networks. Rules or rigid scripted procedures can lock people in so that they don't benefit from the experience they have.

Second, the model of moral networks construes moral choices in a way that captures how we actually make most of our everyday moral decisions—quickly and without a conscious reliance on rules or decision-making procedures. Pattern recognition, a fast and automatic process, gives us the capacity for the kind of rapid and often nonverbal practical reasoning we do.

Third, the features of a moral network help us understand an important source of moral disagreement among people as other than simply a clash of values. Since different experiences will produce different moral networks, we can expect frequent occasions in which good people, with similar values, come to quite different views about what the particular situation before them calls for. From this perspective, the task of moral persuasion will often involve getting another person to *see* the situation as you do, not to *think about* the situation as you do.

Fourth, the moral networks model helps us account for the occasions when pattern recognition is not rapid, when practical wisdom demands careful deliberation. For one thing, learning how to distinguish and recognize important patterns is a long process; it takes a while for sonar devices looking for mines, let alone children and even adults looking for moral guidance, to tune their networks, and none of us can be experts in all domains. Novices always have to deliberate. And experts do too, when they face a new or strange pattern.

Reflective deliberation is a part of moral networks in a second way. We are often faced with situations of moral ambiguity, when moral perception is unclear or conflicted, and the moral network can't settle on a single answer or output. We see this kind of ambiguity all the time in visual perception, as evidenced by Figure 6.3 of the old woman/young woman. In cases like this, small changes in the pattern can tip the balance so that what was ambiguous becomes clear. The fact that we can appreciate moral ambiguity means that there will be circumstances in which we see what morality demands of us in more than one way (i.e., we will appreciate conflict). In such situations, it may take careful deliberation and moral imagination for us to find a way to choose between alternatives (e.g., kindness and honesty) or craft a path that combines them.

FIGURE 6.3 *Ambiguous Figure.* Is the drawing of an
old woman or a young woman? The answer is both.

Finally, the moral network approach helps make sense out of the notion, as old as Aristotle, that practical wisdom can only be learned through experience. A model of moral networks tells us how experience teaches. The patterns we learn come largely from feedback—trial and error. Each of these experiences strengthens certain connections and weakens others, which gives us an increasing ability to identify complex patterns that could not be taught by all the lectures and rules in the world. The capacity to identify patterns is something we're born with, but the patterns we recognize are not. The moral networks of children begin to be tuned by their exposure to moral examples set by parents, teachers, and friends. Moral development is captured by the growing expansion and refinement of the networks.

Aristotle's commitment to science as well as philosophy, ethics, and politics would likely have attracted him to current research on pattern recognition and network theory. As Paul Churchland explains it, moral virtue or excellence, as Aristotle saw it, was not something given by an outside authority and swallowed whole. "It was a matter of developing a set of largely inarticulate skills, a matter of *practical* wisdom." The child is born into a moral community, with detailed social practices already in place. The child's initiation into that community takes time:

> time to learn how to recognize a large variety of prototypical social situations, time to learn how to deal with those situations, time to learn how to balance or arbitrate conflicting perceptions and conflicting demands. . . . This portrait of a moral person as one who has acquired a certain family of perceptual and behavioral *skills* contrasts sharply with . . . accounts that picture the moral person as one who has agreed to follow a certain set of *rules.* . . . Stable rules are not the *basis* of one's moral character. They are merely its pale and partial reflection at the comparatively impotent level of language.
>
> A person might have an all-consuming desire to maximize human

happiness. But if that person has no comprehension of what sorts of things generally serve lasting human happiness; no capacity for recognizing other people's emotion, aspirations, current purposes; no ability to engage in smoothly cooperative undertakings . . . then that person is not a moral saint. He is a pathetic fool, a hopeless busybody, a loose cannon, and a serious menace to society.

CONCLUSION

A child's initiation into a moral community is only the first step in acquiring practical wisdom, a process that continues with experiences we have as we grow up, enter schools and universities, and go to work. Modern cognitive science has given us clues about how such experiences create cognitive networks that give us the categories, emotions, and intuitions we need to be morally skillful. The right experience seems to contain variety, trial and error, and feedback from mistakes. People need to be encouraged to experiment. Doing the same thing again and again may create a powerful network, but not a wise one.

The wrong experience fails to exploit the potential we're born with. So, do the institutions and social systems we live and practice in give us the right experience to cultivate practical moral skill? Do they give us the opportunity to make mistakes and learn from them? As we'll see, all too often efforts to make things better—with carefully developed rules and methodical procedures—actually make them worse. Instead of nurturing practical wisdom, they end up waging a stealth war on it.

PART III

The War on Wisdom

The War on Wisdom

One fine spring day several years ago, a father took his seven-year-old son, Michael, to a Detroit Tigers baseball game. A few innings into the game, the son asked for lemonade. The father dutifully went to a concession stand to get some. Mike's Hard Lemonade was all they had, and the father, a professor of archaeology at the University of Michigan, having never heard of it and having no idea that it was 5 percent alcohol, bought a bottle and brought it to his son.

While father and son were cheering on the Tigers, a security guard happened to notice the child sipping the hard lemonade. The guard called the police, who in turn called an ambulance. The ambulance came to the ballpark, and the child was rushed to the hospital. Doctors found no trace of alcohol in him and were ready to discharge him.

But then the police put the child in a Wayne County Child Protective Services foster home. They hated to do it but they had to follow procedure. County officials kept him there for three days. They hated to do it, but they had to follow procedure. Next, a judge ruled that the child could go home to his mom, but only if his dad left the house and checked into a hotel. The judge hated to do it but he had to follow procedure. After two weeks, the family finally was reunited.

Why did this happen? In telling the lemonade story, NPR's Scott Simon observed: "Procedures may be dumb, but they spare you from thinking. . . . And to be fair, procedures are often imposed because previous officials have been lax and let a child go back to an abusive household." The very rule-following that miscarried in this case might have been exactly what was called for to protect children from continued abuse and neglect when people who should be responsible aren't paying attention. But rules—even good ones—*do* miscarry. They can't substitute for good judgment, and they won't work well without it.

The public officials involved in the hard lemonade case needed practical wisdom and the discretion to exercise it. We may all have the capacity to develop practical wisdom, but it's a capacity that needs to be educated. We can learn to interpret aims and rules in different contexts because we're built with the capacity to see gray and appreciate nuance. A father who unknowingly gives an alcoholic beverage to his son on one occasion is different from a father who regularly supplies his son with such drink or a father who turns a blind eye to a child's alcohol abuse. Our capacity to recognize and interpret significant patterns can be developed if the moral networks we carry in our heads get well trained. But such training in practical wisdom will not happen on its own; it needs institutions that nurture it.

Yet this is not happening. In our ever more corporate and bureaucratic culture, constant demands for efficiency, accountability, and profit have led to an increasing reliance on rules and incentives to control behavior. The policemen, the social workers, and the judge who took Michael away from his family, and then forbade his father to see him, were following rigid procedures that assumed that the judgment of these officials could not be trusted. As institutional practices like these become calcified, we lose our bead on the real aims and purposes of our work and fail to develop the moral skills we need to achieve them. It becomes increasingly difficult for us to develop and to exercise the practical wisdom we need to make the right choices. The result is a stealth war on wisdom: a war no one wants, one that harms us all. It undermines both the moral skill and the moral will that wise practice requires.

How does this assault on wisdom happen? We will look at examples of the obstacles thrown in the way of people who want to practice wisely, and how such obstacles can prevent novice practitioners from ever having the experiences needed to develop the wisdom good practice demands. We will examine how practical moral skills are chipped away by an overreliance on rules and procedures that deprive us of the opportunity to improvise. We will discuss how our will to achieve the proper aims of our practices gets eroded by an overreliance on incentives. And we will explore how some shrewd and brave individuals—"canny outlaws," we call them—find ways to exercise wisdom in spite of organizations whose rules and procedures systematically discourage it.

Ruling Out Wisdom: When Judges Stop Judging and Doctors Stop Prescribing

THE BATTLE OVER DISCRETION

Two years after Judge Lois Forer had sentenced Michael for the toy-gun holdup, Michael had fully complied with the sentence. He had successfully completed his term of imprisonment and probation. He had paid restitution to the taxi driver. He had returned to his family and obtained steady employment. He had not been rearrested. But Forer's sentence had not sat well with the prosecutor. He appealed her decision, asking the Pennsylvania Supreme Court to require Forer to sentence Michael to the five-year minimum sentence for a serious offense committed in or near a public transportation facility that was required by a 1982 Pennsylvania law. Michael's full compliance with Judge Forer's judgment was not relevant to the court's decision. It ordered Judge Forer to resentence Michael to the five years. Forer said:

> I was faced with a legal and moral dilemma. As a judge I had sworn to uphold the law, and I could find no legal grounds for violating an order

of the Supreme Court. Yet five years' imprisonment was grossly disproportionate to the offense. The usual grounds for imprisonment are retribution, deterrence, and rehabilitation. Michael had paid his retribution
by a short term of imprisonment and by making restitution to the victims. He had been effectively deterred from committing future crimes.
And by any measurable standard he had been rehabilitated. There was
no social or criminological justification for sending him back to prison.
Given the choice between defying a court order or my conscience, I
decided to leave the bench where I had sat for sixteen years.

That didn't help Michael, of course; he was resentenced by another
judge to serve the balance of the five years: four years and fifteen days.
Faced with this prospect, he disappeared.

When Judge Forer sentenced Michael, she knew that there were two
standards that could be applied. There were the state's sentencing
guidelines, which gave her the discretion she used. But there was also
the 1982 statute. Five years. No discretion. Forer knew about the 1982
law, but she thought it was unconstitutional and so tried to work around
the mandatory minimum sentencing.

It violated "the constitutional principle of separation of powers," she
said, "because it can be invoked by the prosecutor, and not by the judge,"
and also because "the act is arbitrary and capricious in its application." It
did not allow consideration of "a defendant's previous record or mental
state," and a "hardened repeat offender receives the same sentence as a
retarded man who steals out of hunger." The statute, said Forer, violated
"the fundamental Anglo-American legal principles of individualized
sentencing and proportionality of the penalty to the crime." Mandatory
sentencing laws, Forer concluded, wring the judgment out of judging.
They create a justice system "that operates like a computer—crime in,
points tallied, sentence out—utterly disregarding the differences among
the human beings involved."

The situation Judge Forer faced in Pennsylvania courts was part of a systemic change that affected federal courts too. In 1984, conservatives' concerns that judges were too soft on crime together with concerns about lack of uniformity in sentencing led Congress to pass the Sentencing Reform Act. This led to the 1987 Federal Sentencing Guidelines. Many judges were not opposed to guidelines that would help minimize the disparity in sentencing. But the guidelines weren't really guidelines. They became, in effect, enforceable rules that sentencing judges were legally obligated to follow, especially when combined with other new laws that mandated minimum sentences for crimes like narcotics possession. Judges were basically told to use a grid system. The severity of the current offense is one axis of the grid, past criminal record is the other, and when the data are filled in, the grid precisely determines the sentence. The basic data were quantifiable measures, such as the amount of drugs involved in the crime, or the value of the stolen goods, or the number of past convictions. What was downplayed or ignored was an interpretation of the particular context or motive, the psychological or medical condition of the accused, and her social and economic background. The system aimed to eliminate the need for a judge's wisdom in determining proportionality—the key task of a sentencing judge trying to make the punishment fit the crime. The system also aimed to minimize judgment in balancing the various aims of justice— retribution, rehabilitation, and deterrence. The sentencing formulas prioritized uniformity above balance and made retribution a priority. Judgments about proportionality and balance would be replaced by largely numerical sentencing rules that were to be as precisely calibrated as possible.

The consequences of this systemic assault on the wisdom of judges were not only to squeeze out some wise judges—judges like Lois Forer, who resigned, and many others who took early partial retirement—but also to discourage new judges from developing the wisdom to sentence.

The only experience new judges had was applying rigid rules. By 2006, 89 percent of active federal district court judges had been confirmed after the guidelines had gone into effect. We asked Boston Federal District Court Judge Nancy Gertner about the impact of this change in judicial practice and judicial experience, and she expressed dismay at the number of judges who lack the confidence or competence "to make the sentence fit the circumstances, to be experts in proportionality." She pointed to one federal judge who embraced the guidelines exactly because they relieved him of exercising judgment. Some judges, he wrote, "may have the wisdom of Solomon in figuring out where in that [sentencing] range to select just the right sentence, but I certainly don't." He liked the guidelines because they "are narrow and presumably take into account all those factors I don't feel competent to weigh: punishment, deterrence, rehabilitation, harm to society, contrition—they're all engineered into the machine; all I have to do is wind the key." He was describing a system that forces practitioners to do right by rote—and that was not only squeezing out the wise practitioners but also squeezing wisdom out of the practice.

The battle over eliminating discretion in the name of uniform sentencing hid another struggle over discretion. The new laws didn't so much eliminate discretion as quietly shift the power to exercise it out of the hands of judges and into the hands of prosecutors. *Their* discretion over what charge to bring now determined the final sentence, which was set by the mandatory minimum rules—unchecked by judicial discretion. The threat of mandatory minimums also increased the power of prosecutors to plea-bargain. If a defendant pled not guilty, took a chance on a trial, and lost, she would be guaranteed the stiff, often draconian, mandatory minimum. The interest of prosecutors, unlike that of judges, is not to balance the crime, the circumstances, and the punishment, but to get convictions—ideally, without lengthy and costly trials. Giving prosecutors that kind of unchecked power, says Patricia Wald, former chief justice of the Court of Appeals in Washington, D.C., "dangerously disturbs the balance between the parties in an adversarial system, and deprives defendants of access to an impartial decision maker in the all-important area of sentencing." After an in-depth scholarly study, Professor Kate Stith of Yale Law School concluded that the effect of these laws has been to create in judges "an abject fear of judging" while increasing the discretion of prosecutors.

Efforts by Congress in the 1980s to take the judgment out of judging faced stiff opposition from many judges and lawyers. After the guidelines were created in 1987, many federal judges acted as Lois Forer did, challenging the law in their courtrooms. In 1988, 179 district court judges ruled the sentencing guidelines unconstitutional. The issue seemed to be settled in January 1989 when the Supreme Court, in its *Mistretta* decision, upheld the constitutionality of the guidelines. But the battle over discretion continued. Some judges still tried to bring proportionality to sentencing, to use the guidelines as guidelines, despite the restrictions on doing so. Most of the opposition, however, was outside the courtroom, as organizations of judges and lawyers pressed Congress to revise the new system. The federal judges of all twelve of the circuit courts of appeals publicly opposed mandatory minimum statutes. So did the American Bar Association, representing more than 400,000 lawyers.

For over a decade, the opposition seemed to hit a stone wall. In fact, in 2003, Congress cracked down further on judicial discretion. The argument by the Justice Department and conservative allies in Congress was that judicial discretion was on the rise—that there was increased "noncooperation" on the part of judges with the guidelines. The 2003 Feeney Amendment was justified as needed to resist efforts by judges to "depart downward" from the mandated sentences. This new squeeze on wisdom, we'll see, turned out to be a pyrrhic victory for supporters of the Feeney crackdown because it finally spurred the Supreme Court to reverse its position.

THE DANGER OF A GOOD PRINCIPLE

The problem that judges face is not too many rules per se. A legal system is made up of rules, and the task of judges is to help interpret the rules in particular situations. Judges are prevented from doing this work well when they are required to pick one of the multiple aims of sentencing, like retribution, and prevented from balancing it with other important aims, like rehabilitation and deterrence. They are forbidden from exercising judgment when rigid sentencing rules deny them the discretion to interpret the circumstances, to make *this* punishment fit *this* crime and *this* individual. But it's not only rigid rules like mandatory sentencing laws that discourage the wisdom to balance and interpret. Sometimes good principles, coupled with the best of intentions, can have the same effect.

Principles are valuable guidelines, and we'd be lost without them. We admire principled people. We want our politicians to act on principle and not out of narrow self-interest. Assist the worst off. Protect human rights. Protect national security. Defend free speech. Our codes of professional ethics are all about the good principles that should guide doctors, lawyers, and architects. Respect for client and patient autonomy. Beneficence. Loyalty. Trust. "Unprincipled" is an epithet. But like rules, good principles, unleavened by judgment, can be obtuse and even dangerous. They can make us dumb to the nuances of context. A good principle can blind us to other good principles with which it needs to be balanced. In policy making, the results can be disastrous. In the everyday work of doctors, the results are bad practice.

PRINCIPLED POLICY MAKING

Michael Ignatieff became the leader of Canada's Liberal Party in 2009, but in the run-up to the 2003 war in Iraq, he was a Harvard political science professor, an influential liberal commentator, and a highly respected human rights activist. In January 2003, he wrote an article in the *New York Times Magazine* that strongly supported military intervention in Iraq. And for a highly principled reason—Saddam Hussein's vicious repression of the Iraqi people. Ignatieff did not challenge what was then the official justification for the war, the charge that Saddam Hussein had, or soon might have, weapons of mass destruction. But Ignatieff's major argument was the human rights imperative for intervention. Ignatieff had his facts right about Hussein's tyrannical rule. And he learned, firsthand, the consequences of the repression when he visited northern Iraq in 1992. "I saw what Saddam Hussein did to the Kurds. From that moment forward, I believed he had to go." The United States had the right and the responsibility to intervene to protect human rights and to build democracy. "There are many peoples," wrote Ignatieff, "who owe their freedom to an exercise of American military power." The Japanese and the Germans. The Bosnians and the Kosovars. The Afghans. The Kurds. Removing Saddam Hussein was part of the burden of empire.

In August 2007, Ignatieff wrote a second article for the *New York Times*, in which he recognized that things were not going well in Iraq, and that figuring out what to do next "requires first admitting that all courses of action thus far have failed." The unfolding events in Iraq, and his own experience and self-reflection, led Ignatieff to think differently about how to make such choices. About what you need to know. About the danger of a good principle. And there was something else that transformed Ignatieff's thinking: he was no longer sitting in the abstract world of academia.

He had left teaching and policy analysis, returned to his native Canada, been elected a member of Parliament in 2006, and had made a strong but unsuccessful run to be prime minister. "Politicians," he wrote in 2007, "cannot afford to cocoon themselves in the inner world of their own imaginings. They must not confuse the world as it is with the world as they wish it to be. They must see Iraq—or anywhere else—as it is." Improving our grasp of reality, said Ignatieff, means confronting the world every day and learning—"mostly from our mistakes."

When Ignatieff had supported the Iraq war on humanitarian grounds in 2003, he had a lot of experience in the field of human rights and as a university teacher and a public commentator. But his experience in Iraq was largely limited to his visit to the northern Kurdish area and he did not understand the circumstances on the ground elsewhere. He was not an expert on Iraq, or the Middle East. He knew the principles, but not the particular context. He lived, as many university sages do, in the world of the abstract and theoretical, a world that often eschews practical wisdom. "As a former denizen of Harvard, I've had to learn that a sense of reality doesn't always flourish in elite institutions." In politics, says Ignatieff, good judgment is "messy" because it "means balancing policy and politics in imperfect compromises that always leave someone unhappy—often yourself." He now argues that "knowing the difference between a good and a bad compromise is more important in politics than holding on to pure principle at any price." In Iraq that would have meant balancing the need to stop the human rights violations of a tyrant like Saddam Hussein against the consequences a U.S. occupation would have for human life and for stability in a postinvasion Iraq and in the region.

Ignatieff does not reject the high moral principles that led him to support the war in the first place. "Fixed principle matters," he says, but "fixed ideas of a dogmatic kind are usually the enemy of good judgment." He has learned to admire the kind of wise statesmen that British philosopher Isaiah Berlin describes as having "understanding rather than knowledge"—the kind of intimate involvement with the relevant facts that enables them to figure out what can and cannot be done in particular circumstances. Ignatieff now sees such wisdom as far better than "ideological thinking," which "bends what Kant called the 'crooked timber of humanity' to fit an abstract illusion. Politicians with good judgment bend the policy to fit the human timber."

THE PRINCIPLE OF AUTONOMY

It's not just in politics and war that good principles are dangerous to the exercise of wisdom. It's common in our everyday life and work—for example, on a trip to the dentist.

Carl Schneider, a University of Michigan law professor, recounts a conversation with his endodontist that followed an examination of a dental problem for possible root canal treatment. The endodontist presented the facts, and Schneider asked if he needed a root canal procedure. It was Schneider's decision, the dentist told him.

> I replied that I understood that, but that I would be glad of a recommendation. He made it clear that he could not and should not decide this medical issue for me. I asked what he would do if it were his tooth. He told me that his values might not be my values, so that what he might do could not be relevant for me. I was baffled (even after hearing all his information, I had no idea how to think about the question), morally reproved (why was I so debased as to refuse responsibility for this important decision?), irritated (why was I being required to make a basically technical decision?).

No matter what Schneider asked, the endodontist remained "sturdy in the righteousness of his cause" and adamantly refused to say what he thought best.

Balancing autonomy and beneficence is the kind of ethical challenge doctors face every day. The norms of the medical profession have, in recent decades, increasingly prioritized the principle of patient autonomy, and that emphasis has been reinforced by the field of medical ethics. This principle has marginalized the once-dominant principle of beneficence—that doctors should do what they think most benefits the patient. In actual practice, good doctors have always balanced these two principles. The balance is so integral to good practice that it's hard to avoid. But the language for even talking about balancing these aims according to the context—a wisdom language—has become overshadowed with rules talk about the sanctity of patient autonomy.

Unlike Schneider's endodontist—and it should be noted that Schneider was working on a book about the principle of autonomy at the time of his visit—many doctors look for ways to balance patient choice with what they think is best for a particular patient in a particular circumstance. We've already seen that all information is framed and that no frame is neutral; this is perhaps nowhere more stark than in medicine. For example, patients have been shown to be more likely to choose the treatment if the information is presented as survival rates than if it is presented as mortality rates. And more than that, how information is framed will affect not only a patient's decision, but also a patient's hope, her will to fight on. And what if the patient seems too ill or confused to understand? Take the not uncommon situation of a patient's refusal of treatment. A doctor with the wisdom to balance autonomy and beneficence will not simply accept that refusal as "patient choice." She will want to ask and know more. What kind of decision-making capacity does the patient have? Does the patient suffer from dementia? Is it mild or serious? Who should speak for him, and how much should his own opinions be respected? To talk of patient autonomy as *the* principle to follow is to hide the need for balance and interpretation, and to exclude the importance of wisdom to finding that balance and making that interpretation. When Schneider's dentist clung to the principle, he forsook the need for wisdom.

Empirical research indicates that often the very people upon whom autonomy is urged don't actually want it. If you ask patients how much choice they want, different people want different amounts of choice, and even the same person wants different kinds of choice in different circumstances. W. M. Strull, at the University of California San Francisco Medical Center, studied 210 hypertension patients and found them avid for information about their condition, but "they did not equivalently want to participate in medical decisions." He found that "nearly half (47%) of patients preferred that the clinician make the therapeutic decisions 'using all that is known about the medicines' but without the patient's participation." And Carl Schneider reports on evidence that the elderly are less likely than the young to want to make medical decisions, and the graver the illness, the less likely the patient is to want to decide. A story in the *New York Times* titled "Awash in Information, Patients Face a Lonely, Uncertain Road" reported that patients often feel abandoned when they are forced to make difficult medical decisions. One thirty-nine-year-old woman with ovarian cancer that had spread to her liver was asked whether she wanted to undergo a new chemotherapy treatment about which the five consulted oncologists disagreed. She asked her doctor and he said he didn't know what to tell her and that she would have to make the decision based on her own values. The patient, "bald, tumor-ridden and exhausted from chemotherapy, was reeling. 'I'm not a doctor!' she shouted. 'I'm a criminal defense lawyer! How am I supposed to know?'"

It often turns out that even doctors don't want to make these choices when they, themselves, are patients. Dr. Alfred Tauber remembers how stuck he felt when he had a kidney stone and was struggling to decide whether to have surgery or wait out the ordeal. "I was in such distress that I could not think. I had no clear idea of what was happening to me. Between the narcotic-induced grogginess and the intermittent agony, I could barely understand my predicament, my options, or the possibility of a resolution." But Tauber's urologist gave ambiguous counsel and insisted Tauber—who was, after all, a physician—make the decision. "I was immobilized. . . . I knew the risks of surgery, the postoperative recovery, etc., and still I procrastinated. . . . They probably didn't take me seriously—the guy who always made decisions couldn't decide whether he was in enough discomfort to have surgery." During the sixth pain episode, Tauber's urologist finally made the decision. "'Well, Fred, it's time. You've had enough.' I nodded numbly."

When doctors' accounts of their own illnesses were put together in an anthology, the editors reported that Dr. Tauber's response was actually quite common. This was a group that often tried to "exert control beyond the bounds of reason." This was a group with special, expert knowledge. Yet almost all the sick doctors who expressed an opinion "suggest[ed] that they want to be taken care of so that they can give up their lonely vigil. Most of them want[ed] to be cared for, have decisions made for them."

There is a strange disconnect here. The reality most doctors face demands balancing the principles of autonomy and beneficence; when patients and doctors themselves are seriously ill, they do not want to abide by the principle of autonomy; and few doctors are, in practice, radical autonomists like Schneider's endodontist. But despite the balancing act that many doctors still do, patient autonomy has become the dominant principle of medical ethics and an official professional norm. Why so much autonomy talk and so little wisdom talk?

In the context of this argument, it is tempting to look back to prior decades as a kind of golden age of wisdom in the medical profession, a time when doctors wisely dispensed advice to soon-to-be-satisfied patients. And indeed, until the late 1960s and early 1970s, the norm of physician paternalism—the doctor knows more and knows best— dominated. But the paternalism of earlier forms of medical care was no exemplar of practical wisdom. The faith placed in the absolute knowledge of the doctor was just as unwise a rule as is the principle of radical autonomy.

The rise of the principle of patient autonomy was an attack on such paternalism. The idea of "doctor knows best" might have made sense as long as close, personal links between doctors and patients allowed doctors to know their patients well and doctor-patient trust to be built. But the replacement of small practices and local hospitals with large bureaucratic organizations and a growing reliance on specialists made treatment more impersonal. Doctors and patients were gradually turned into strangers, corroding both detailed knowledge and trust. This estrangement came at exactly the time when new medical technologies were creating choices that demanded even closer bonds between patients and doctors: organ transplantation, kidney dialysis, and respirators allowed life to be prolonged, but this often demanded that patients and their families figure out how to balance sustaining life with the anguish and suffering of a life prolonged by machinery and drugs. If anything, doctors needed not more pressure to adhere to one principle or another but more practical wisdom to counsel and guide patients in making such choices. But more pressure is what they got.

Citizen groups and judges pressed state legislatures to pass laws regulating end-of-life medical decisions. States gave legal standing to "advance directives" or "living wills," allowing individuals to direct their doctors not to use heroic measures to sustain their lives if they were terminally ill. In 1990, Congress passed the Patient Self-Determination Act, mandating that health care institutions inform their patients of their rights to make advance directives.

The aim of these court decisions and legislative acts was a legitimate one: expand patient choice and restrict physician paternalism. Informed consent became the legal expression of patient autonomy. But simply replacing one principle with another marginalized the need for practical wisdom and balance. Moreover, legal concerns created pressure for institutions to conform. Shifting responsibility to the patient who had consented shifted some of the legal liability as well. The fear that hospitals and doctors had of litigation—the dark shadow of malpractice suits—created an incentive to support "patient choice." And at the same time, doctors' authority to make decisions was being wrested from them by insurance companies and HMOs, much as the mandatory sentencing laws reduced the authority of judges.

Institutionally, autonomy became a centerpiece of new medical ethics courses that were required in medical schools. The idea also had popular appeal among patients in an era of demands for civil rights, women's rights, and consumer rights. It was easy, if ultimately misleading, to adopt the "patient as consumer" frame. The patient as consumer had the right to choose his or her own treatment. In choices about treatment, it was the patient and not the doctor who should rule. The doctor should fully inform, but the patient had the right to choose among the possible treatments, to go against physician recommendations, and to choose how long to continue life support. The doctor "proposes," the patient "disposes."

Despite these pressures to conform, frontline doctors still understand how impractical it is to adhere rigidly to the principle of autonomy—or to the principle of paternalism, for that matter—if they are going to do their work well. And among experienced doctors the debate is far from settled. Dr. Donald Berwick tells a revealing story of an encounter he had in a subcommittee on the quality of health care in America that he was asked to chair by the prestigious Institute of Medicine in 2000 (the IOM is one of the three bodies that make up the U.S. National Academy of Sciences). The subcommittee was tasked with writing national guidelines for professional care, and that meant, first, clarifying the aims of health care. "Patient control" was one of the most contested issues. This committee of practicing doctors found itself torn between a traditional notion of professionalism—"Trust us, we know best what will help you"—and the consumerist view of quality—"Let us know what you need and want, and that is what we will offer." Compromise terms emerged—partnership, sharing, respect for patients. The group settled on "patient centeredness": health care should honor the individual patient and respect the patient's choices, culture, social context, and specific needs.

But agreeing on a term did not settle the differences. Berwick called "patient centeredness" a verbal analgesic that masked the real pain felt by doctors who wanted one principle or the other. But perhaps not settling the issue definitively was exactly the right result because it is not an issue that should be "settled." The principle of patient centeredness moves the discussion toward wisdom talk exactly because of its unsettled ambiguities.

Berwick's committee was not the first to use the term "patient centered," but the principle's endorsement by the IOM in its 2001 report, *Crossing the Quality Chasm*, and by medical school deans in 2004, and its promotion by respected doctors like Berwick, have added to its prominence in medical school curricula and in recent professional discussions about the aims of health care. The language used by advocates of patient-centered care has a clear bias toward patient choice, but it tends to avoid the principled extremes. Instead there is talk about things like "shared decision making," "collaboration," the "customization of health care" according to a patient's needs and circumstances, and "partnership" among the physician, patient, and family. Physicians are to work with the patient to "help the patient" make care—and end-of-care—decisions. One prominent guide for making hospitals more patient centered talks about encouraging patients and their families to "participate in care and decision making at the level they choose." It talks about listening to and honoring patient and family perspectives and choices and incorporating beliefs and cultural backgrounds into care planning and decision making.

Such language and guidelines promote practices that are more likely to nurture practical wisdom than an ethic that simply prioritizes the principle of autonomy. "Patient-centered" doctors are encouraged to interpret the patient's circumstances and needs, to balance the patient's desire and capability to choose with the doctor's experience and expertise. In some institutions, it has become more than simply a rhetorical guideline. The Dana-Farber Cancer Institute in Boston, for example, has deliberately restructured its entire organization to make it more patient centered.

Whether or not patient-centered care will become a dominant model for health care is still an open question. But it does begin to reframe discussion away from autonomy versus paternalism. There is no good way to settle such a debate. The hegemony of either principle would be harmful to the goals of medical care. Finding a Rules-Talk or Principles-Talk solution is simply not practical. Doctors must develop the wisdom to balance these two legitimate principles, and the right balance will be different at different bedsides.

CONCLUSION

Judge Forer, Michael Ignatieff, Carl Schneider's dentist, and Dr. Tauber's doctor all remind us of how important rules and principles are, but how damaging they can be absent practical wisdom. We want judges who obey the rules: their job, after all, is to uphold the rule of law. Sentencing guidelines can usefully tell judges what to look for and help assure greater fairness in sentencing. We want policy makers and doctors who are principled: such principles point them—and us—toward doing the right thing and remind us of our responsibilities, of the aims of our practices. Principles that call on us to respect human rights, seek political stability, assure national security, respect patient autonomy, and do what we judge to be best for a patient's health and well-being are invaluable in guiding our choices. But rules can't be applied without interpreting the context. Principles are often in conflict with one another and need to be balanced. If rigid rules and dogmatic principles marginalize the practical wisdom we need to interpret and balance, we are prevented from choosing well.

8.

Eroding the Empathy
to Be Wise

Empathy is critical for practical wisdom. So is detachment. We can't figure out how to do the right thing unless we understand what the people we are interacting with are feeling and thinking, but if we get too involved in their perspective we can't help them step back to see more clearly. It is not only Rules Talk that discourages us from learning how to balance these seeming opposites. Powerful institutional forces drive out empathy and discourage balance.

DOCTORS YOUNG AND OLD: DRIVING OUT EMPATHY

THE EROSION OF EMPATHY IN PROFESSIONAL TRAINING

Dr. Jerome Lowenstein, whom we met earlier as Mr. N.'s doctor, was not only a physician at New York University Medical Center, but also a teacher. He was deeply involved in the Humanistic Medicine Program and met weekly with his students and other house staff in small-group seminars on the wards to discuss their experiences and responses to patients. He understood that empathy was at the heart of good practice and saw the seminars as a way to teach empathy and compassion to young doctors. In one seminar, the question was directly put to the students: Do you think we can teach you compassion? An uncomfortable silence. Then a young intern, in a voice that conveyed both anger and shame, said, "I don't know if you can teach compassion, but you surely can teach the opposite."

Exactly so, Lowenstein realized. The questions of empathy he discussed in the afternoon seminar were not what he modeled in the patients' rooms when he led morning rounds with his students. How patients understood and responded to their illnesses was rarely discussed. Lowenstein realized that he approached clinical practice by focusing only on the underlying pathophysiology—just the way he remembered doctors doing it in his student days. Subliminally, he said, he learned to feel "a deep discomfort, during my rounds, whenever I heard myself deviating from the image of one of my rigorous scientific role models." Today, medical students are cautioned by house staff against "becoming too involved" with individual patients. They are counseled that time spent with books will get them farther than learning about any single patient. The huge body of knowledge physician-teachers must transmit encourages them to narrow their focus and deal only with the part of the disease they know best, focusing on just this specific problem and directing attention "away from the patient, where all problems intersect." Students are hardened, Lowenstein observes. They learn an insensitivity to suffering and pain—an insensitivity to the needs of patients. Doctors-in-training witness a dehumanization of patients by their teachers—the staff or "attending" physicians and residents—who describe patients as "homeless," "undomiciled," "an IVDA," a "shooter." Worse, they sometimes refer to patients "in order of decreasing humanity, as "MIs," "hits," "crocks," "gomers," and "shpozes." A survey of 665 students at six Pennsylvania medical schools showed that 98 percent had heard physicians refer derogatorily to patients. Lowenstein sees this process as a kind of *psychic numbing* (a term he borrows from psychiatrist Robert Jay Lifton's work) that occurs with remarkable speed, often during the early years of clinical training.

Lowenstein's observations, shared by many other medical school teachers, have been corroborated by recent research. At Jefferson Medical College in Philadelphia, Dr. Mohammadreza Hojat and his colleagues measured the changes in empathy among 456 students as they moved through four years of medical school. The researchers found a significant decline in empathy during the third year—the very time when students move out of the classroom and begin to work with patients. The decline was sustained in the fourth year. Other research confirms these findings. And there is further evidence that empathy continues to decline during the residency that follows medical school. Along with this erosion of empathy, there is evidence of an ethical erosion too. The study of Pennsylvania medical students found that 61 percent witnessed what they believed to be unethical behavior by other medical team members, and of these students, 54 percent felt like accomplices. Sixty-seven percent felt bad or guilty about at least one thing they had done as clinical clerks, and 62 percent believed that at least some of their ethical principles had been eroded or lost.

It's not that medical school teachers don't talk to students about empathy. They do. But Dr. Lowenstein's experience is common: there is a gap between what is said in courses and what students see modeled by the doctors on hospital rounds. In the lectures, explained one medical student, we hear about the loss of empathy, but "we stop having these discussions when they actually apply to us." When rounds begin students are "all scared and confused, but the general consensus is that you are supposed to put on your big, brave doctor face and not talk about what you're seeing. . . . We see upper-level residents who have seen so many codes [indicating hospital emergencies] that they're no longer affected by them. . . . We also see people make fun of patients or roll their eyes at them and, since we want to be included, we do it too. It's a classic example of little kids watching big kids and acting like the big kids to be cool. We don't know what we are doing so we mimic what we see."

Dr. Frederic Hafferty, at the University of Minnesota's School of Medicine in Duluth, calls what Lowenstein was seeing the "hidden curriculum" of medical school. While academic concern with ethics is focused on how to improve the formal ethics courses, the real teaching is happening outside the classroom and is often in direct conflict with what is being touted in formal medical ethics courses. What doctors do on rounds, as opposed to what they say in class, is part of this hidden curriculum, but it goes deeper. It is embedded in daily training and in the very organization of the medical schools themselves. Time pressures and sleep deprivation, built into the training, make students feel "overwhelmingly tired and unempathetic at times," explained one student in Hojat's survey. "I am thinking more about getting through the encounter expeditiously than about making a connection with the patient. And, I have always considered myself an empathetic person." Deans, provosts, and hospital administrators often establish frames that distort wise practice by the very metaphors they use. Patients are "insured lives" or "consumers," health care is a "product," and what the administrators are doing is "right-sizing" departments, improving the "total quality" of faculty, and creating new programs as "ventures" or "strategic investments," with a potential "return on equity."

This official embrace of a language that frames patients as customers buying the services of providers further discourages empathy, or any ethical considerations for that matter, even if the opposite is being taught in the formal curriculum. The same problem occurs in other professions where the preaching and practice of empathy are disconnected. University faculty may be told to pay attention to each student as an individual, to be sensitive to each student's way of learning. But if junior faculty are judged for promotion by the number of student "customers" who are enrolling in their classes—so many that it is impossible to empathize with them as individuals—and by multiple-choice customer-satisfaction surveys administered to these students, the real message desensitizes teachers and erodes their empathy.

Lowenstein was turned into what we might call a canny outlaw by his experiences and self-reflection. He bucked what were then accepted practices. Unlike many of his colleagues, and those who had taught him, he tried to model what he taught in class. In his teaching during rounds, for example, he began encouraging the students to see the subtle and distorting effects that shorthand ways of describing patients had on diagnosis and treatment. When an intern opened his presentation with "This is the first hospital admission of this thirty-five-year-old IVDA," Lowenstein interrupted and asked, "Would our thinking or care be different if you began your history by telling us that this is a thirty-five-year-old Marine veteran who has been addicted to drugs since he served, with valor, in Vietnam?" Lowenstein found ways to integrate details about patients' perceptions and responses without sacrificing attention to other aspects of clinical medicine. "The time and place to teach compassion," he says, "are the time and place in which all of the rest of medicine is taught."

DISCOURAGING EMPATHY IN PRACTICE

When Joseph H. was referred to Stanford physician Allen Barbour at the Stanford Diagnostic Clinic—a last-resort diagnostic facility for tough cases—he complained of feeling "light-headed, dizzy." His case had already stumped a variety of doctors and stymied an even wider variety of diagnoses and treatments. He had no vertigo, faintness, disequilibrium, or other symptoms. For eighteen months, his doctors had been trying to determine what his disease was. He had been given a careful and systematic workup that included an electrocardiogram, electroencephalogram, aortic arch and cerebral arteriography, consultations in neurology and ENT (ear, nose, and throat) with electronystagmography, audiometry, and other special tests. All the studies were negative and his doctors ultimately settled on the working diagnosis of "dizziness of unknown etiology, possibly arteriosclerosis." So for three months they tried therapeutic trials of Hydergine, vasodilators, the "anti-vertigo" antihistamines . . . and anticoagulants (warfarin), but Joseph failed to respond. They considered a new diagnosis of his disease: depression. They put him on tricyclic antidepressants for two more months, but his illness continued unabated.

Joseph was desperate, and Dr. Barbour was the ideal person to turn to for one last opinion. A crackerjack diagnostician and teacher, he was revered by his colleagues and students. His book *Caring for Patients: A Critique of the Medical Model* draws on 403 of the difficult cases referred to him at the clinic by doctors who could not figure out what was happening with their patients. This was his specialty.

When Joseph came to his office, Dr. Barbour began by asking Joseph to describe exactly what he meant by "feeling dizzy."

"Doctor, I feel dizzy nearly all the time since my wife died. I'm confused. I watch TV, but I'm not interested. I go outside, but there's no place to go."

Barbour observed that "Joseph looked sad indeed as he told of the emptiness of his life. He had moved to California with his wife after retirement. He had no children, no close friends, no special interests." Joseph's story gave Dr. Barbour the clue to the diagnosis. "'Dizzy' was Joseph's way of expressing his confusion. . . . [His] personal situation was the clinical problem, and the key to its solution. . . . What Joseph needed was personal understanding rather than biomedical treatment." With the help of a social worker, Joseph was guided to accept and surmount his grief and to establish new friends and activities. The "dizziness" abated.

Why was the heart of Joseph's problem missed for so long by so many smart doctors doing so many sophisticated medical tests? Barbour thoroughly read all of Joseph's medical files. There was no mention of his recent loss or how he felt about it. Had the doctors not asked, or not listened, or not written it down? After all, Dr. Barbour had simply asked Joseph: What do you mean by "feeling dizzy"? And Joseph had handed him the diagnosis. It seems so straightforward. But it seems this way because Dr. Barbour was an experienced, expert listener. In his book, he reports on evidence that good listening is not simple, and not as common as one might hope. One study, for example, showed that the "mean elapsed time between the moment patients began to express their primary concern and the doctor's first interruption was 18 seconds." Thereafter, the doctors took control of the interview by asking increasingly closed-ended questions, like this:

RESIDENT: What's troubling you?

PATIENT: I have this pain in my stomach (indicating with his hands the entire abdomen).

RESIDENT: Where is it?

PATIENT: Pretty much all over.

RESIDENT: Is it here (pointing to the patient's epigastrium)?

PATIENT: Yes, I feel pain there.

RESIDENT: When do you get it?

PATIENT: A lot of the time.

RESIDENT: Before meals?

PATIENT: Yes, before meals, but I get it any old time.

Good listening often demands interrupting a patient. But this resident's second question—"Where is it?"—cut off the patient's own description, and from there on the patient only answered the doctor's questions. Instead of encouraging the patient ("tell me more about it"), the doctor asked questions designed to probe for specific conditions. He diagnosed probable peptic ulcer disease and ordered a GI series. Had he known how to listen, and not looked so quickly for confirming evidence, he might have discovered that the patient had functional bowel disorder. But like many doctors, the resident prematurely objectified a symptom "before understanding what the patient really feels." This is what happened to Joseph. His dizzy feeling was objectified as "vertigo," "faintness," or "disequilibrium." To get the correct diagnosis, Barbour had to clarify "*how* Joseph felt."

The wisdom to know when and how to interrupt is not something that only doctors need to learn. How to balance listening quietly and interrupting someone (and how to interrupt when we do) is a quandary we face so frequently that we don't even think of it as a puzzle we are always solving. Except, maybe, in catastrophic cases where we get it wrong. That it is ordinary does not, however, mean that it's unimportant. Will we learn what we need to know by letting our upset child work through her feelings or our friend stumble through his current confusion, or are they going around in circles, lurching in the darkness, needing us to ask them the right questions or to help them frame their confusion usefully? If we are too quick to interrupt or to solve what we think is their problem, we may, like the novice doctor, miss what the real problem is. But if we wait too long, our friend may dig himself into a hole.

We also need practical wisdom even to know whether solving a problem is the point of listening. Maybe our friend simply wants us to listen so that she can unburden herself or get reassurance or get clarity on her own. And when we *do* interrupt, we need to know how to do it—with a raised eyebrow, a gentle question, a blunt suggestion? For doctors and the rest of us, good listening is the window into empathy and into wise choice making. If we lack the wisdom to know when and how to be silent and when and how to talk, we cut ourselves off from the good listening our social and work relations demand. There is a virtuous circle between practical wisdom and good listening: you need to be practically wise in order to listen well, and learning to listen well enables you to be more practically wise.

The empathetic skills that doctors—and the rest of us—need are not simply verbal. An empathetic doctor has the perceptiveness and imagination to hear subtle emotional clues, and the sensitivity to read body language and facial expression in order to hear what is not said. Pediatricians need to "listen" to babies who can't talk. The elderly are often forgetful, confused, demented—not the most reliable witnesses to their own condition. And adolescents are often tough, troubled, suspicious, fearful, and closed.

A wise doctor also needs the wisdom to control his empathy, and so do we all. The physician, Barbour explains, has to "identify with the patient and enter into his world as the patient experiences it, but simultaneously be objective about it." Barbour was a good listener because he could simultaneously enter the patient's world and stand outside it, because he could balance empathy and detachment.

Beyond diagnosis, the empathy to listen well is also critical if doctors are to advise and treat wisely. Dr. Barbour needed to understand Joseph's perspective in order to determine an effective treatment. There was no pill or other quick fix for Joseph's dizziness. It took several months before Joseph even accepted the fact that loneliness following his wife's death was the whole source of his illness. He was reluctant to get involved with a seniors' group and when he did, he was slow to open up to new relationships. Treating Joseph meant helping him change his life. Treatment as life change has become increasingly common in the United States, as modern medicine is less about responding to acute conditions than it is about managing chronic conditions, like arthritis, congestive heart failure, hypertension, obesity, diabetes, AIDS, low back pain, or osteoporosis. Patients who feel vulnerable, frightened, hopeless, depressed, and confused must be encouraged to participate actively in often arduous life changes. Doctors and nurses—like any good professionals—need to assess what the particular person in front of them can manage, and how to motivate him. Is it feasible to tell this patient that he needs to lose fifty pounds? Or that he needs to walk at a brisk pace for thirty minutes a day? Will it do any good to tell him he needs to lower the stress level of his job? If the doctor enlists the help of the patient's family, will the patient find that encouraging or demeaning? Knowing how to treat patients demands balancing what is scientifically sound with what the patient can or will do, and that demands understanding the perspective and life circumstances of the patient. What's right for one patient may be disastrous for another.

Barbour thought that teaching doctors techniques for good listening—for example, providing guides for intake interviews and rules of thumb for using them—was helpful. But technique alone can't replace empathy. If novice doctors are going to learn to be empathetic, they need to see empathy modeled, they need to be mentored and coached. The erosion of empathy in medical training is exacerbated by the organization of medical practice itself. Institutional forces dissuade doctors from understanding how a patient is feeling and thinking, thereby discouraging the practical wisdom to know when to deviate from standard operating procedures.

Some of the culprits are well known. There are the time pressures. Doctors are pressured to move patients in and out of their offices so quickly—often every fifteen or twenty minutes at best—that they don't have time to put on the bifocals of empathy and detachment even if they have the inclination. We know from our own experiences as overloaded parents or overbooked friends what such time binds do to our ability to be empathetic, let alone compassionate. We saw what happened to the divinity students Darley and Batson studied at the theological seminary. When they were put in a time bind by being told they were late for the lecture they had to give, most of them hurried by the man slumped in the alleyway as they rushed to deliver their talk about the parable of the Good Samaritan. Even if we assume that most doctors have both the disposition to care for their patients and the know-how to do it well—that they have the capacity for practical wisdom—imagine the effect of an organizational structure that is always whispering to the doctor, "You're late."

The effect of time pressures on empathy is compounded by the bureaucratization of medicine and the explosion of specialization. And absent explicit efforts to protect and encourage empathy, the sophisticated, "efficient" diagnosis and treatment that come with these changes have a dark side—impersonalization. Except in cases where the specialist ends up becoming, for all intents and purposes, a primary care physician who knows the whole patient as a person—as, for example, oncologists often do for their cancer patients—specialists know only their specialties, and patients are more organ systems than people. It is thus not surprising that all the specialists examining someone like Joseph, each testing or ruling out different possibilities, would miss the fact that he did not have a disease at all.

The computerization of medical records being urged by the government and professional organizations is unlikely to alleviate the corrosive effects of time pressure and bureaucratization on empathy, and some doctors worry it may make things worse. Dr. Howard Spiro, emeritus professor at Yale Medical School, observes how diagnosis has turned from the ear to the eye. Doctors, who used to listen to their patients, now look for disease on a screen or in a number. "Laptop docs," patients name them. Case presentations at physician conferences "now include a token history, physical findings, laboratory data, and *the images*." The patients remain unseen and unheard, no longer appearing at the conferences. There is "no empathy for CAT [computerized axial tomography] scans!" says Dr. Spiro. The eye, he says, can discern diseases on screens or films, "but the ear hears complaints of patients. Even more than examining the body, listening to patients taps our sense of empathy. When we take the time to listen, we begin to do so."

The estrangement created by time pressure and bureaucratization drops empathy into a powerful, corrosive brew. It is hard for doctors who want to resist these pressures to be empathetic, canny outlaws, though many try. Dr. Barbour had it relatively easy, because he worked in a protected haven for just such outlaws. The Stanford Diagnostic Center was a relatively well funded university institution whose very purpose was to have high-powered diagnosticians take the time to diagnose what had baffled other doctors. Yet even in that context, there was another, more subtle culprit eroding empathy, one of particular concern to Dr. Barbour. It was the model of diagnosis and treatment that underlies common practice.

Barbour argued that this model was primarily a "disease model," and the very way it framed a person's illness discouraged empathy, balance, and wisdom in the doctor-patient relationship. The presumption within this frame is that a symptom is caused by a specific malfunction of part of the living system that is a human being. The main aim of diagnosis is to understand the locus and the nature of the malfunction so it can be treated and cured. Often the model is right. But illnesses like Joseph's cannot be reduced to a specific malfunction. "His symptoms reflected a human situation—the problem of a person rather than the disease of a part." Such human situations are often the major causes of illnesses: recurrent headaches; backache, muscle tension, and chronic pain; gastrointestinal disorders like irritable bowel syndrome; chronic weakness and fatigue; eating, sleeping, and sexual disorders. They are a major cause of psychiatric disorders like panic, anxiety, and depression. Personal situations and lifestyles are often at the root of diseases and common clinical problems associated with tobacco, alcohol, and drug abuse.

Barbour thought that 70 percent of the patients coming through the Stanford Clinic demanded an understanding of just such things in order to be properly diagnosed and treated. The disease model, however, encourages doctors to look for a disease with a specific biological cause, not a systemic human one. It thus marginalizes empathy and good listening. It's not that doctors think empathy is a bad thing. Patients want doctors who are empathetic, many doctors would like to be more empathetic, and even hospital administrators know that empathetic doctors get better "customer satisfaction" ratings and fewer lawsuits. Administrators sometimes even encourage courses that teach doctors empathy and listening skills. But Barbour's point is that the disease model itself ignores the practical importance of empathy for diagnosis and treatment. It conveys the message that there is no medical necessity to listen to stories, understand the anxieties of growing up, notice the tension in a family's marriage, or recognize stress at work. This frame makes it hard to mount a counterattack to protect and nurture the empathetic skills that a practically wise doctor needs. If empathy is regarded as an optional add-on—something that "nice" doctors do to please patients—the medical defense of empathy against the powerful pressures of time, efficiency, and bureaucratization is weakened.

So too in other professions. Simon's lawyer colleague framed Mrs. Jones's "problem" as how to avoid a trial and get her the lightest sentence possible. This model of lawyer-as-advocate sounds as reasonable as the "disease model" of medicine—until we realize that a more person-centered model would have also considered Mrs. Jones's life story, and her own sense of how to balance the desire to seek justice and the risks of a trial. School systems that urge teachers to frame students as products to be tested and evaluated using standardized, multiple-choice tests are aiming to create an efficient, fair, and uniform way to measure learning. But we'll see that a model like this can also sideline the empathy a practically wise teacher needs. A good teacher is always trying to figure out how a particular student is thinking and feeling and how this creates obstacles to learning, or perhaps encourages a different, nonstandardized kind of learning.

MARGINALIZING THE WISDOM
TO COUNSEL

Good counseling is often at the heart of serving people or working on their behalf, whether we are hairdressers, architects, lawyers, marriage counselors, mediators, or good friends. At the heart of such good counseling is the ability to balance empathy and detachment. Good counseling almost always involves helping others clarify their goals, assess their interests, resist acting impetuously, and make difficult choices. Such counseling is what a good doctor needs to do to balance paternalism and patient choice when helping patients figure out how to customize a complex or difficult treatment regimen, or when nudging patients to overcome fear and choose to do what the doctor knows to be in their best interests. To counsel well, we need to understand the other people's perspectives—to get inside their hearts and minds. But we also need to move outside their perspective, detach ourselves from what they are thinking and feeling at the moment, so that we can help them detach too—so that we can help them gain perspective. Much of our ability to counsel wisely comes from lessons we learn from friends and family as we make mistakes by being too detached, or even too empathetic. But the institutions that structure our work environments also teach us.

WISE COUNSEL ON CHICAGO'S MEAN STREETS

On the morning of August 23, 2007, a relative phoned Martin Torres in Austin, Texas. Emilio, his seventeen-year-old nephew, had been murdered on Chicago's South Side. Torres immediately took off his cook's apron and rushed back to his home turf. He had been close to Emilio. "I thought, man, I'm going to take care of business. That's how I live. I was going hunting. This is my own blood, my nephew." Torres, then thirty-eight, had once headed a small Latino gang in Chicago and the two silver studs in his ear are signs of his affiliation. He himself had been shot six times. He borrowed two guns. He asked around and soon thought he knew who killed his nephew. He planned to track the killers down after the funeral.

Alex Kotlowitz, a teacher and writer at Northeastern University, pieced together the story for an article he was doing on CeaseFire, an organization that employs "violence interrupters" to reduce violence on the streets by intervening early in conflicts like this. Its goal is to prevent violence from spreading by preventing shootings. One of those violence interrupters, Zale Hoddenbach, also thirty-eight, thought he might have some leverage in this case. When he was younger, Hoddenbach had belonged to a gang under the same umbrella as Torres's, and they had become friendly seventeen years earlier when they both served time at Pontiac Correctional Center (Hoddenbach for armed violence, Torres for possession of a stolen car and a gun).

Hoddenbach got a call from Emilio's father—Torres's brother—who told Hoddenbach that he was worried that Torres was preparing to seek revenge and that the last thing he wanted was for his son's death to precipitate more violence. He asked if Hoddenbach would try to speak with him. Torres was thrilled to talk to Hoddenbach—he assumed his old prison mate wanted to help exact revenge. But Hoddenbach spent the next days trying to talk Torres down—sitting with him, talking with him, urging him to respect his brother's wishes. Hoddenbach let Torres vent, says Kotlowitz, but then laid into him with every argument he could think of. "Look around, do you see any old guys here? I never seen so many young kids at a funeral. Look at these kids! What does the future hold for them? Where do we fit in? Who are you to step on your brother's wishes?"

"Because of our relationship, I thought there was a chance," Hoddenbach told Kotlowitz. "We were both cut from the same cloth." And Torres did finally relent, but admits that he still feels shame. In the past, he had sought revenge for "people who weren't even no blood to me." But now, he said, looking more puzzled than comforted, "Something made me do what Zale asked me to do. Which is respect my brother's wishes."

Chicago's CeaseFire was founded by physician and epidemiologist Gary Slutkin, who sought to bring the methods he had learned when managing tuberculosis and AIDS to managing the spread of violence. (Similar programs have since been started in Baltimore, Newark, Kansas City, and Providence, Rhode Island.) Slutkin believed that violence spreads like a disease, with one instance causing another. Stopping Torres's revenge would help stop the spread. So would stopping gang members from arming themselves to avenge an egging of their freshly painted cars (one interrupter prodded them to go to a car wash instead and then persuaded them it wasn't worth risking their lives over a stupid prank).

Doing this kind of counseling demanded a great deal of courage and wisdom. The starting point was recruiting the right kinds of people. Recruiters often went looking for former gang members, signing up some while they were still in prison. They sought people who regretted their pasts, who wanted to find work and stay out of prison, who wanted to atone for their wrongdoing. I want "to give back, be a blessing," "to make penitentiaries go bankrupt," to "stop the self-inflicted genocide," were the kinds of explanations new recruits gave. The new recruits came to their jobs with the contacts, the respect, and the street smarts to sniff out cases that might escalate. They spoke the language. They had a storehouse of examples and stories, including their own, to guide them. But that wasn't enough to give them the practical wisdom they needed to "talk down" a revenge-seeking Martin Torres.

The interrupters were tasked with counseling people who had not asked to be counseled. They had to know how to get inside the hearts of the people seeking revenge, to listen and empathize, to know when to let them vent and when and how to talk with them. They needed the courage to walk into dangerous situations, unarmed, and confront violent gang members. They needed the dedication and commitment to want to stop the violence. They needed the know-how to frame what they said so that those they counseled could retain their status and manliness even if they walked away from revenge. Gary Slutkin put it this way: "The interrupters have to deal with how to get someone to save face. In other words, how do you not do a shooting if someone has insulted you, if all of your friends are expecting you to do that?"

The daily balancing acts built into their work also demanded practical wisdom. There was a constant tension between accepting their "clients" as they were and pushing them to become someone else. "We can't act like we're lifesavers," one interrupter explained. "We have to act at their level." That meant being sensitive to gang culture and having the ability to withhold judgment of the young people they worked with. At the same time, the interrupters were expected to act as role models, a positive presence in the lives of high-risk young adults. A detailed study of the program carried out at Northwestern University found that many clients said the interrupters did serve as models, mentors, even father figures in their lives, helping them stay off drugs, find employment, get out of gangs, or avoid being pressured into joining them. Another constant balancing act the interrupters faced was the need to uphold the law while simultaneously upholding the logic of the streets. "They're not meant to be a substitute for the police," says Kotlowitz, "and indeed, sometimes the interrupters negotiate disputes involving illicit goings-on. They often walk a fine line between mediating and seeming to condone criminal activity."

So the past criminal and prison experience the interrupters brought to their jobs was important. But it was not enough. How did they develop the practical wisdom they needed to bring this experience to bear on the risky, high-stakes counseling and mediation they signed up to undertake? CeaseFire worked hard to create an organizational structure and ethos that helped them learn. Its centerpiece was hands-on experience. The violence interrupters were encouraged to work in pairs or small groups and to teach each other on the job. They learned much of what they needed to know watching those they worked with model counseling and seeing what worked and what didn't. They got informal coaching. They also learned from their own mistakes and taught one another by sharing their stories and discussing them.

The on-the-job training was supplemented by a required weekly meeting with their supervisors and the other interrupters—fifteen to twenty-five men and a couple of women sitting around tables arranged in a circle in a public health building at the University of Illinois. They shared information on current hot spots and potential upcoming conflicts. They discussed how to handle tough dilemmas they faced. At one meeting Kotlowitz attended, the interrupters argued over "whether they could dissuade stickup artists from shooting their victims" (although "persuading them to stop robbing people didn't come up for discussion"). They often reported on what they did and how well it worked, or didn't, and the stories they told helped them teach and motivate one another. "One of them, Calvin Buchanan, whose street name is Monster and who just recently joined CeaseFire, showed the others six stitches over his left eye; someone had cracked a beer bottle on his head while he was mediating an argument between two men. The other interrupters applauded when Buchanan told them that, though tempted, he restrained himself from getting even." Sometimes Cease-Fire provided them with more formal training at the meetings: stress management, legal aid for clients, substance abuse awareness, conflict resolution. They were also taught about what kinds of things can't be asked, how to network, how to see things as the disputants see them, and how to have a confrontation if it can't be avoided. Such sessions were most successful when led by people with street experience, like former gang members.

CeaseFire also worked hard to create a larger community environment that encouraged their counseling efforts. CeaseFire not only needed the local gangs to tolerate and trust the interrupters but also needed the support and collaboration of local police, community organizations, churches, schools, service agencies, and merchants. Getting police support was the most difficult, and it took discretion—and wisdom—to manage. The police were an important source of information for the work violence interrupters do. They required a heads-up from local stations when violence occurred, and information—like gang involvement—about the victims and circumstances.

So CeaseFire recruited violence interrupters who already had the kind of experience they would need to succeed on the job. But then it created an organizational and community structure that gave the interrupters experiences that encouraged them to develop the practical wisdom needed to counsel well. This is exactly what many big corporate law firms fail to do.

Marginalizing the "Lawyer as Counselor"

Though we often think of lawyers as hired guns—as paid advocates zealously arguing for whatever the client wants as long as it's not illegal—there is a long tradition in the law to think of lawyers as counselors. That's because one of the purposes of legal practice is helping clients to understand what their interests are: counseling them in ways that help them look past the heat of the moment, as when a lawyer tries to get a couple battling angrily over the financial terms of a divorce to consider the harm it would do to their children.

But this tradition of "lawyer as counselor" has been marginalized in recent years by the growing dominance of zealous advocacy as the norm. This shift was energized by transformations in the world of big corporate law firms: increased specialization, market competition, and

growing bureaucratization encouraged the corrosion of good counseling and the practical wisdom it demands.

Beginning in the 1970s, business corporations began to change their
long-term relationships with the large law firms upon whom they had
depended. The corporations started setting up their own in-house legal
departments and putting routine work in the hands of their own lawyers.
This challenged the traditional relationships between the corporations
and the independent law firms. These long-standing relationships had
established trust and confidence among the lawyers and their clients;
the lawyers often had a deep knowledge of the historical experiences
and aims of their clients and knew the key actors well. This kind of
relationship established bonds of loyalty that encouraged good counsel,
like "tough love" in a good friendship. Lawyer-counselors did not expect the clients to walk away if their questions and advice were not
what the clients wanted to hear.

The in-house lawyers working for the corporations were in a very
different position. Whatever their professional judgment, they were
permanently and directly beholden to only one client—the corporate
boss who gave them their paycheck. It was difficult to be detached from
the hand that fed them, and there was a built-in temptation to temper
independent judgment, to avoid being the counselor who delivers un-
wanted news.

As in-house lawyers began to do much of the work that had been
done by independent law firms, the relationship between the corporate
clients and the law firms changed. Corporations with their own legal
staffs were less likely to maintain a long-term ongoing relationship with
an independent firm. They were more likely to look at legal services as
commodities to be bought on a project-by-project basis. They shopped
for the firm that offered the most expertise on the specific problem at
hand and offered it for the best price. The traditional bonds between
law firms and their corporate clients frayed as they were increasingly

replaced by market relationships. And the big law firms themselves changed in response to this market competition.

The law firms began to focus on providing the kind of specialized knowledge in-house lawyers couldn't provide, aggressively marketing specific services. Lawyers became like medical specialists who see only one kind of problem, over and over again, and have short-term relations with each client. That made it difficult for lawyers to understand the history of their clients' firm in a way that would enable them to put the current matter in appropriate context. They no longer knew their clients well enough to do anything but accept the clients' definition of the problem and give the narrow advice being sought. With a microscopic view of isolated problems, these lawyers were less able to help clients reconsider their immediate goals in light of their long-term interests.

The erosion of long-term relationships between law firms and their corporate clients also made it more difficult for the independent lawyers to say hard things. Giving tough advice risked alienating a client who only came for short-term, specialized service and who would be willing to go elsewhere. Even if you're a wise counselor, and want to supply more than technical expertise, you still need to think twice. If there is no long-term relationship, your client may decide to shoot the messenger and go back into the market and buy another commodity—hire another law firm.

Professor Kimberly Kirkland at Franklin Pierce Law Center looked inside large law firms to see what impact this growing specialization and market competition had on the younger lawyers coming up in the firm. She did in-depth interviews with twenty-two lawyers (primarily litigators) in ten large firms. What she found was a kind of organization that squeezed out wise counsel and discouraged the experiences that teach wise judgment. The lawyers Kirkland interviewed painted a picture of a large bureaucracy in which the very busy senior partners—the "finders" who generate the new business and the "binders" who work to keep existing clients—delegate the actual legal work to the "cheaper" mid-level lawyers—the "minders." These "minders" manage many of the cases and, in turn, have young associates who work for them. The competition of the young associates to "make partner" is fierce. Many more are hired than will be promoted to partner. This "promotion-to-partner tournament" and the bureaucratic hierarchy of the work combine to encourage shrewd thinking about survival strategies but not wise judgment about counseling.

As the law firm took on the traits of any big bureaucracy, the norm for the lawyers was not the exercise of independent judgment, but a stance of "looking up and looking around" in which "morality becomes indistinguishable from the quest for one's own survival and advantage." It was not appropriate for junior lawyers to worry about figuring out right and wrong. They were trained to "look up the food chain and ask, 'What would the lawyer I'm working for think is right here?'" And what Kirkland found is that "the lawyer at the top of the food chain will ask what the client wants"—not "How can I give good counsel?" Not surprisingly, one fifth-year associate explained to her, that's what most of the lawyers further down on the chain will think too:

> To make partner in litigation you need to be seen as really aggressive. Your partners need to know that you are not going to be pushed around or bullied out there. . . . The client wants to know that you won't be pushed around; that you will do what you need to, to defend them. You have to create the impression that you are looking out for the client in every way. Internally, [inside the firm] you need to be a yes person.

The supervising lawyers, reported Kirkland, "expect 'service' from their junior associates in the same way clients expect service from their lawyers." In fact the lawyers who worked for other lawyers understood "that their supervisors are their primary 'clients.'" Kirkland found that the habit of mind being cultivated in the firm was to do whatever you guessed your supervising lawyer wanted. "The final arbiter of the quality of your work is not the client, the judge, or any external truth," one junior associate told Kirkland. "It's the partner you're working for." The effect is not only to discourage wise counseling. It also upends the very purpose of legal practice.

MARGINALIZING PUBLIC SERVICE

One important challenge for a lawyer is to be an advocate *and* a wise counselor; another is the lawyer's responsibility to be a client advocate and a public servant. Quite often such balancing of client interests and the public interest also demands the wisdom to counsel well. Alexis de Tocqueville's nineteenth-century metaphor of lawyers as the natural aristocracy captures this aim of law. He saw the professional lawyer as a practitioner with the disposition and wisdom to be responsible for encouraging justice and for protecting the norms of fairness, decency, and integrity upon which the legal system is based.

Balancing these goals with serving one's clients is part of the everyday work of lawyers, not something reserved for occasional dramatic moments. Trial lawyers, for example, often must decide whether to "impeach" the credibility of a witness they know to be telling the truth in order to win their client's case. It may be legal, but it violates a significant purpose of the law and threatens the system that makes fair trials possible. If lawyers routinely did this, the testimony of most witnesses could be undermined or thrown into doubt, making it more difficult for judges and juries to reach fair and just decisions, or perhaps any decisions at all. So lawyers must always balance their responsibility to their client with their responsibility as "officers of the court."

There is no rule or principle to settle this tension between being the partisan champion of a client and upholding the integrity of the law as an impartial officer of the court. The tension is built into the American legal system, based as it is on the presumption of innocence until proven guilty and on a procedure that demands that plaintiffs and defendants argue their cases before juries who will make this decision. "[The] real challenge," wrote former Yale Law School dean Anthony Kronman, "is not to overcome the dilemma (for that cannot be done), but to resist the temptation to resolve it by always putting the client's well-being before the law's."

Traditionally, many big-firm lawyers prided themselves on their will and ability to balance the private interests of their clients with the public good, on wisely counseling their clients in this regard and not simply serving as hired guns. What enabled them to maintain this balance were the long-term relationships they had with their clients. When Professor Robert Nelson, a sociologist at Northwestern University, interviewed senior partners in some of the "mega–law firms" that were emerging in the 1980s, they avowed the highest ethical standards for their firms, and a majority of them asserted that lawyers should act as the conscience of their clients when counseling them.

Ralph Fine, once a senior partner at a large corporate law firm in Boston, told us about watching one of his clients on a collision course with the public school system because of stalled negotiations with striking Boston school bus drivers. His law firm was representing a company that owned all the school buses in Boston. The company was refusing to yield on salary and benefits issues in talks with the union. School was starting, the buses weren't rolling, news of the failed negotiations was in the headlines, and his client was refusing to sweeten its offer to the union. It wasn't Fine's case, but he knew a continued strike wasn't going to be good for anybody. He went downstairs to see the lawyer in charge, who assured him not to worry: "We've got them in a corner. If we just hang tough for a few more days we can break the union. They're going to give in at any moment." Ralph asked his associate for the phone number of the client and permission to call. "This wasn't my field of expertise," said Fine, "but I knew this was not in the long-term interests of either the client, or the city, or the schoolkids, or the union. I talked with the head of the company the next day. I spent an hour there, suggesting reasons that hanging tough, even if they won, would create bad press for them and have bad long-term consequences. They settled the strike in a day."

Nelson's research and the work of other scholars and observers indicate that the Ralph Fines may increasingly be the rare exceptions in big firms. Despite the verbal commitments to ethical concerns and good counseling that Nelson heard, his research showed that these "large-firm lawyers are above all committed advocates." The senior partners almost never seriously disagree with what a client proposes to do, and they hold positions about law and policy that are very close to those of their clients. Far from encouraging a stance of detachment or balance among the lawyers below them, the partners encourage subservience to client interests. The researchers who worked on the American Bar Association's report *Ethics: Beyond the Rules* in the late 1990s similarly found that the dominant view among large-firm litigators about the "moral thing to do" was zealous representation of client interests, not acting as counselors or attempting to balance client interests with public ones.

The marginalization of lawyers as public servants may also explain current public opinion about lawyers. Polls that measure popular respect for various occupations consistently rate lawyers well below nurses, doctors, and teachers, and only slightly ahead of insurance salesmen, HMO managers, professional admen, and used-car salesmen. Supreme Court Justice Sandra Day O'Connor warned law students and their professors at Washington University in St. Louis that "few Americans recall the trust that our society once placed in its lawyers." She said that more than half of all practitioners report dissatisfaction with the profession, and in society at large, "lawyers are compared frequently, and unfavorably I might add, [to] skunks, snakes, and sharks." She urged her audience to turn this situation around, to commit themselves to their role as public servants. Quoting John W. Davis, a former U.S. solicitor general, she reminded them of their humble but professional role: "True, we build no bridges. We raise no towers. . . . But we smooth out difficulties; we relieve stress; we correct mistakes; we take up other men and women's burdens and by our efforts we make possible the peaceful life of men and women in a peaceful state." She concluded: "You should make it the Law School's commitment to teach the importance of doing good while doing well."

9.

Right by Rote: Overstandardization and the Rise of the Canny Outlaw

WISDOM IN THE LINE OF FIRE

Lieutenant Colonel Chris Hughes had a delicate mission in the religious center of Najaf on the morning of April 3, 2002. The Iraq War was in its early weeks, and he had been trying to get in touch with the most important Shiite cleric in Iraq, Grand Ayatollah Ali al-Sistani. The soldiers in his small unit were walking along a street when suddenly hundreds of Iraqis poured out of the surrounding buildings, waving fists, shrieking, frantic with rage. They pressed in on the Americans, who looked at one another with terror. Lieutenant Colonel Hughes, impassive behind surfer sunglasses, stepped forward, rifle high over his head, barrel pointing to the ground. "Take a knee," he ordered his men. They looked at him as if he was crazy. Then, one after another, swaying in their bulky body armor and gear, they knelt before the angry crowd, pointing their guns at the ground. The Iraqis fell silent. Their anger subsided. Hughes ordered his men to withdraw.

Journalist Dan Baum called Hughes after seeing this incident live on CNN and asked him who had taught him to tame a crowd like that. Hughes said that no one had prepared him for an angry crowd in an Arab country, much less in Najaf. Officers learn certain techniques like using the rotor wash from a helicopter to drive away a crowd or firing warning shots. "Problem with that is, the next thing you have to do is shoot them in the chest," said Hughes. The Iraqis already felt that the Americans were disrespecting their mosque. For Hughes, the obvious solution was a gesture of respect.

But what made this solution obvious? Hughes had to read the context—what this crowd was thinking, what they understood or more likely misunderstood, how he might get through to them. He had to imagine the consequences of any steps he took and make a decision in a complex and unpredictable situation with competing goals (protect his men, not harm civilians, make contact with Sistani). He had never trained for this situation. He had no rules to follow. Like the wildland firefighters, he had to improvise. And quickly.

Even before the Iraq invasion, the U.S. Army had become concerned that many of its officers lacked the ability for this kind of improvisation. In 2000, the Army Chief of Staff, General Eric Shinseki, wanted to figure out why, and what could be done about it. He sought help from retired Lieutenant Colonel Leonard Wong, a research professor of military strategy at the Army War College and a professional engineer. Wong had directed the army's Office of Economic and Manpower Analysis and taught leadership at the U.S. Military Academy.

In the army, wartime experience is considered the best possible teacher, at least for those who survive the first weeks. Wong found another good one—the practice junior officers get while training their units. The decisions these officers have to make as teachers help develop the capacity for the judgment they will need on the battlefield. But Wong discovered that in the 1980s, the army had begun to restructure training in ways that had the opposite results.

Traditionally, company commanders had the opportunity to plan, execute, and assess the training they gave their units. "Innovation," Wong explained, "develops when an officer is given a minimal number of parameters (e.g., task, condition, and standards) and the requisite time to plan and execute the training. Giving the commanders time to create their own training develops confidence in operating within the boundaries of a higher commander's intent without constant supervision." The junior officers develop practical wisdom through their teaching of trainees, but only if their teaching allows them discretion and flexibility. Just as psychologist Karl Weick found studying firefighters, experience applying a limited number of guidelines teaches soldiers how to improvise in dangerous situations.

Wong's research showed that the responsibility for training at the company level was being taken away from junior officers. First, the time they needed was being eaten away by "cascading requirements" placed on company commanders from above. There was, Wong explained, such a "rush by higher headquarters to incorporate every good idea into training" that "the total number of training days required by all mandatory training directives literally exceeds the number of training days available to company commanders. Company commanders somehow have to fit 297 days of mandatory requirements into 256 available training days." On top of this, there were administrative requirements to track data on as many as 125 items, including sexual responsibility training, family care packets, community volunteer hours, and even soldiers who had vehicles with Firestone tires.

Second, headquarters increasingly dictated *what* would be trained and *how* it would be trained, essentially requiring commanders "to follow a script." Commanders lost the opportunity to analyze their units' weaknesses and plan the training accordingly. Worse, headquarters took away the "assessment function" from battalion commanders. Certifying units as "ready" was now done from the top.

The learning through trial and error that taught officers how to improvise, Wong found, happens when officers try to plan an action, then actually execute it and reflect on what worked and what didn't. Officers who did not have to adhere to strict training protocols were in an excellent position to learn because they could immediately see results, make adjustments, and assess how well their training regimens were working. And most important, it was this kind of experience that taught the commanders how to improvise, which helped them learn to be flexible, adaptive, and creative on the battlefield. Wong was concerned about changes in the training program because they squeezed out these learning experiences; they prevented officers from experiencing the wisdom-nurturing cycle of planning, executing the plan, assessing what worked and didn't, reevaluating the original plan, and trying again.

Wong's research supports the findings of other researchers exploring the essence of professional judgment. MIT professor Donald Schön dubbed it "reflective practice." Schön, an expert on how professionals and organizations learn, argued that good professionals are always adjusting their actions to the particular context in order to achieve a general aim (health, education, justice), and the way they learn how to do this is by assessing the particular actions they choose (their words, their advice, their framing), and reevaluating, often rapidly, what they have said or done so they can improve upon it. This process of reflective practice—of trial, error, reassessment, and trial again—allows them to get better and better at what they do. They learn the moral and technical expertise to do their work well.

The top-down approach in the army's new training model did have benefits. The higher echelons, for example, could provide more information than any individual commander about the lessons being learned from worldwide deployments. Training was more uniform and standardized. It seemed to promise quality control. In fact, the assumption beneath this way of organizing training is one that has long underpinned much modern thinking about efficient industrial organization and management. It is assumed that an organization is most efficient if there is a division of labor between those who conceive and plan the work and those who actually execute the plans. There are the specialists in "theory" and the specialists in "practice." Similarly there is a presumption that assessment is best left in the hands of the planning specialists. They have more information and objectivity; they will look at the outcomes, alter their plans, and then give new orders to those who execute them.

But Wong found a distinct downside to this division of labor. "Put all the directed requirements together and the life of a company commander is spent executing somebody else's good ideas." Too many rules and requirements "removes all discretion" and stifles the development of flexible officers, resulting in "reactive instead of proactive thought, compliance instead of creativity, and adherence instead of audacity." These are not the kinds of officers the army needs in unpredictable and quickly changing situations where specific orders are absent and military protocol is unclear. The army is creating cooks, says Wong, leaders who are "quite adept at carrying out a recipe," rather than chefs who can "look at the ingredients available to them and create a meal." Wong found a number of top brass who agreed. Retired General Wesley Clark observed that senior army leaders have "gone too far in over-planning, over-prescribing, and over-controlling." The consequence, according to retired General Frederick Kroesen, is that "initiative is stymied, and decision making is replaced by waiting to be told. . . . There is no more effective way to destroy the leadership potential of young officers and noncommissioned officers than to deny them opportunities to make decisions appropriate for their assignments."

The same thing can be said about public school teachers.

DISCOURAGING WISDOM IN TEACHERS

Overall, Deborah Ball was pleased with the progress being made by her third-grade math class in Lansing, Michigan, as the term drew to a close. The students in her class had not only learned the rudiments of fractions but also had learned to think and reason for themselves. But teaching them to reason and problem-solve wasn't rote work. And this afternoon, as the clock ticked toward the end of the day, she had a problem.

It started when Mei, a small Taiwanese girl, noticed that the larger the "number on top" of a fraction, "the bigger the piece you'll end up [with]." Ball asked the class to figure out if Mei's conjecture was correct. One student suggested 4/4 and 5/5. Ball could simply have told the class that these two fractions were the same. But instead, Ball had the students draw two rectangles in their notebooks, one divided into four parts and the other into five, and then to shade in the numerators.

"I was confident that everyone would soon realize that 5/5 did not have 'a bigger piece' shaded in." But when she asked the students, she was astonished. Mei changed her position and saw they were the same, but some of the students chorused: "YES! Five-fifths did have a bigger piece shaded." Cassandra, a tall African-American student, older than the rest and a frequent class participant, began to argue with Mei's new claim that they were both the same. "Five-fifths is not the same [as 4/4]," said Cassandra, "because they are different numbers just like three and two are different numbers. So how could they be the same?" "I'm not *saying* the *numbers* are the same!" Mei replied, her voice rising. "I am saying that they—the part you shade *in*—are the same."

Ball tried again, reframing the question: "If Mei has 4/4 of a cookie and Cassandra has 5/5 of an identical cookie, who has more cookie?" Sheena jumped into the fray. She went to the board and drew two cookies, one in four parts and one in five. Emphatically, she made her point: "With 5/5 there is enough to pass out one piece to each of your five friends, but with 4/4 one friend will not get a cookie."

For Ball to figure out what to do at this moment clearly demanded some knowledge of math—something that Ball, originally a French major who went back to school to learn math, thinks is a fundamental starting point for good teaching. But it demanded something more. She had taken the class through this material before. It had seemed as if they had understood it. But now Ball wasn't sure. To teach the students, it was not good enough that Ball understood the math for herself. She had to get inside the thinking of those who concluded that ⅗ was bigger than ¼ and figure out how to get them to see the equivalence.

Ball distinguishes mathematical knowledge from what she calls "mathematical knowledge for teaching," which demands the skill to understand a student's confusion and then help her overcome it. Ball practices doing this by regularly asking the students how they come to the conclusions they do. She also has the students keep journals in which they write down their thinking and questions. She reads the journals regularly. In this case of fraction confusion, Ball sought to determine whether this really was confusion about the mathematics or whether something else was going on.

"I worried about Mei and Cassandra," says Ball. "Each was so sure she was right. Each restated her position, a little more definitely, almost defiantly. Was this dispute mathematical or social?" It was difficult to know, said Ball, because her third-graders are sometimes motivated "out of stubbornness" and sometimes "out of confidence. Sometimes their ideas drive the discussion, sometimes their relationships. More often than not, it is some combination of the two." Ball knew that Cassandra often relished disagreeing with classmates, not always attending to the evidence they were giving. Mei often maintained a particular view while others in the class argued with her. So Ball wasn't sure that mediating a disagreement between these two girls would resolve the issue.

The moment also presented Ball with a classic, practical, ethical quandary of the sort that is embedded in almost any moment of teaching. She needed to balance the equal treatment of all students with the special needs of one or two. Should all students "share equally"—get the same amount of time and attention from a teacher, or should time "be distributed according to need" or perhaps "according to merit."

These different notions of fairness—Aristotle would say justice—are legitimate, but often in radical conflict with each other. Yet to teach well, Ball needed the wisdom to balance these competing notions.

Only four of the children "were waging this battle, all girls," says Ball. "I wondered what the others were thinking. Were they engaged with this argument, and, if so, what was their position?" If only a handful of students were confused, maybe Ball should just work with them later and not take time from all the other students. Ball decided to see where the rest of the class was on this issue. "How many people think that ¼ and ⅖ are the same amount? . . . Okay, who thinks that ⅖ is more?" The class was split, seven to eight. Ball then wondered if there was any pattern in who was taking which position, but there was roughly equal distribution among the African-American, white, and international children, and between the boys and the girls. This was clearly a discussion that the whole class needed to have.

But how should she proceed? Should she correct the students or let them figure it out by helping them discuss it among themselves? How should she balance critique with support, correction with encouragement? Determining how to correct anyone's mistake always raises quandaries like this for teachers—and for parents, friends, supervisors, and colleagues. Ball has thought a lot about the hows and whys of correcting students, about whether she should ask them to figure it out or tell them the correct answer, and how to prod them.

As a general principle, Ball leans toward the position of American philosopher John Dewey, who believed that students could only really learn if teachers encouraged them to practice working things out—making conjectures, defending their answers, and arguing with each other—as opposed to memorizing. Teachers who disagree with Dewey and who generally favor telling over asking are critical of what they sometimes call "discovery learning" or "child-centered learning." Instead, they emphasize the importance of accumulating a wide range of information—a knowledge base or a cultural literacy, as E. D. Hirsch has dubbed it. Ball, herself a teacher of teachers at the University of Michigan's School of Education (and appointed dean in 2005), was more of an "asker" than a "teller." But for her, this was a balancing act. She wanted her students to have the competence and confidence to think for themselves, but they also had to have a knowledge base. She tried to encourage other teachers to learn how to do this balancing. And in this class, on this day, the question for her was how long she should indulge wrong answers for the sake of teaching critical thinking— especially given only three days until the end of the term.

"We need to stop for a moment," Ball told the class. Balancing principle and expediency, she decided just to tell them directly—"something impatient observers sometimes urge me to do." She would show them that Cassandra and Sheena were right that the number of pieces would be more but that mathematically the size was the same so that $\frac{1}{5}$ and $\frac{1}{4}$ were the same. Ball pulled out two large white envelopes, turned them into imaginary cookies, and cut one into four pieces and one into five. She and the students talked about pieces and then taped the pieces back together to make the original "cookies"—both the same size. But Ball discovered that this telling and showing still did not quell the disagreement. Lucy argued that "they both have the same," but Daniel responded, "I disagree because that one ($\frac{1}{4}$) has lots less 'cause it's got four, and [the other] five." Ball pressed insistently. "I didn't ask which one had more pieces. I asked which one had more cookie." But there was only five minutes until recess. Ball asked the students to write in their notebooks what they thought about the comparison of $\frac{1}{4}$ and $\frac{1}{5}$. She would take it up again tomorrow.

Ball has generally had great success teaching students to think mathematically by encouraging them to figure things out. Films of her third-grade class show the day students derived the concept of infinity ("You would die before you counted all the numbers," one girl said) and how one eight-year-old girl proved that adding two odd numbers would always yield an even number. For teachers to learn how to do this, they need to learn the math, they need to learn how to think about math the way their students do, and they need mentors who can model effective teaching and coach them. But a necessary condition for any of this to work is that the teachers have the opportunities to learn through the same kind of practical, trial-and-error experiences they are encouraging their students to have. Like the army officers training their units, they need to learn from their own mistakes. But just as the army officers Wong studied were often prevented from having these kinds of experiences, so too are many public school teachers.

———

Donna Moffett teaches first grade at Public School 92 in Brooklyn. At forty-six, brimming with idealism and enthusiasm, she abandoned her $60,000-a-year job as a legal secretary to earn $37,000 teaching in one of New York's most troubled schools. When she began her "literacy block" at 11:58 one Wednesday in May, she opened the textbook to Section 1, "Pets Are Special Animals." Her mentor, veteran teacher Marie Buchanan, was sitting in. When Ms. Moffett got to a line about a boy mischievously drawing on a table, she playfully noted, "Just like some students in here." Ms. Buchanan frowned. "You don't have to say that." When Ms. Moffett turned to a page that suggested an art project related to the story and started passing out paper, Ms. Buchanan chided: "You're not going to have time to complete that." After the lesson, Ms. Buchanan pulled her aside. "You have to prepare for these lessons and closely follow your teacher's guide. We're going to do this again tomorrow, and you're not going to wing it."

The teacher's manual Ms. Moffett was using (which includes an actual script and specifies the time to spend on each activity, from thirty seconds to forty minutes) was also being used in hundreds of schools nationwide and was required in New York's low-performing schools. Schools using it have shown some improvement in scores on standardized tests. The manual's fixed routines and careful instructions are sometimes helpful to novice teachers like Ms. Moffett; they can act as training wheels on a bicycle, helping them keep their balance when they first start teaching in the chaotic environment of an inner-city public school. Ms. Moffett admits that the step-by-step script, and the instructions from Ms. Buchanan, have helped ease her transition into the classroom. But Ms. Moffett would like to learn to teach more like Deborah Ball does.

When she applied to the teaching program in New York she wrote: "I want to manage a classroom where children experience the thrill of wonder, the joy of creativity and the rewards of working hard. My objective is to convey to children in their formative years the sheer pleasure in learning." Now she rankles under the tight script she has to follow. "I don't think the [city's] call for help was to have people come into these schools and say 'Open your book to page blah-dee-blah.'" She is facing the same problems Wong noticed among the military officers: she is not being given the kind of experience she needs to learn to improvise like Ball does. And worse, many school systems make it difficult to take the training wheels off, no matter how much experience the teacher has.

The New York Board of Education required teachers in low-performing schools like P.S. 92 to follow a lockstep curriculum, and this is common in many school systems. In some systems, teachers' annual evaluations, and even pay, are based on their students' performance on standardized tests (the scripted curricula are written to prepare students to pass these tests). In other systems, the kind of micromonitoring of teacher behavior that Ms. Buchanan was doing as a temporary mentor is permanently built into the system. When Texas, for example, began experimenting with mechanisms to hold teachers accountable in the 1980s, teachers were scored to determine their place on the "Career Ladder," and their pay increments. School administrators were sent in to observe teachers, armed with a generic checklist applicable to all subjects, all grade levels, all children, and all teachers. An hour's teaching was broken down into forty-five observable, measurable behaviors.

Teachers earned points for required behaviors such as maintaining eye contact with the students, having a "catchy opener" and definite closure to the lesson, having the objective for the day written on the board for all to see, and "varying verbal responses" to students. To ensure that all teachers knew a variety of "positive verbal responses," the teachers were supplied with a list of one hundred approved "praise words." Some teachers kept lists of praise words on the lectern and tried to slip them in as often as they could. When a similar system was tried in Florida (Florida Performance Measurement System, or FPMS), the 1986 Teacher of the Year (also a runner-up in NASA's Teacher in Space program) failed to earn a bonus because the principal observing his laboratory lesson found a deficiency of required behaviors. Teachers in Florida were downgraded for asking questions that "call for personal opinion or that are answered from personal experience," although students often learn best exactly when they can make these connections. Teachers were also marked down for answering a question with a question. Socrates, the scholars of the Talmud, and Deborah Ball would all have been in trouble.

Current educational reforms aimed at improving performance through standardization are rooted in early-twentieth-century attempts to impose "scientific" organization on factory workers, using techniques developed by Frederick Winslow Taylor (1856–1915), the father of what came to be known as "scientific management." In the early 1900s, Taylor encouraged American managers to improve efficiency by carefully breaking down the movements of workers on the shop floor, timing and analyzing each one to the hundredth of a second, and then using these "time-and-motion" studies to reorganize the workplace to get the same results in less time. Planning and assessment would be in the hands of management. Assembly lines would run more quickly, efficiently, and profitably. When these efficiency experts went into the schools in the early 1900s, they used stopwatches to figure out the number of arithmetic problems students should be able to do and at what speed, the facts they should be able to recall, and the words they should know how to spell. In 1913, management expert Franklin Bobbitt observed, "having these definite tasks laid upon her, she [the teacher] can know at all times whether she is accomplishing the things expected of her or not."

Standardized scripted curricula tied directly to high-stakes tests are today's version of such scientific management. "High stakes" means schools and teachers are rewarded (more money) or punished (funds denied, schools closed, staff dismissed or reassigned) based on student test performance. Most states have such systems and the No Child Left Behind Act of 2001 required all states to administer standardized reading and math tests in third and eighth grade. School systems risk losing federal funding if students consistently fail to meet the standards. Standardized tests gave birth to standardized, scripted curricula. If schools and teachers would be rated, funded, or paid based on student test performance, it made sense to mandate that teachers use materials explicitly designed so that students could pass the tests. In fact, novice teachers, quite reasonably, often appreciated the scripts. If they and their students were to be judged by test scores, here was a set of routines that promised to make their students better test takers. Many educators countered that giving novice teachers the needed guidelines did not have to be a choice between *no* curriculum materials and *lockstep* curriculum materials— that there were curriculum materials that encouraged teacher autonomy and practical wisdom by helping teachers learn about content, pedagogy, and student learning. But this third way was rarely an option. Most schools simply purchased standardized materials from private vendors, complete with texts, lesson plans, lockstep scripts (with appropriate student responses), and the standardized tests coordinated with these materials.

On "Day 53," Ms. Jabbari joined all the other kindergarten teachers in the Chicago system in teaching the letter *b* to her students. The binder she used identified the section of the Iowa Test of Basic Skills to which that day's lesson plan corresponded, and provided step-by-step questions and conversation starters.

SCRIPT FOR DAY: 053

> TITLE: Reading and enjoying literature/words with "b"
> TEXT: *The Bath*
> LECTURE: Assemble students on the rug or reading area. . . . Give students a warning about the dangers of hot water. . . . Say, "Listen very quietly as I read the story." . . . Say, "Think of other pictures that make the same sound as the sound bath begins with."

Her students sat cross-legged on a corner rug. The children's book *The Bath* was not available, so Ms. Jabbari chose *Jesse Bear, What Will You Wear?* But no matter. She still began with the script, reminding them: "It's always safe to have an adult around when you take your bath."

Supporters of lockstep curricula and high-stakes standardized tests were not out to undermine the wisdom, creativity, and energy of good teachers. The scripted curricula and tests were aimed at improving the performance of weak teachers in failing schools—or forcing them out. If lesson plans were tied to tests, teachers' scripts would tell them what to do to get the students ready. If students still failed, the teachers could be "held accountable." Equality would seemingly be achieved (no child left behind) by using the same script, thus giving the same education to all students. But this also meant that all teachers, novice or expert, weak or strong, would be required to follow the standardized system.

Teachers on the front lines often point to the considerations left out of the teach-to-test paradigm. Tests are only one indicator of student learning, and poor performance on tests has other causes aside from poor teaching—poorly funded urban schools, students from poor or immigrant backgrounds with few resources at home and sometimes little or no English, overcrowded classrooms with not enough teachers, poor facilities, lack of books and equipment, students with learning problems or other disabilities. But one of the chief criticisms many teachers make is that the system is dumbing down their teaching. It is de-skilling them. It is not allowing them—or teaching them—the judgment they need to do good teaching. They are encouraged, says education scholar professor Linda Darling-Hammond, "to present material that [is] beyond the grasp of some and below the grasp of others, to sacrifice students' internal motivations and interests in the cause of 'covering the curriculum,' and to forgo the *teachable moment,* when students [are] ready and eager to learn, because it [happens] to fall outside of the prescribed sequence of activities." Sooner or later, "turning out" kids who can turn out the right answers the way you turn out screws, or hubcaps, comes to seem like normal practice. Worse, it comes to seem like "best practice."

ENTER THE CANNY OUTLAW

When education professor Linda McNeil and her research team from Rice University Center of Education in Texas began their 1980s study of urban magnet schools in Houston, they planned to study innovation, not standardization. The three magnet schools they picked for their research seemed like promising models for responding to failing Houston schools.

Talented and dedicated teachers, with very limited resources, had reorganized their academic programs to help a diverse inner-city student body make it in the world. One school, for example, aimed to prepare minority youth to enter medical careers. Far from using a standardized curriculum created by outside "expert" planners, the teachers updated and reworked their courses year to year and often day to day, as their knowledge and students' experiences grew. Walking into Ms. Watts's ninth-grade physical science class, McNeil's team might have dodged the clay ball she was throwing against the wall. Why was it flat on one side? Ms. Watts wanted to know. Had it changed when it hit the wall? Had the wall changed? Mass, weight, gravity, resistance, and velocity were all at work and she wanted the students to figure out how. Walking into Mr. Drew's economics class, researchers might have interrupted a board meeting of the student-run start-up company that was at the heart of his course. Drawing on his own experience in industry, Mr. Drew taught students economic principles in a way that made sense to them because they were researching potential products they would actually sell (a mug with the school logo; a T-shirt designed by a student graphics team). They were conducting market surveys, accumulating capital, making decisions about the scale of investment, the risk, the profits.

McNeil wanted to figure out whether and how these teachers were improving the education of the inner-city students. But these magnet schools were about to be swept up by larger political forces. In mid-1980s Texas, pro-education Democratic governor Mark White teamed up with conservative billionaire H. Ross Perot to promote educational reform. White had promised voters to raise teacher salaries more than 20 percent, but he needed the support of recalcitrant state legislators. He turned to Perot and asked him to chair a task force heavily weighted with business leaders. The compromise they crafted was more funding for schools in return for a business model of efficiency and accountability. Scripted curricula tied to high-stakes testing would allow bad teachers to be identified—by the consistently bad scores of their students—and removed. It was the same kind of compromise that Massachusetts's Senator Ted Kennedy, Arizona's Senator John McCain, and President George W. Bush would forge in 2001 to create the No Child Left Behind Act.

In Houston, the magnet schools were forced to reorganize to prepare for the coming White-Perot reforms. McNeil changed her study. The new question was: How would these teachers cope with a curriculum that was test-driven? The concepts that Ms. Watts was teaching, like mass and velocity, were part of the new "proficiencies" that would be tested. But they were presented as vocabulary terms to memorize, not as phenomena to be observed and explained. Throwing clay balls against brick walls was not on the district's new proficiencies list, nor was dropping objects from different heights and calculating the speed at which they fell. Neither was testing out different paper airplane designs and observing stability, speed, and resistance. Mr. Drew's economics class did not conform to the proficiency sequence and he had to drop the course, except as an elective. The paperwork required by such new requirements—to assure the bureaucracy that teachers were teaching by the rules—discouraged individualized time spent with students and robbed time previously devoted to planning and assessing lessons. The requirements created the same kind of time bind Wong observed when such requirements were imposed on military trainers. And, as in the case of the new military training model, the new requirements discouraged flexibility, adaptability, and creativity.

McNeil found that many of the experienced teachers fought back. They became canny outlaws, or creative saboteurs, dodging the "law," finding ways to cover the "proficiencies" with great efficiency and squirreling away time to sneak real education back in at the margins of the standardized system, sometimes even conspiring with their students or teaching them how to "game" the system. Mr. Drew taught his students that economic cycles vary in length and intensity, but in the test prep period, he told them to forget this because the official answer was that each cycle lasts eighteen months. There was a danger that students who learned to look beyond the obvious, to ask "what if," to look for the exceptions to the rules, would do badly on the tests. One history teacher prepped his students for the exam by telling them: "You just have to think, 'What's the least dumb answer here.' Do not try to use your mind on those [proficiency questions].'"

The ability of wise teachers to operate as canny outlaws is most seriously constrained when a highly scripted curriculum comes riding into town on the heels of high-stakes standardized tests. By prescribing, step by step, what to say and do each day to prepare students for these tests, such lockstep curricula pose a serious challenge to professional discretion. Yet even under these adverse conditions, in many schools there are canny outlaws who find ways to avoid being channeled.

Rebecca Joseph spent fourteen months carefully observing and interviewing six first-grade teachers in California schools who were required—as were many teachers across the country—to use the highly scripted Open Court literacy curriculum to teach their students to read and write. These teachers, who had two to eleven years of experience and held solid teaching credentials, all worked around the scripts, abandoning them when the techniques they mandated did not work and creatively introducing other methods and materials to help their students learn. None eschewed the entire curriculum; rather, they used it critically. One teacher, Catherine, had students engage with partners to predict story plots and brainstorm adjectives for a collaborative story. Vicky allowed her students to speak Spanish when they assisted each other in such off-script collaborations because "they flesh out their ideas in their native language and then translate it back into English. Their writing is much better." Open Court's emphasis on phonetics excludes ongoing spelling development, but Catherine and her fellow first-grade teachers implemented a spelling program that tremendously improved the students' reading and writing. At the same time, they also allowed the students to spell phonetically in their daily journals because some students' writing benefited from inventing spelling. The Open Court script demanded multiple rereadings to teach students comprehension, but the teachers recognized the resulting student boredom and rejected this. One of the teachers instead had the students do skits based on the reading, knowing the students would have to refer back to— and "comprehend"—the text in creating the skit. Open Court focuses solely on *reading* for first-graders. All six teachers concluded that *writ-*

ing was critical too. And that first-graders loved it. Some teachers introduced daily journals. Four of them developed writing workshops that included components like brainstorming, drafting, editing, and publishing, and supplemented the workshops with individual conferences. Such canny outlaws treated Open Court as a useful guide and improvised around it. They abandoned the lockstep script.

But there were schools that closed down even this improvisation, using strict enforcement to prevent teachers from turning the scripts into guidelines. Open Court was introduced in California's Downer Elementary School in fall 2002. The first year, a number of teachers looked, quietly, for ways to work around some of its less workable rules. In 2003, enforcement tightened. Outside consultants, including trainers from McGraw-Hill, the company that sells Open Court, began entering classrooms at will, says Ms. Jaeger, then the school's literacy coordinator. Teachers' lessons were interrupted, and some teachers were chastised in front of their students. The principal threatened disciplinary action against teachers who veered from the script. The administration grew rigid, "focusing on things like whether teachers had posted sound/spelling cards in the correct place." Most of the teachers spoke privately about their frustrations. Ms. Jaeger and a few of her colleagues were more outspokenly opposed to Open Court, but they nevertheless offered to help with in-service trainings, with organizing student study teams, and with mentoring new teachers. They also tried to negotiate modifications in the curriculum. Their help was refused.

In October 2005, Ms. Jaeger and four other teachers wrote an open letter to their colleagues stating their opposition to particularly egregious aspects of the program and said they would no longer participate in these practices. They all received letters of reprimand, and two of them, including Ms. Jaeger, were removed from their classrooms and transferred to other sites. There were local protests from parents and teachers, and support from educators around the country.

In 2006 the University of Arizona College of Education awarded the

"Downer Five" its annual "In Defense of Good Teaching" Award, established to "honor educators who have stood up to laws, policies, and practices that are threatening to students and teachers."

At times such protests against screw tightening have been even more widespread. In Los Angeles, for example, school district efforts to supplement once-yearly standardized state tests with periodic or "benchmark" tests, administered three to ten times a year, were vocally opposed by the teachers' union (the UTLA, United Teachers of Los Angeles) and more quietly resisted by some teachers who simply refused to give them. Then, in January 2009, during contract negotiations, the chairs of five hundred union chapters unanimously called for a boycott, refusing to administer the next round of tests. The boycott was widespread and lasted throughout the school year. Interestingly, the union members in some of the schools run by Green Dot Public Schools, a charter school group with a solid educational track record, did not boycott the benchmark tests. The reason that they refused is revealing. Green Dot's exams are created by a panel of teachers from its schools and are regularly reviewed for effectiveness and modified by the teachers. The tests have more credibility with the teachers than the tests for the rest of the district's schools, which are written by an outside company, imposed from above, and don't mesh with year-round schedules.

The quiet resistance of canny outlaws and the vocal protests of others are signs that teachers dedicated to preserving and encouraging discretion and wise judgment are not going quietly into the night. These teachers are not people who simply rebel at rules or who are just committed to their own ways of doing things. They are committed to the aims of teaching, a practice whose purpose is to educate students to be knowledgeable, thoughtful, reasonable, reflective, and humane. And they are brave enough to act on these commitments, taking the risks necessary to find ways around the rules. We suspect that many of our readers are canny outlaws themselves or know people who are: practitioners who have the know-how and courage to bend or sidestep formulaic procedures or rigid scripts or bureaucratic requirements in order to accomplish the aims of their practice. We admire canny outlaws in the stories we tell ourselves about such people and even in some of our children's stories. We read the Harry Potter tales to them because Harry, Ron, and Hermione are canny outlaws who gain the guts and skill to break school rules and stand up to illegitimate power in order to do the right thing to achieve the aims of wizardry, indeed to save the practice itself.

We depend on teachers who are canny outlaws to sustain the practice of teaching. But we need to recognize that these teachers are operating in a system in which the practical wisdom to improvise is discouraged by design. Some standardization is essential in any institution: predictability, uniformity, and hierarchy enable institutions to function, and can assist in quality control. But standards can be achieved without this kind of standardization. The overstandardization created by lockstep curricula and high-stakes testing risks driving the practical wisdom out of the practice of teaching, undermining a crucial trait that teachers need to do their work well.

A consequence of overstandardization is that novice teachers like Ms. Moffett and Ms. Jabbari are prevented or discouraged from having the experiences that teach them practical wisdom. And experienced teachers are forced to swim against the current to do their work well. Teachers who do not have the energy to become canny outlaws and fight the routinization can resign themselves to the new methods or just plain resign. Some flee to schools where standardization is less rigidly enforced—usually more affluent suburban or private schools. Others, demoralized, leave teaching altogether. Chapman University in California graduates more credentialed teachers each year than any other California university. A study of why experienced teachers are leaving the profession surveyed 114 teachers who had graduated from the Chapman program and been teaching six to ten years. The pressures of high-stakes testing, test preparation, and standardized curricula was the number one reason for leaving. Teachers complained about not being able to use the lessons they prepared because of mandated materials or about their "creative talents" going "by the wayside" because of the "drill and kill" tests they were required to do.

Thus, the de-skilling of teachers produces a kind of "de-willing." It risks taking the fight out of some good teachers and takes other good teachers out of the fight. The danger here is a downward spiral. Good, experienced teachers leave, and idealistic and talented prospective teachers are discouraged from entering the classroom. Administrators interpret the lack of experience or commitment as evidence that more stringent procedures and rules are needed and ratchet up the standardization, demoralizing and turning away more promising teachers. Forcing teachers to do right by rote risks driving the wisdom out of the practice and driving out the wise practitioners.

10.

The War on Will

ON THE BUBBLE

Mrs. Dewey teaches third grade at Beck Elementary School in Texas. Many of the students are economically disadvantaged and most are Hispanic—longtime residents of Texas as well as first-, second-, and third-generation immigrants. The principal wants to get the test scores up. So do the teachers. Scores on these high-stakes tests are the metric of evaluation under the Texas Accountability System. Since 1992, Beck Elementary has been doing okay, but only okay. The state rates it "acceptable," but the administration and most of the teachers are anxious to achieve the more prestigious "recognized" status, which requires that more than 80 percent of the students pass the state tests. The system is, in the words of administrators, "data-driven," and there is only one kind of data that ensures officially sanctioned success: scores on a standardized test. All third-grade students must pass the reading test to move on to fourth grade. The teachers regularly administer "practice" tests throughout the year. The goal is to get 80 percent of the students to pass the test, moving the school from "acceptable" to "recognized."

Mrs. Dewey, a twenty-year-veteran, listens as a consultant hired by the district explains how to use the data from practice tests:

Using the data, you can identify and focus on the kids who are close to passing. The bubble kids. And focus on the kids that count—the ones that show up after October won't count toward the school's test scores this year. Because you don't have enough special education students to disaggregate scores for that group, don't worry about them either.

To make this concept tangible for teachers, the consultant passes out markers in three colors: green, yellow, and red. Mrs. Dewey hears someone mutter, "What is this? The traffic light theory of education?"

Take out your classes' latest benchmark scores, and divide your students into three groups. Color the "safe cases," or kids who will definitely pass, green. Now, here's the most important part: identify the kids who are "suitable cases for treatment." Those are the ones who can pass with a little extra help. Color them yellow. Then, color the kids who have no chance of passing this year and the kids that don't count— the "hopeless cases"—red. You should focus your attention on the yellow kids, the bubble kids. They'll give you the biggest return on your investment.

Mrs. Dewey stares blankly into the hallway. Focus on the bubble kids. Tutor only these students. Pay more attention to them in class. This is what most of her colleagues have been doing, and test scores have gone up. The community is proud, and the principal has been anointed one of the most promising educational leaders in the state. At every faculty meeting, the principal presents a "league table," ranking teachers by the percentage of their students passing the latest benchmark test. And the table makes perfect fodder for faculty room gossip: "Did you see who was at the bottom of the table this month?"

Mrs. Dewey has made compromises, both large and small, throughout her career. Every educator who's in it for the long haul must. But this institutionalized policy of educational triage weighs heavily and hurts more. Should she really focus only on Brittney, Julian, Shennell, Tiffany, George, and Marlena—the so-called bubble kids—to the exclusion of the other seventeen students in her class? Should Mrs. Dewey refuse to tutor Anthony, a persistent and eager little boy with no chance of passing the state test this year, so that she can spend time with students who have a better shot at passing? What should she tell Celine, a precocious student, whose mother wants Mrs. Dewey to review her entry for an essay contest? Celine will certainly pass the state test, so can Mrs. Dewey afford the time? What about the five students who moved into the school in the middle of the year? Since they don't count toward the school's scores, should Mrs. Dewey worry about their performance at all?

In her angrier moments, Mrs. Dewey pledges to ignore this test-centered approach and to teach as she always has, the best way she knows how. Yet, if she does, Mrs. Dewey risks being denounced as a traitor to the school's effort to increase scores. This is what stings the most.

PRIZES FOR READING

Swarthmore, Pennsylvania, is an affluent community populated largely by highly educated professionals. Residents of the community teach their kids from a very early age to value education and take it seriously. Many of the kids are reading even before kindergarten, and those who aren't reading by then are being read to constantly. Whatever problems the elementary school teachers may have in running their classes, motivating the kids to read is not one of them. One year, a long-term substitute teacher came to the school to teach fourth-graders. She came from a school in which discipline and motivation had been a major challenge for students. In Swarthmore, she introduced a technique that had been quite effective for her previously. Every time one of her students read a book, the student would get a point. By accumulating a certain number of points, the kids could win prizes. And whichever kid accumulated the most points would win a grand prize. The results of this procedure were amazing. The kids were reading like demons. Some were reading more than a book a day. We learned this from a colleague, whose daughter was in the class. When we told him how impressed we were, he told us that things were not as impressive as they seemed. His daughter, who had already been a pretty voracious reader, was now choosing books to read on the basis of two criteria: how long they were—the shorter, the better—and how big the print was—the bigger, the better. And the young girl seemed unable to remember what was in the books. The only point to her reading seemed to be to get to the end of one book so that she could start another.

———

Incentives may get you what you pay for, but they often will not get you what you want and need. Sure, we (parents and society more generally) want more kids to pass the reading tests. But not at the expense of the kids who most need our help. We want to encourage kids to read. But we want them immersed in books, and changed by them, not trudging through them to get the next gold star.

There are two problems with incentives. First, they are often too blunt an instrument to get us what we need. In situations that call for scalpels, incentives are sledgehammers. Second, when incentives are introduced into a situation, they can undermine other, better motives to do the right thing. Different kinds of motives can compete, and financial or other material incentives often win the competition. The result, as we'll see, is that such financial incentives can lead to demoralization—in two senses. First, they take the moral dimension out of our practices; second, they risk demoralizing the practitioners themselves.

A BLUNT INSTRUMENT

When a consultant tells teachers to concentrate on the bubble kids and ignore the kids who are most in need of help, something has gone wrong. And if gold stars turn reading from an adventure into a job, something has gone wrong. But what? The typical response to examples like these is not to blame incentives but to blame "dumb" incentives. The presumption is that "smart" incentives, or at least "smarter" incentives, will do the job.

This is a mistake. In many situations, for many activities, no incentives are smart enough. Teachers like Deborah Ball and Mrs. Dewey spend their day figuring out how much time to spend with each student and how to tailor what they teach to each student's particular strengths and weaknesses. They are continually balancing conflicting aims—to treat all students equally, to give the struggling students more time, to energize and inspire the gifted students. Along comes the incentive to bring up the school's test scores, and all the nuance and subtlety of Mrs. Dewey's moment-by-moment decisions go out the window. And what "smarter" incentive is going to replace judgment in making sensitive choices in a complex and changing context like a classroom?

Or what, exactly, would you incentivize to encourage hospital custodian Luke to seek the kind and empathetic response to the distraught father who wanted his son's room cleaned? Incentives are always based on meeting some specific, measurable criterion: read more books; raise more test scores; wash more floors. Left to his own devices, Luke asks himself, "What can I do to be caring?" and because he has moral skill, he comes up with a good answer. With "caring" incentivized, Luke might ask, "What do I have to do to get a raise or a bonus?" "Reclean the room" might be a right answer. "Look sympathetic" might be a right answer. "Be caring" surely is not. Aristotle thought that good people do the right thing *because* it is the right thing. Doing the right thing because it's the right thing unleashes the nuance, flexibility, and improvisation that moral challenges demand and moral skill enables. Doing the right thing for pay shuts down the nuance and flexibility.

Consider health care. How do we reduce the cost of health care without reducing its quality? The future financial security of the United States may depend on finding an answer to this question. The Patient Protection and Affordable Care Act (PPACA), signed into law by President Obama on March 23, 2010, aims to reduce cost *and* maintain or even improve quality. One obvious problem with the current system is that doctors are paid for procedures: the more they do, the more they earn. This is not a formula for quality care or for cost containment. What, then, should be done? The PPACA will begin pilot programs leading to a Medicare physician payment program by 2015 that is aimed at rewarding quality of care rather than volume of services. The specific implementation details have yet to be worked out, but this sounds just right. We want physicians to aim at quality of care, not at how to earn more by doing more. The devil, however, may well be in those implementation details. When Massachusetts, which in 2006 introduced a health care program that insures virtually all residents, grappled with a similar problem, a blue-ribbon commission suggested a system of "global payments" to doctors to incentivize treating patients well rather than treating patients more. Again, this sounds just right. But the commission went further when it suggested that if it turned out that the costs of treating a patient were *less* than the global payment, the provider network could keep what remained, as profit. A moment's thought should make clear that a scheme like this will incentivize doing *less*. We, as patients, don't want doctors doing more than is needed, but we don't want them doing less than is needed, either. Like Goldilocks, we want them doing what is "just right." Incentives are far too blunt to encourage this kind of balance.

In the best of circumstances, it is difficult for doctors to get the mix between too much and too little "just right." Historically, the ethical standards in the medical profession sought to keep financial conflicts of interest out of such decisions because of concern that they would warp the good judgment of doctors. Rewarding doctors for denying service sidelined such judgment and risked turning doctors into "double agents" "committed to patients but beholden to third-party payers." If patients ended up well treated, it was an accidental by-product of an incentive system designed to produce something else. You don't incentivize "better medicine" by kicking unspent fees back to the doctors. How *do* you incentivize better medicine?

It seems feasible to be able to develop a complex measure of quality of care and incentivize that, rather than how many procedures are done. But beware. As cardiologist Sandeep Jauhar has pointed out, such efforts often have unintended consequences. He cites the development, in the 1990s, of "surgical report cards," intended to help patients choose hospitals and surgeons. Seems like a good idea. But what happened, as with the bubble kids, is that both hospitals and surgeons started cherry-picking surgical candidates. In a survey conducted in New York State, some 63 percent of cardiac surgeons admitted that the introduction of report cards had induced them to accept only relatively healthy patients for coronary bypass surgery. Instead of making the difficult judgment of when, and for whom, surgery might be the best option, doctors worried primarily about their "grades." The unintended consequence of incentivizing success was that those most in need of help were the ones who didn't get it.

We must have ways of evaluating the performance of doctors. How else are they to learn from their mistakes? But incentives are not the only way to motivate and evaluate performance. If we assume that doctors *want* to be good at what they do, and almost all people who begin the study of medicine do so inspired by the telos of the practice, a program of careful and systematic evaluation can help them without inducing them to distort what they regard as best practice in pursuit of financial incentives. Indeed, hospitals around the country have been discovering that the way to make so-called mortality and morbidity conferences—the reviews of cases that have gone wrong—really useful is to make them less about credit and blame and more about a communal effort to improve medical care. You can de-incentivize and get doctors to sign on to a common project rather than covering up for themselves and one another.

PERFORMANCE VERSUS MASTERY

Why is it that incentives seem to have these perverse effects? We can begin to answer this question when we appreciate that incentives have two distinct components. First, they provide feedback; a bonus or a gold star says, "You've got it right. Good job! Keep up the good work." Second, incentives provide people with something that they want and like—money, status, or glory, for example. That is, they are hedonically positive. It's the hedonic kick that's the source of the problem.

Think about two different tennis pros giving you tennis lessons. The first pro says things like "good shot" and "good swing" all the time, to encourage you. The second one says "good swing" only when you make a good swing. If hearing "good swing" gives you a hedonic charge, then you will prefer the first instructor to the second (more gold stars, more encouragement). But if what gives you the charge is getting better at tennis, you will prefer the second instructor to the first. That's because the second instructor's feedback to you is much more informative than the first one's. You're not after "good swing" gold stars; you're after a better tennis game. So feedback is essential to the development of a complex skill—whether it be empathy or a strong forehand. But he-

donic feedback, in the form of incentives, is not. It may even be counterproductive, as in the case of instructor number one.

In schools, tests provide an extremely important source of feedback—
of information—to the teacher and the student—about how things are
going. Tests, or something like them, often offer the best way to diagnose problems and correct them. So tests as a source of *information* are
good and important. The problem is that in addition to providing information, tests provide outcomes that students, and their parents, and
their teachers, want and like—outcomes like approval, prizes, awards,
honors, special privileges, and school ratings. The hedonic character of
these outcomes is what gets students and teachers to orient their work to
passing the tests, and to regard what they do in the classroom as merely
instrumental, as merely a means to various rewarding ends.

There are important differences between children oriented to getting A's and children oriented to learning from their mistakes. Psychologist Carol Dweck and her associates have spent thirty years
studying the incentive systems that govern the learning of children
throughout the educational process. They have uncovered two funda-
mentally different approaches to learning in kids that can often lead to
profound differences in how well kids learn. One group of kids has
what Dweck has called *performance goals*; the other group has what she
has called *mastery goals*. Children with performance goals are primarily
interested in gaining favorable judgments of their competence. They
want to do well on tests. They want social approval. They want awards.
Children with mastery goals are primarily interested in *increasing* their
competence rather than in demonstrating it. They want to encounter
things that they can't do and to learn from their failures. As Dweck puts
it, performance-oriented children want to *prove* their ability, while
mastery-oriented children want to *improve* their ability. Children with
performance goals avoid challenges. They prefer tasks that are well
within the range of their ability. Children with mastery goals seek challenges. They prefer tasks that strain the limits of their ability. Children

with performance goals respond to failure by giving up. Children with mastery goals respond to failure by working harder. Children with performance goals take failure as a sign of their inadequacy and come to view the tasks at which they fail with a mixture of anxiety, boredom, and anger. Children with mastery goals take failure as a sign that their efforts, and not they, are inadequate, and they often come to view the tasks at which they fail with the kind of relish that comes when you encounter a worthy challenge.

Dweck has shown that when classroom tasks become moderately difficult, mastery-oriented kids do better than performance-oriented kids. That's one reason to inspire a mastery orientation in our children. But there is more. A mastery orientation that encourages people to continue to seek new challenges is likely to keep people intellectually engaged throughout their lives—to keep them involved and learning—because they find things of intrinsic interest and value, and not because of possible payoffs and punishments. It is this kind of mastery orientation that enables people to develop practical wisdom. Such wisdom, we have seen, can only be learned through trial and error. That means having the motivation and courage to take on difficult tasks and experience failure, and to see failure as a challenge to try again and learn more. The more we rely on incentives that only encourage performance goals, the more likely we are to discourage the mastery goals that practical wisdom demands.

None of this is meant to suggest that it is desirable, or even possible, to develop in kids a single-minded pursuit of knowledge that has them completely indifferent to grades and teacher (and parent) approval. We want students who want to do well *and* want to learn. The point is that these two motives will not always complement each other. What it takes to *do* well and what it takes to *learn* well won't always be the same. When they aren't, we need to find a way to balance the two.

Some school systems have largely given up the effort to maintain the balance. A vivid example is New York City's pilot program, now being copied in one form or another in many other cities, in which children of all ages will get substantial cash rewards for doing well on standardized tests. A score of 5 (the top score) on Advanced Placement tests will win high school students $1,000. There has been no outcry in response to this initiative. The only questions in people's minds seem to be, "Will it get test scores up?" and "Can we afford to offer these rewards to everybody?"

What we have said about students is also true of their teachers. Good teachers will be motivated by the desire to do what is best for their students. Their aim will be to teach their students to read, write, and compute, and to teach their students how to teach themselves and how to be enthused when they face an opportunity for mastery. The teachers will also want to do well—to get all the accolades, the promotions, the bonuses, and the awards that the system makes available. If the system within which teachers work could find a way to arrange the accolades and promotions so that they merely amplified the desire to be good teachers, all would be well. But making the desire to do good and the desire to do well compatible is difficult. The standardized tests on standardized curricula that have become the measure of all things are at best imperfect indices of the learning objectives we really care about. When teachers like Mrs. Dewey are encouraged by incentives to teach just to improve test performance, the big tests stop being indices of anything—except student ability to do well on big tests. When teachers adopt methods that completely routinize instruction, again with an eye toward high test performance, their own incentive-driven behavior gets transferred to their students. There is nothing exciting—for students or teachers—about "test and drill," and students exposed to a relentless diet of test and drill become performance-oriented rather than mastery-oriented. When teachers or administrators are incentivized to focus entirely on the tests, the real aims of teaching aren't served at all, no matter how high the test scores get.

INCOMPLETE CONTRACTS

Why are incentives such a blunt instrument? The main reason is that most jobs—and certainly all jobs involving substantial interactions with other people—are organized around what are called "incomplete contracts." Some of the job duties are specified explicitly, but many are not. Doctors prevent disease, diagnose it, treat it, and ease suffering. But exactly how they do these things is left to them to figure out—with guidelines, of course, but only guidelines. And how they interact with their patients is left for them to figure out. Lawyers serve their clients, but as we saw with William Simon and Mrs. Jones, how to counsel, how to advocate, and how to balance the two is up to them. Teachers impart knowledge, but the best way to reach each child is left for them to judge. Being caring and sensitive to patients and their families is not part of Luke's "contract," nor are there any rules or procedures that specify how to be caring.

Detailed scripts and rules may enable us to make contracts that are more complete, but moving in that direction will compromise the quality of the services that doctors, lawyers, teachers, and custodians provide. More complete contracts allow us to incentivize what we think we want ("Perform tasks A, B, and C in the manner X, Y, and Z and you get a bonus"). But what we really want is "Make a good-faith effort to do whatever it takes to achieve our objective." We can have confidence that our service providers will do "whatever it takes" only if they have the will to do the right thing. How much we depend on this good faith on the part of employees, even in factory, assembly-line settings, is revealed by a kind of union protest that used to be popular many years ago. When a dispute with management arose, instead of going out on strike, unions would sometimes resort to "working to rule." Employees did exactly what was specified in their contracts—and nothing more. Such work-to-rule actions paralyzed production.

When we lose confidence that people have the will to do the right thing, and we turn to incentives, we find that we get what we pay for. Teachers teach to the test, so that test scores go up without students learning more. Doctors do more, or fewer, procedures (depending on the incentives) without improving the quality of medical care. Custodians just "do their jobs," leaving unhappy, uncomfortable patients in their wake. As economist Fred Hirsch said thirty years ago, "The more that is written in contracts, the less can be expected without them; the more you write it down, the less is taken, or expected, on trust." The solution to incomplete contracts is not more complete ones; it is a nurturing of moral will.

Why can't we leave incomplete contracts incomplete, and just incentivize "doing the job well," leaving it to the discretion of the supervisors to judge whether a doctor, lawyer, teacher, or janitor *is* doing the job well? In theory, we could. But the problem is that much of what is left incomplete (e.g., Luke's caring) is extremely difficult to quantify. Is Mrs. Dewey a good teacher, worthy of praise, a bonus, and tenure? In the absence of clearly identified criteria for "goodness," we have to trust the judgment of Mrs. Dewey's supervisor. Would another supervisor, from another school, agree? If we are unwilling to trust the judgment of Mrs. Dewey, why would we be willing to trust the judgment of her supervisor? Complete contracts seem attractive because they promise uniformity, fairness, and objectivity. They identify objective metrics by which the performance of employees can be scored. And especially when money is on the line, people feel the need for this objectivity. So incentives don't *inevitably* lead to standardizing and objectivizing criteria for evaluation, but they exert a powerful push in this direction.

When incentives misfire, as they so often do, the temptation is always to try to make them smarter. When we think we've licked the problem of doctors doing too many tests with an incentive scheme that encourages them to do too few, we adjust. And when we find problems with the new, adjusted scheme, we adjust again. What we hope and expect is that over time, incentives that get us ever closer to what we want will evolve. Manipulating incentives seems easier and more reliable than nurturing moral will.

And what's the harm? If incentives can't do the job by themselves, perhaps they can contribute to improving performance, both by telling people (doctors, teachers) how they're doing and by motivating them to do better. They can't hurt. Or can they? As it turns out, there is harm in incentives, and the harm can be quite considerable.

MOTIVATIONAL COMPETITION

An Israeli day care center was faced with a problem: more and more parents were coming late—after closing—to pick up their kids. Since the day care center couldn't very well lock up and leave toddlers sitting alone on the steps awaiting their errant parents, they were stuck. Exhortation to come on time did not have the desired effect, so the day care center resorted to a fine for lateness. Now parents would have two reasons to come on time. It was their obligation, and they would pay a fine for failing to meet that obligation.

But the day care center was in for a surprise. When they imposed a fine for lateness, lateness *increased*. Before the imposition of a fine, about 25 percent of parents came late. When the fine was introduced, the percentage of latecomers *rose*, to about 33 percent. As the fines continued, the percentage of latecomers continued to go up, reaching about 40 percent by the sixteenth week.

Why did the fines have this paradoxical effect? To many of the parents, it seemed that a fine was just a price (indeed, that was the title of the article reporting this finding). We know that a fine is not a price. A price is what you pay for a service or a good. It's an exchange between willing participants. A fine, in contrast, is punishment for a transgression. A $25 parking ticket is not the price for parking; it's the penalty for parking where parking is not permitted. But there is nothing to stop people from interpreting a fine as a price. If it costs you $30 to park in a downtown garage, you might well calculate that it's cheaper to park illegally on the street. Any notion of moral sanction is lost. You're not doing the "wrong" thing; you're doing the economical thing. And to get you to stop, we'll have to make the fine (price) for parking illegally higher than the price for parking in a garage.

That's exactly what happened in the day care center. Before the imposition of fines, parents knew it was wrong to come late. Obviously, many of the parents did not regard this transgression as serious enough to get them to stop committing it, but there was no question that what they were doing was wrong. But when fines were introduced, the moral dimension of their behavior disappeared. It was now a straightforward financial calculation. "They're giving me permission to be late. Is it worth $25? Is that a good price to pay to let me stay in the office a few minutes longer? Sure is!" The fine allows parents to reframe their behavior as an exchange of a fee (the "fine") for a "service" (fifteen minutes of extra care). The fines *de*moralized what had previously been a moral act. And this is what incentives can do in general. They can change the question in people's minds from "Is this right or wrong?" to "Is this worth the price?"

Once lost, this moral dimension is hard to recover. When, near the end of the study, the fines for lateness were discontinued, lateness became even more prevalent. By the end of the study, the incidence of lateness had almost doubled. It's as though the introduction of fines permanently altered parents' framing of the situation from a moral transaction to an economic one. When the fines were lifted, lateness simply became a better deal.

There is certainly nothing dumb about imposing a fine for lateness. Any one of us might have reached for exactly this tool. But it is only a small step down a slippery slope from the Israeli day care center to teachers who teach to the test and doctors who treat with their eyes firmly fixed on the bottom line.

Another example of the demoralizing effects of incentives comes from a study of the willingness of Swiss citizens to have nuclear waste dumps in their communities. In the early 1990s, Switzerland was getting ready to have a national referendum about where it would site nuclear waste dumps. Citizens had strong views on the issue and were well informed. Bruno Frey and Felix Oberholzer-Gee, two social scientists, went door-to-door, asking people whether they would be willing to have a waste dump in their community. An astonishing 50 percent of respondents said yes—this despite the fact that people generally thought such a dump was potentially dangerous and would lower the value of their property. The dumps had to go somewhere, and like it or not, people had obligations as citizens.

Frey and Oberholzer-Gee then asked their respondents whether, if they were given an annual payment equivalent to six weeks' worth of an average Swiss salary, they would be willing to have the dumps in their communities. They already had one reason to say yes—their obligations as citizens. They were now given a second reason—financial incentives. Yet in response to this question, only 25 percent of respondents agreed. Adding the financial incentive cut acceptance in half.

These studies of Israeli parents and Swiss citizens are surprising. It seems self-evident that if people have one good reason to do something, and you give them a second, they'll be more likely to do it. You're more likely to order a dish that tastes good and is good for you than one that just tastes good. You're more likely to buy a car that's reliable and fuel efficient than one that's just reliable. Yet when the parents at the day care center were given a second reason to be on time—the fines—it undermined their first reason, that it was the right thing to do. And the Swiss, when given two reasons to accept a nuclear waste site, were *less* likely to say yes than when given only one. Frey and Oberholzer-Gee explained this result by arguing that reasons don't always add; some-times, they compete. When the Swiss respondents were not offered in-centives, they had to decide whether their responsibilities as citizens outweighed their distaste for having nuclear wastes dumped in their backyards. Some thought yes, and others, no. But that was the only question they had to answer.

The situation was more complex when citizens were offered cash incentives. Now, they had to answer another question before they even got to the issue of accepting the nuclear wastes. "Should I approach this dilemma as a Swiss citizen or as a self-interested individual? Citizens have responsibilities, but they're offering me money. Maybe the cash is an implicit instruction to me to answer the question based on the calculation of self-interest." Taking the lead of the questioners, citizens then framed the waste-siting issue as just about self-interest. With their self-interested hats squarely on their heads, citizens concluded that six weeks' pay wasn't enough. Indeed, they concluded that no amount of money was enough. The offer of money undermined the moral force of people's obligations as citizens. Morality is for suckers, the offer of money seemed to be saying, even if only implicitly.

A substantial body of research done with children and adults con-firms these findings. In a typical adult example, people are asked to solve various imaginative and engaging puzzles. Many of the participants like solving these types of puzzles. So they're looking forward to participat-ing in the experiment. The experimenter sits the people down and explains that they will be paid $5 for each puzzle they solve. Then the people dig into the puzzles. Afterward, the experimenter returns. The participants are asked to fill out a form that asks about how much they liked participating in the task. They are also given several additional puzzles and told to feel free to work on them while they are waiting for the experimenter to return.

What researchers have found in experiments like this is that, in com-parison with other people who do the same task but are not paid $5 for each puzzle, the people who are paid report that they liked the task less. In addition, they are less likely to work on any of the extra puzzles while they are waiting. The monetary payoff seems to have communicated to them that this activity, which they thought they enjoyed, wasn't really fun after all. "People get paid only for work, not for play," they seem to be saying to themselves. "So this task must have been work."

Similar results were obtained in a study of nursery school children. The children were given special felt-tipped drawing pens, and they used the pens with great enthusiasm. After a period of observation, in which the psychologists measured the amount of time the children spent drawing with the pens, the children were taken into a separate room, given the pens, and asked to draw pictures. Some of the children were told they might receive "Good Player" awards for their drawings; others were not. A few weeks later, back in the regular nursery school setting, the drawing pens were again made available, this time with no promise of any award. The children who had received awards previously were *less* likely than the others to draw with the pens at all. And if they did draw, they spent less time at it than other children and drew pictures that were judged to be less complex, interesting, and creative. Without the prospect of further awards, their interest in drawing with the special pens was now only perfunctory.

A series of studies by social scientists James Heyman of the University of Saint Thomas and Dan Ariely of Duke University makes a similar point. In one study, people were asked if they would be willing to help load a couch onto a van. Some were offered a modest fee and some were not. As Heyman and Ariely explain their findings, participants in the studies can construe the task they face as either a social transaction (doing someone a favor) or a financial one (working for a fee). Absent the offer of a fee, they are inclined to view the situation in social terms and agree to help. The offer of a fee induces the participants to reframe the transaction as financial. Now, the fee had better be substantial.

It might seem that if you are inclined to do someone a favor, the offer of compensation should only give you a second reason to do what you were inclined to do already. Again, two reasons are better than one. Except that they're not. The offer of money tells people implicitly that they are operating in the financial/commercial domain, not the social domain. The offer of money leads them to ask, "Is this worth my time and effort?" That is not a question they ask themselves when someone asks them for a favor. Thus, social motives and financial ones compete.

These examples help us answer the question "What's the harm in using incentives?" There *is* potential harm, even if the incentives work. Incentives like money, prizes, or awards can "crowd out" the pleasure people get from an activity (drawing or solving puzzles). They can crowd out the moral motives that drive an activity (day care or nuclear waste). And they can crowd out the inclination people have to be helpful to others. Whether this crowding out will matter depends on the situation. If you're working as a dishwasher in a diner, chances are that there are no incentives operating other than financial ones (but based on the attitude that Luke and some of his colleagues have toward their work, we shouldn't be too quick to assume that any employment is, by its very nature, "just a job"). If you're working as a lawyer, a doctor, or a teacher, there are obviously reasons for doing the work, and doing it in a particular way, other than just the paycheck it provides. Financial incentives only corrupt performance if there is something to corrupt.

You may think that lawyering, doctoring, and teaching are special cases, that typically people work to get paid, and only to get paid. Our view, in contrast, is just the reverse: people almost always have multiple reasons for doing their work, with the result that their motivation and performance can be corrupted by the wrong financial incentive structure. Incentivizing doing more procedures or doing fewer procedures will certainly affect the nation's medical bills. If your aim is to lower costs, it's clear which way to go. But if your aim is to improve quality, the two incentive schemes may be equivalent in diverting doctors from asking, "What does my patient need?" and getting them to ask instead, "What's best for me?" The doctors' behavior will thereby be demoralized. The will to do the right thing will be replaced, or at least weakened, by the will to maximize income.

Not everyone who is subjected to incentive schemes will be demoralized by them. Some doctors, lawyers, and teachers will do what they think is right and be impervious to the financial consequences of their behavior. But many will not. Furthermore, as incentive schemes come to dominate practices, they will reshape what the practices are like, making it increasingly difficult for the handful of canny outlaws to do their work as they think it should be done. Not only will they have to find clever ways to work around the constraints on good practice imposed by the system or its administrators, but they will have to do so in pursuit of a set of objectives that everyone around them seems to have abandoned. This is what stung Mrs. Dewey the most. It is hard to maintain the morale, the courage, and the confidence that being a canny outlaw requires in the face of a tidal wave of colleagues and supervisors who are moving in a different direction.

11.

Demoralizing Institutions

But tell me, your physician . . . is he a moneymaker, an earner of fees, or a healer of the sick?" This challenge by Socrates, in fourth-century B.C. Athens, is a challenge that sounds startlingly modern. In one sense the answer to Socrates' question is simple: the aim of being a doctor is *not* to make money, and if one practices for that reason, one will not practice well. But the answer is not *that* simple: doctors, teachers, lawyers—all professionals—aim to serve others, but they also make their livelihood by doing so. This builds temptation into any professional practice. A practitioner can often make more money by doing things that do not serve clients well—the extra medical test, the extra appointment, the extra billable hour—and the client will not know. We trust that the majority of professionals who serve us are not like this.

But the challenge to professionals is not simply to resist the temptations of greed and profit. A professional, no matter how dedicated, can't avoid the business of making money. Decisions have to be made within financial constraints. Even the canny outlaws are frequently challenged to balance dollars and devotion. They must balance matters of money and time with what's good for their patients or clients. A doctor or a lawyer must decide when to say no to a client who can't pay. Should there be adjustable fees, and if so, how adjustable and for whom? How much pro bono work should you do?

If you are a newspaper editor, doing your work well means telling readers the truth about things that matter. That demands supporting a staff of reporters who dig up important stories about corruption in local government and neglect of needy children by social service agencies. But if circulation and advertising income is driven by people who read stories about celebrity romances and weight-loss programs, how much "real" news do you cut and how much fluff do you add?

Dedicated college professors demand that students do the difficult reading and writing necessary to become skillful in understanding the complexities of the world. But the university distributes resources like research funds and new faculty positions based in part on how many students populate classes and how positively students evaluate courses. How much do you simplify to keep up enrollment and keep resources flowing into your department?

Professionals face questions like these all the time. They are challenged to find the balance between commitment to doing things that are true to the "soul" of their profession and willingness to do things that keep their institution alive and afloat. The wisdom to find the right balance demands skill *and* will. And the burden for finding this balance does not reside entirely on the shoulders of individuals. Institutions can ease the burden or exacerbate it. It is easier to do the right thing when people around you are also so inclined. And that's more likely when your school, your law firm, or your hospital encourages and nurtures doing the right thing.

This was one of the problems with the financial incentives we explored in the last chapter. Organizations that rely heavily on such incentives can undermine the will of practitioners to do the necessary balancing. The incentives can tilt them toward being makers of money. Incentives can crowd out other motives, undermining the moral will to do the right thing. But even if we wanted to, there is no way to remove financial incentives entirely. No owner, manager, or supervisor can count on all employees to want to do the right thing, all the time, and they certainly can't design an organizational structure as if all employees were motivated to serve the aims of the organization. Besides, people do have to make a living, and institutions do have to pay their bills.

The challenge is to find a way to enable people to earn their livelihoods and create a viable organization without having payoffs completely control what people do—without having payoffs demoralize both the people and the practices in which they engage. When the managers of professional institutions focus only on the bottom line—when considerations of efficiency, accountability, and profit permeate the whole organization—practitioners themselves are discouraged from getting the balance right. If the whole aim or purpose of a professional organization is changed to moneymaking instead of service, it risks corroding the practical wisdom of practitioners by demoralizing the entire practice. This danger is latent in the commercialization of any profession, but it is perhaps starkest in medical practice.

DOLLARS VERSUS DEVOTION

The commercialization of medicine demoralizes the practice of medicine and, in doing so, it threatens to "de-moralize" doctors. The problem is not so much that doctors act in blatantly immoral ways. Rather, commercialization upsets the balance between dollars and devotion. It also demoralizes doctors in another sense, sapping their morale, their patience, their energy, and their drive to do the right thing. Doctors like David Hilfiker resisted the effects of commercialization, but it was an uphill battle.

Dr. Hilfiker was a skillful and devoted doctor who chose to work for a nonprofit practice (directed by a board elected from the community) in a small town in northern Minnesota. He and his colleagues had significantly lower salaries than the average physician, and they worked hard to try to neutralize the issue of money. They had a sliding scale of fees that provided discounts for poorer patients, and no one who could not pay was turned away. Dr. Hilfiker was devoted to his patients and they trusted him. He was acutely conscious of the inflated salaries of physicians and of what he thought was "the obvious, yet seldom discussed, tension between the physician as entrepreneur and the physician as servant." Yet, he had difficulty escaping the ways in which money was driving the movement for productivity and efficiency in medicine. The language of business—cost/benefit analyses, time management, and financial profiles—had become the language of medicine. Try as he might to resist these pressures, he felt himself sucked in.

> The fee schedule had made procedures much more lucrative than in-depth interviews, counseling sessions, or time taken to comfort a hospitalized patient. There were also many important services I performed which had no charge attached whatsoever . . . giving emotional support to a family after a death, going to medical staff meetings, to mention only a few. But despite my conscious disagreement with many of the values assigned by price, I noticed that surgery, procedures . . . and emergency-room work slowly became a more and more important part of my practice. Dealing with emotionally hurting patients, taking time to educate patients about the course of their disease and the nature of their treatment, even obtaining a comprehensive interview history, became less central. Not that I consciously changed my routines; but money had powerful ways of bending my perceptions. . . . It is not an exaggeration to say that money seeped into every crack in my life.

Despite his efforts to resist the pressures around him, Hilfiker realized that he was learning to aim at the wrong things. He describes the deep pain he began to feel as work began to change his values in ways he could not control.

> Clinical detachment, efficiency and productivity, prestige, authority, the medical hierarchy, and wealth are all phenomena based on a common value structure in which people are treated as if they were not fully human, as if they were no more than objects to be manipulated. I did not consciously choose that value structure; indeed I rejected the notion of it, but so much of my life as a physician was spent in its service that it inevitably became mine. . . . Paradoxically, as I did my best to manipulate patients into conforming to the needs of an efficiently run office, it was I who became the object, the machine. . . . I measured myself at the end of the day by what I had produced. I hung on to my authority and power, since they seemed so integral to my work. I certainly recognized the limited power of money to satisfy me, yet since much of my day was structured around charges and costs and since my income level had become emotionally important to me, money was an important value. Patients' diseases and my service became commodities that were bought and sold at a price.

Hilfiker feared that the way he was forced to practice medicine was de-moralizing him. He took a leave of absence and began to write. It became clear, he said, "that mine had not simply been a personal struggle, nor was what happened to me simply 'my fault'; and I started to dream of finding ways of restructuring medical practice to make life as a physician more possible for me." Eventually he found a way, when he accepted an invitation to work in an inner-city clinic in Washington, D.C., that served the urban poor. He knew the pressures would be great but he was attracted by the community of health care providers who ran the clinics. They were part of a small, ecumenical Christian church involved in a many-sided mission to the poor that included housing, jobs, child care, and spiritual guidance, as well as health care. He was drawn to a community of health care providers who not only shared their emotional and spiritual lives but saw their work as a calling.

The doctors who professionalized medicine in the early twentieth century understood the kinds of concerns Hilfiker experienced. They knew that doctors' dependence on medicine as a livelihood introduced the making of money into the aim of healing the sick. They were concerned about the effect of moneymaking on doctors and the resulting erosion of the public's trust in doctors. Because practicing well depended on such trust, making medicine a profession depended on encouraging and protecting the commitment to medicine as a calling. The solution was to recruit people of character who were dedicated as well as smart, and then certify them only after they went through rigorous training and licensing. By certifying doctors, and imposing and policing standards, the profession aimed to protect patients from being deceived and exploited by unprincipled charlatans. But these early professionals realized that more was needed: the very regulation of those allowed to enter the profession also gave doctors a monopoly on medical care. Steps had to be taken to protect patients from the potential abuse of this monopoly power.

In asking for and getting monopoly power over their profession, doctors were in effect asking their patients for trust, trust that they would adhere to professional standards, that they would judge one another, that they would never let their monopoly position allow them to become either greedy or careless. Organizations like the American Medical Association (AMA) tried to nurture this trust by developing norms and guidelines to keep medicine professional—to prevent it from becoming a business. Conscious of the temptations built into the "fee for service" payment system, and the risk that dollars could undermine devotion, the AMA sought to convince physicians and assure patients that medical professionals were dedicated first to patient health, not to the fees they charged for their services. This was reflected in the AMA's 1957 *Principles of Medical Ethics*, which declared that medical judgment should be free of financial interest: "a physician should not dispose of his services under terms or conditions that tend to interfere with or impair the free and complete exercise of his medical judgment and skill or tend to cause a deterioration of the quality of medical care." The AMA successfully pushed for separating the prescribing of pharmaceuticals from their sale, so that patients would know that their doctors saw no profit from the prescriptions they wrote. Physicians were expected to refrain from advertising and from entering into financial arrangements with device and drug manufacturers. As the AMA put it, "Where physicians become employees and permit their services to be peddled as commodities, the medical services usually deteriorate, and the public which purchases such services is injured." The doctors and the AMA knew that medical professionals wanted to earn a good livelihood, but no matter how good this livelihood became, they wanted to ensure that money-making was not the purpose of a doctor's work. The professional ideal was to make doctors confident that their hard work and commitment would lead to a calling in which they served humanity with dedication and compassion, and would be rewarded with both the successes of their ministry and the respect, admiration, even love of their community.

In practice, some doctors gave in to the temptations of the "fee for service" system, trading in their calling for greater fees. But public and professional standards labeled such practices unacceptable; revelations of doctors making money at their patients' expense were treated as scandalous. Until the 1980s, says political scientist and health policy expert Deborah Stone, the discovery of such financial incentives was presented "with a tone of muckraking horror and read by news media as well as government agencies as fraudulent and unethical." It was considered immoral to let money influence medical judgments. It was sometimes grounds for dismissal from the profession.

New practices, however, began to erode this norm. Ironically, these practices were often well-intentioned attempts to get doctors to cut costs, often by doing and prescribing less. Cost-cutting policies were motivated by government and public concern with rising health care costs. The high fees charged by some doctors were only a small part of the problem. Technological advances in health care (computerized axial tomography, or CAT, scans; magnetic resonance imaging, or MRI; dialysis, bypass surgery, new drugs) were extremely costly. Medicine's ability to keep people alive longer meant that more people needed expensive, long-term care for chronic illnesses. The solution to these rising costs was to create prepayment systems, like HMOs. The fixed cost per patient gave HMO managers the incentive to control costs by discouraging doctors from prescribing unnecessary tests and treatments. But in doing so, many of these policies had the effect of openly bringing moneymaking into the heart of medical practice by creating incentives that rewarded doctors for doing less. Patients protested when HMOs refused to pay for certain treatments. But there was little outcry over the normalization of moneymaking as a legitimate consideration for doctors in deciding on patient care.

In prepaid treatment plans, insurance companies and HMOs made money by using doctors as gatekeepers. The gatekeepers got, or lost, money by regulating who got access to the medical care on the other side of the gate. In "capitation" systems, HMOs paid their doctors a per capita fee for each patient they contracted to treat. Because doctors were paid a fixed fee no matter how many services they performed, physicians had no incentive to overuse services. But the dark side of the system was that doctors had an incentive to see as many patients as they could, as quickly as possible. The more patients they contracted for, the more money they made. In addition, if they prescribed too much, the costs came out of their pre-negotiated fixed fee per patient. Integral to the system was getting doctors to think about the money involved in all their medical choices—the time they spent with each patient and the tests and treatments they prescribed.

There were also "risk-sharing" agreements forced on doctors by the HMOs and insurance companies, a subtle mechanism often hidden from public view. Soon after joining her HMO in Washington, internist Devra Marcus referred two of her diabetic patients to an ophthalmologist because diabetes puts people at risk for blindness. A colleague took her aside and explained that such referrals would reduce her referral fund and could reduce her salary. How could this be? Dr. Marcus discovered that her group had a risk-sharing agreement with the HMO. A portion (as much as 20 percent) of each doctor's pay per patient was withheld until the end of the fiscal year. How much of the "withhold" the doctor eventually got back was linked to the costs of the treatments the doctor recommended or performed. The risk sharing did not *forbid* doctors from prescribing tests and treatments, but each doctor was given a financial reward for cutting back. Too many referrals and there would be financial penalties for all the doctors in the medical group. If, however, Dr. Marcus and her colleagues limited the referrals, they became eligible for bonuses. The distortion of good practice introduced by these financial incentives was unacceptable to Dr. Marcus. "I pulled out [of the HMO]. I didn't want to think about whether I would be losing money if I ordered an ophthalmologic consultation. I wanted to think about what was best for the patients."

Commercializing doctors' motives in the new prepayment HMO system did not encourage greed or drive doctors' salaries up. On the contrary, HMOs often tried to drive doctors' salaries down, in the name of efficiency, accountability, and HMO profits. But encouraging moneymaking in doctors' choices about patient care tilted the balance between dollars and devotion toward the dollars.

As HMOs shifted the balance, there was also a relaxation of laws and norms that discouraged the temptations of moneymaking. Take the rise of "self-referrals"—doctors prescribing treatments and tests in medical facilities they themselves own or in which they have investments. Depending on the region of the country, doctors have a financial stake in 25 to 85 percent of ancillary medical facilities. There is good evidence that these financial interests warp doctors' judgments. Physicians with such investments order many more tests, at much higher cost, than physicians without a stake in diagnostic facilities, with no evidence of better diagnostic or treatment outcomes. Indeed there is some evidence that there are more cases of inappropriate procedures in facilities that are physician owned. Physician Sandeep Jauhar recently observed that "a doctor who owns a scanner is seven times as likely as other doctors to refer a patient for a scan."

The AMA, which once tried to prevent the commercialization of medical practice, has pulled back. The professional norm disapproving of the practice of self-referral has eroded. The AMA also once regarded advertising and entrepreneurial activities by physicians as unethical; now it officially sanctions both. After medical organizations lost some costly antitrust trials in 1980 (they were accused of such "offenses" as limiting doctors' fees), the AMA changed its ethical guidelines. It declared medicine to be both a profession *and* a business.

Economic necessity is another pressure that encourages young doctors to be more motivated by moneymaking. Many budding physicians undergo grueling training because they are interested in the intellectual challenges of medicine, or because they want to ease pain and suffering and cure the sick, or both. But the financial pressure hits home early. Medical school education, though heavily subsidized by various types of federal granting agencies, is still incredibly expensive. The average private medical school bill was about $50,000 in 2009. The typical medical school graduate begins practice with a six-figure debt. The annual cost of malpractice insurance can exceed $100,000. Medical associations estimate that in order to meet debt payments and various overhead expenses, many doctors will have to be earning more than $200,000 a year within five years of beginning to practice. Such pressure can't help but shift moneymaking to a more central place in a doctor's choice making.

In medical centers that train new doctors and conduct research, a different but related problem appears. Such teaching hospitals have encouraged their faculty to forge partnerships with industry—drug companies or device makers. The industry gets access to the best minds in medical science and the institution gets substantial financial support that it uses to run labs and defray the costs of training new doctors. In theory, everybody wins. But then it turns out that some doctors who are supported by these drug companies and device makers earn hundreds of thousands of dollars a year giving speeches that tout company products. For example, Pfizer, the world's largest drug maker, paid about $20 million to forty-five hundred doctors and other medical professionals for consulting and speaking on its behalf in the last six months of 2009. Merck, Eli Lilly, and GlaxoSmithKline revealed similar practices. Some doctors have their names on journal articles that were written not by them but by professional writers employed by the drug companies. For example, between 1998 and 2005, Wyeth produced some twenty-six ghostwritten articles, with prominent scientists identified as authors, that cast drugs Wyeth produced for the treatment of symptoms of menopause in a positive light. Are the lectures telling the "whole" truth about the drugs or devices? Are the articles in journals accurate? Are other articles that might report data less favorable to the product not being written? Often, it's hard to tell. The commercialization of research in medical centers creates a blatant conflict of interest, tempting research doctors to be motivated far too much by gain and glory and not enough by devotion to solid, accurate, and medically useful research. The medical centers welcomed the win-win partnerships with industry, trusting that the integrity of their scientists would just take care of itself. But integrity does not take care of itself.

The pressures of economic necessity, the payoffs to doctors to be gatekeepers, and the weakening of professional norms are exacerbated by the local "culture of care" in different regions and in different hospitals. In recent years, researchers at the Dartmouth Medical School have been tracking regional variation in the cost of health care in the United States. They have found significant variation in costs from place to place, largely owing to variation in the culture of care. Sometimes motivated by the aspiration to high fees, but sometimes not, standards of practice develop in particular communities and then become entrenched.

An example is the contrast between the culture of care created by the Mayo Clinic in Rochester, Minnesota, and that created by the Doctors Hospital in McAllen, Texas. An August 2009 case study supported by the Commonwealth Fund looked at how well Mayo displayed the attributes of an ideal health care delivery system. It details some of the specific measures the clinic has taken to improve the quality of care like team-based coordination of care, a physician-led governance structure, and an organizational and technological infrastructure that encourages physicians and other caregivers to excel at the clinical work they were trained to do. But animating it all, the soul of the clinic, is the "cultural philosophy of doing the best for the patient." The touchstone for decisions of all sorts, ranging from conducting research to establishing the dress code or designing a new hospital, is captured by the words of founder William J. Mayo: "The best interest of the patient is the only interest to be considered." The doctors are not paid fees for services, but salaries, and this compensation scheme "fosters team-oriented patient care and peer accountability." The result has been some of the lowest-cost and highest-quality health care in the United States.

In Rochester, Minnesota, where the culture of care is shaped by the huge Mayo Clinic, Medicare spending per patient is in the lowest 15 percent of all regions in the United States. When Atul Gawande, a surgeon and a writer, visited McAllen, Texas, he discovered that the culture of care there was very different. The result was striking. As Gawande noted in an article in *The New Yorker* that attracted widespread national attention, including the attention of members of Congress and of President Barack Obama's administration (then in the midst of developing health care legislation), in McAllen, Medicare spending per patient is the highest in the country, about twice the national average. When Gawande compared the people in McAllen with those in nearby El Paso, where per capita costs were half as much, he found that patients weren't older, sicker, fatter, poorer, or less educated. Nor was the health care in McAllen better than in the United States in general (or in El Paso). The doctors in McAllen did more than the doctors in El Paso—more tests, more specialist visits, more procedures, more surgery. Gawande concluded that what happened in McAllen is that a culture of treatment evolved so that overtreatment was standard practice. When there was a clear and unambiguous protocol for "best care" for a given disease, McAllen doctors looked like doctors everywhere. But wherever there was any ambiguity, McAllen doctors reliably did more—a lot more. So overtreatment was largely about conforming to community standards. Where do these standards come from?

They are encouraged in part by the fact that doing more earns doctors more. In McAllen, the newest, fanciest hospital has a reputation for recruiting "high-volume" doctors. They are paid a fee for service, and the hospital is physician owned, which means it returns a percentage of hospital profits from tests, surgery, and other care to the doctor-owners. One hospital administrator explained to Gawande that over time a "culture of money" had developed in McAllen. He knew of doctors who owned apartment complexes and strip malls as well as surgery centers or imaging centers or other medical facilities that they directed their patients to. The doctors had "entrepreneurial spirit," he said, and were aggressive and innovative in finding ways to increase revenues from patient care. Gawande found that McAllen doctors were not like the Mayo doctors. They had created a culture that "came to treat patients the way subprime-mortgage lenders treated home buyers." And in such a culture, says Gawande, doctors are likely to start thinking of patients in the same way—"as profit centers."

Once the making of money inserts itself as a central aim in the daily life of doctors and the institutions where they work, it begins a spiral of ever greater demoralization. Sandeep Jauhar says:

> [The marketplace is] creating a serious and deepening anxiety within the profession. Among my colleagues I sense an emotional emptiness created by the relentless consideration of money. Most doctors went into medicine for intellectual stimulation or the desire to develop relationships with patients, not to maximize income. There is a palpable sense of grieving. We strove for so long, made so many sacrifices, and for what? In the end, the job has become for many only that—a job.

Surveys indicate that a significant minority of doctors would not go to medical school if they had it to do over again.

Medicine has always involved both human (and humane) relationships and commercial considerations. And there has always been a concern to prevent the second from spilling over and washing away the first. But walls built to prevent the spillover in the twentieth century, however insufficient, have now been weakened further as financial incentives are touted as a cure to prevent escalating health care costs. We can't take it for granted that such financial incentives—in the service of efficiency, or cost reduction, or even quality of care—will leave the humane motives unaltered. Yet the challenge of finding a balance between the humane and the commercial is being neglected. The result, say Pamela Hartzband, veteran endocrinologist and internist, and Jerome Groopman, physician, cancer and AIDs researcher, and noted author, is that

> many physicians we know are so alienated and angered by the relentless pricing of their day that they wind up having no desire to do more than the minimum required for the financial bottom line. In our view, this cultural shift risks destroying some essential aspects of the medical pro-

fession that contribute to high quality health care, including pride in profession, sense of duty, altruism, and collegiality. Extending oneself to patients, families, trainees, and colleagues not only is a traditional element of medicine but translates into more effective care.

Dr. Hilfiker would certainly agree. The commercialization of modern American medicine and medical research is, by and large, not the doctors' fault. How doctors practice is largely driven by how third-party payers—insurance companies—reimburse. How doctors do science is driven largely by what funding agencies are willing to support. Most doctors would love to be able to spend thirty minutes with each patient, so as really to get to know the people they are treating. They don't like being discouraged from ordering tests and specialist consultations that they think appropriate because the tests and consultations cut into profits. They don't like being thought of as greedy and untrustworthy. But their hands are often tied.

Medical diagnosis and treatment doesn't have to be this way. It can be reorganized so doctors continue to be motivated more by care and quality than by money. That is what the Mayo Clinic has done, and the Cleveland Clinic, and even small organizations like Bassett Medical Care in Cooperstown, New York, and the Ben Taub General Hospital in Houston, both of which run on the Mayo model. The shift from devotion to dollars is not inevitable. But the current pressures are great. And not just in medical practice: the commercialization of other professions illustrates the danger of organizations' losing their souls and undermining practitioners' will to be wise.

CASHING IN AT THE BAR

In 1987, Patrick Schiltz finished his prestigious clerkship for Supreme Court Justice Antonin Scalia and took a job at a large Minnesota law firm. Making money was not his main aim: he thought he was choosing a balanced, ethical life by turning down the high-paying, big-city, big-firm jobs. But the culture of moneymaking soon began to seep into his life. In the lower-middle-class neighborhood in which he grew up, Schiltz never met anyone who could be called wealthy. "I almost never talked about money or thought about money," he remembers, but despite his best intentions "all that changed when I started practicing law. . . . Slowly, imperceptibly, the things I cared about and the way I thought about others and the way I thought about myself changed." The culture that slowly began to change Schiltz's purpose in practicing law was not always the culture that dominated law. It is the product of changes in the last decades of the twentieth century.

The legal profession, like medicine and all professions, was long concerned with keeping the making of money secondary to the aims of the practice. Lawyers had to balance the business of law with service to clients and the public. Though there were always lawyers for whom work was simply a way to make money, the norm of the profession was to aim at service. In the frequently quoted words of prestigious jurist Roscoe Pound: "the term [profession] refers to a group . . . pursuing a learned art as a common calling in the spirit of public service—no less a public service because it may incidentally be a means of livelihood. Pursuit of the learned art in the spirit of public service is the primary purpose."

In the 1980s, there was a dramatic increase in the commercialization of legal practice in large law firms. Growing market competition spurred a consolidation of medium-size firms into today's mega-firms. Advertising and marketing of firm services grew. New fee-setting practices linked a firm's income to its clients' profits, and lawyer compensation was tied more to economic performance and less to seniority. Talk about income and clients' fees, even within the large Wall Street firms, just wasn't done before the 1980s, says Schiltz. But today, lawyers talk of little else. Trade publications like *The American Lawyer* began to report regularly on lawyer incomes, publishing extensive surveys that focused on the incomes of associates and partners in big firms. "These surveys are pored over by lawyers with the intensity of kids poring over the statistics of their favorite baseball players." In 1986, the American Bar Association (ABA) was concerned enough to create a Commission on Professionalism, whose report called on the judiciary, the practicing bar, and law schools to take steps to promote public service and "resist the temptation to make the acquisition of wealth a primary goal of law practice." When Justice O'Connor spoke to the Washington University faculty and students in 1997, she warned that the economic pressures of the legal marketplace have escalated to a point where, as one lawyer put it, legal practice is "like drinking water from a firehose." "Clients," she said, "increasingly view lawyers as mere vendors of services, and law firms perceive themselves as businesses in a competitive marketplace."

What happens when law school graduates actually go to work is often gradual and subtle. The culture of moneymaking seeps in slowly. No one takes a young lawyer aside and says, "Jane, we here at Smith and Jones are obsessed with money. From this point forward the most important thing in your life has to be billing hours and generating business. Family and friends and honesty and fairness are okay in moderation, but don't let them interfere with making money."

Schiltz, who, like Dr. Hilfiker, fled his job because of what it was doing to him, went into teaching (at Notre Dame Law School) and tried to prepare his students for what to expect. You will become unethical, Schiltz warns his students, "a little bit at a time." Not by "shredding incriminating documents or bribing jurors" but "by cutting a corner here, by stretching the truth a bit there." It will start, says Schiltz, with your time sheets and the extraordinary pressure to achieve the mandatory number of billable hours.

One day, not too long after you start practicing law, you will sit down at the end of a long, tiring day and you just won't have much to show for your efforts in terms of billable hours. . . . You will know that all of the partners will be looking at your monthly time report in a few days, so what you'll do is pad your time sheet just a bit.

The billable-hours system that Schiltz is referring to is relatively new (it was not common in the 1960s) and has both a bureaucratic and a market logic to it. Billable hours provide a numerical indicator to help rank lawyers in the fierce competition for position and money that has become a hallmark of corporate law firm life—the "promotion-to-partner tournament." Senior partners hire many more associates than there are partnership seats to accommodate, and then challenge the young associates to compete to keep their jobs and to "make partner." The system encourages hard work and generates greater profits for the partners than they can make by themselves. Billable hours are easy-to-monitor indices of hard work. And the system motivates associates to generate extraordinarily large numbers of billable hours, putting money-making and promotion at the center of their concerns. Each day, this system makes the merry-go-round of work spin faster, with associates looking over their shoulders to outwork their peers, hoping to improve their chances at grasping the brass rings of affluence and job security that "making partner" promises.

One effect of the system, says Schiltz, is to undermine the young lawyer's devotion to the interests of the client. To pad your time sheet:

Maybe you will bill a client for ninety minutes for a task that really took you only sixty minutes to perform. However, you will promise yourself that you will repay the client at the first opportunity by doing thirty minutes of work for the client for "free." In this way, you will be "borrowing," not "stealing." . . . And then what will happen is that it will become easier and easier to take these little loans against future work. And then, after a while you will stop paying back these little loans. You will convince yourself that . . . you did such good work that your client should pay a bit more for it.

Another consequence is that the young lawyer's devotion to the truth, and to his colleagues in the firm, will also suffer. The little lies on the time sheets will create the habit of little lies.

> You will get busy and your partner will ask whether you proofread a lengthy prospectus and you will say yes even though you didn't. And then you will be drafting a brief and you will quote language from a Supreme Court opinion even though you will know that, when read in context, the language does not remotely suggest what you are implying it suggests. . . . And then you will be reading through a big box of your client's documents—a box that has not been opened in twenty years— and you will find a document that would hurt your client's case, but that no one except you knows exists, and you will simply "forget" to produce it in response to your opponent's discovery requests.

After a couple of years, Schiltz tells his students, you'll stop even noticing that lying and cheating have become part of your everyday practice. "Your entire frame of reference will change" and the dozens of quick, instinctive decisions you make every day will "reflect a set of values that embodies not what is right or wrong, but what is profitable, and what you can get away with."

Putting this commercialization of time at the heart of legal practice undermines a lawyer's motivation in other ways. Michael Trotter is a Harvard-trained Atlanta corporate lawyer who has worked for, or been a senior partner in, some of that city's largest law firms. In his experience, exercising the qualities lawyers need to serve clients well— imagination, creativity, sound judgment, real concern for clients' welfare, pride in quality workmanship—"runs against the drive for billable time." Not only are lawyers not encouraged to gain these habits, but the billable-time machine discourages the very mentoring that young lawyers need from their senior colleagues to develop these qualities. "A partner who stops his work to explain to an associate (or a younger partner) why something is the way it is, or to share a war story and the lesson it entails, is providing a service to the firm in training its young lawyers." But if he is thinking about billable hours, what is he to do? "He would be dishonest if he charged a client for the time, and so would the associate if he put it on his time records." Indeed, there is empirical evidence that lawyers and other professionals (e.g., management or computer consultants) who bill for their time increasingly come to think that "time is money," and this attitude starts to leak into the time they spend with friends and family. They start asking, "Is it worth it? Is it worth the billable hours I'm giving up?"

These same factors discourage wise deliberation, says Yale law professor Anthony Kronman. Such wisdom does not always go with being an outstanding moneymaker. As the deal maker and business getter have become the new heroic figures of the law firm, the wise counselor and statesman are no longer models for success that young associates can look to. Dedication to public service is another likely victim. In *Partners with Power*, his mid-1980s study of mega-firms, sociologist Robert Nelson found that some of the same lawyers who built large law firms into mammoth bureaucratic organizations openly expressed fears that "the economic pressures have become so intense that partners and associates are driven to specialize narrowly, bill 'too many' hours, and forgo activities in bar associations, civic institutions, and pro-bono litigation that would serve the public interest."

The demoralization of lawyering is not just the result of the billable hour system per se. As the culture of moneymaking becomes embedded in a law firm and changes the soul of the practice, it slowly permeates everyday life, transforming what the lawyers themselves are aiming at. This demoralization of lawyers, this loss of purpose beyond making money, is part of what explains why so many lawyers are dissatisfied with their work. Multiple studies document the growing unhappiness of lawyers—both at work and in their lives outside of work. There are unusually high levels of depression, substance abuse, career dissatisfaction, and suicide.

Patrick Schiltz, who was appointed a federal judge for the district court in Minnesota in 2006, hoped that his students would do better in private practice than he had done. But he wouldn't count on it. In 1999, while he was still teaching at Notre Dame, he wrote, "No matter how pure a young lawyer's intentions, no matter how firm his resolve, when he goes to work at a firm, the culture will seep in. I got sucked into playing the game, and even today, four years after leaving the big firm, I still find myself playing the game at times."

WHAT DO BANKERS DO?

Elouise Manuel had lived in her home in Decatur, Georgia, for half her life. At sixty-eight, she was retired from a career in food service, where she had worked as a line server and made salads. In 2004, her only income was $527 a month in Social Security. But she owned her house free and clear. She needed a loan to pay off home repairs and other bills. She went to a mortgage broker and explained that she wanted a loan with a monthly payment of no more than $120. The broker told Ms. Manuel that she would not have to pay more than that and promised the lowest fixed rate possible. He got her a loan at IndyMac Bank.

The loan turned out to be quite different from what she expected. It was an adjustable-rate mortgage. The initial teaser rate of 3.875 percent lasted only one month, then jumped to 6 percent and eventually to 10.25 percent. Ms. Manuel's monthly payments climbed to about $200 a month. She had to get help from her family and apply for food stamps to keep up with the growing expenses. She was not sophisticated about complex financial matters. It wasn't until she called IndyMac that she learned she had an adjustable-rate loan.

The lawsuit she filed with the help of Atlanta's Legal Aid Society said that IndyMac purposely ignored her financial circumstances in structuring the deal. IndyMac specifically instructed the mortgage broker to send copies of Ms. Manuel's Social Security award letters with the dollar amounts blacked out. Furthermore, IndyMac should have known from the paperwork that she wanted a fixed, not an adjustable-rate loan. But IndyMac's bankers didn't care about Ms. Manuel's financial well-being. And they weren't worried they would lose money if she defaulted. Her loan was quickly packaged with countless others and sold to investors. Seducing a senior citizen into taking on debt at impossible terms was just in a day's work for an IndyMac banker. How did this come to be?

IndyMac was one of the early casualties of the 2008 banking crisis. It was taken over by the FDIC in July 2008 to prevent bankruptcy. Michael Perry, IndyMac's CEO, and the others who ran the bank didn't think they were doing anything wrong in writing the kinds of risky, dubious loans they were writing. They blamed IndyMac's demise on the bursting of the "housing bubble." The bankers at IndyMac were not the only ones making these types of loans. IndyMac was hotly competing with other banks to sell as many of these risky loans as possible because they were so profitable. Between 2003 and 2006, IndyMac more than doubled its profits, to $343 million. In such banks, profiting from risky loans came to seem normal. And it might even seem normal to many Americans now reading about the behavior of such bankers in the aftermath of the crisis. These bankers seemed like any businesspeople, and isn't the business of business to make money—by any (legal) means possible? Isn't that what the bankers did—just "business as usual," though this time with millions of people all over the world losing their jobs, their houses, and their retirement incomes? It might even seem strange that President-elect Barack Obama would say at the height of the crisis in December 2008 that "everybody from CEOs to shareholders to investors are going to have to be asking themselves, not only is this profitable . . . but is it right? Does it conform to some higher standards, in terms of how we operate?"

Actually, it's not so strange. The norm for bankers was never just moneymaking, any more than it was for doctors or lawyers. Bankers made a livelihood, often quite a good one, by serving their clients—the depositors and borrowers—and the communities in which they worked. But traditionally, the aim of banking—even if sometimes honored only in the breach—was service, not just moneymaking.

In the movie *It's a Wonderful Life*, James Stewart plays George Bailey, a small-town banker faced with a run on the bank—a liquidity crisis. When the townspeople rush into the bank to withdraw their money, Bailey tells them, "You're thinking of this place all wrong. As if I had the money back in a safe. The money's not here." He goes on. "Your money's in Joe's house. Right next to yours. And in the Kennedy house, and Mrs. Backlin's house, and a hundred others. Why, you're lending them the money to build, and they're going to pay you back, as best they can. . . . What are you going to do, foreclose on them?"

No, says George Bailey, "we've got to stick together. We've got to have faith in one another." Fail to stick together, and the community will be ruined. Bailey took all the money he could get his hands on and gave it to his depositors to help see them through the crisis. Of course, George Bailey was interested in making money, but money was not the *only* point of what Bailey did.

Relying on a Hollywood script to provide evidence of good bankers is at some level absurd, but it does indicate something valuable about society's expectations regarding the role of bankers. The norm for a "good banker" throughout most of the twentieth century was in fact someone who was trustworthy and who served the community, who was responsible to clients, and who took an interest in them. A good banker worried about helping farmers get this year's seed into the ground.

He worried about helping a new business get off to a strong start or a thriving one to expand. He worried about making sure that a couple in their fifties would have enough to retire on, that a couple in their forties would be able to pay for college for their kids, and that a couple in their thirties would buy a house with a mortgage that wouldn't swamp them. Their work served the dual masters of community service and profitability. They shared the essential characteristics of a professional: a commitment to the interests of their clients and society in general, and the capacity and motivation to render judgment with integrity.

At the heart of banking is a relationship between the banker and his clients based on mutual trust and responsibility. The depositors need the trust and confidence that the bank will not put their money at undue risk, and the bank needs to know and trust the borrowers enough to lend that money out, safely and profitably. Laws and regulations restrain bankers from acting irresponsibly, but the banking system depends on bankers knowing whom to trust, being trustworthy themselves and being perceived as such. That was J. P. Morgan's point when he testified at congressional hearings in 1912 and explained how he decided to make a loan or investment: "The first thing is character," he said. But how about the hard facts, like collateral? the congressmen asked him. "A man I do not trust could not get money from me on all the bonds in Christendom."

Knowing whom to trust in today's complex banking world has to depend on more than personal relationships. There are the credit checks, the credit ratings, the algorithms, the risk models. But without the trust, the bank and the banking system as a whole are vulnerable to collapse. And trust depends on practical wisdom. A good banker needs the practical wisdom to figure out who is creditworthy and what risks are worth taking. A good banker needs the wisdom to manage the bank's finances and to give good advice to clients. And a good banker needs the wisdom to balance the interests of depositors and borrowers, and the community as a whole, with the interests of the bank itself.

Such wisdom is quite practical. The whole banking system depends upon it.

The growing size and complexity of modern banking institutions has inevitably led to some depersonalization of the banker-client relationship. Banks like IndyMac take such depersonalization to extremes. They have become mortgage factories. Mortgages are produced, packaged, and sold to borrowers whom the bankers barely know. They are then repackaged into bundles and sold on Wall Street to buyers who have no idea who took out the loans and scant knowledge of the creditworthiness of borrowers. The bankers have lost their traditional bearings and have forgotten what they need to aim at.

For years investment banks like Goldman Sachs enabled their clients to build their businesses by helping them sell bonds and raise capital. Goldman prided itself on its close relationships with its clients, on its ability to service their particular needs. Goldman bankers aimed to be honest brokers between the investors with the capital and the clients who needed it. Integrity and trust were cultivated because this was what investment banking was about. Goldman bankers made money. Lots of it. But moneymaking per se was not their business. Their business was investment banking. "No firm better resisted the temptations than Goldman," says Roger Lowenstein, author of *The End of Wall Street*. From its founding in 1869 through recent decades, Goldman Sachs "epitomized, with only rare slip-ups, the best of American finance. Serving the client was its lodestar, and its bankers were pillars of society, more conversant in literature than in the vagaries of, say, mortgage securities." But then it changed its aim and decided to become an investor and trader itself. Instead of aiming at a socially useful function—helping others raise capital to build their businesses and earning money while doing it—the main goal became simply earning money.

Goldman Sachs did this, says Lowenstein, by inventing "rearrangements—new permutations, new alignments of risk—on flows of cash that already existed." The most notorious of these was the trading that stemmed from complex derivatives that had only a remote connection to the underlying assets from which they were "derived." Capital raising became a sideshow at Goldman, accounting for only 11 percent of its business. In 2009, trading and investing for the firm's own account produced 76 percent of its revenue. With moneymaking as the major aim of banking, let the client beware.

In April 2010 the Securities and Exchange Commission accused Goldman of fraud, charging it with misleading investors to whom it sold one of its bundled home-loan derivatives. The prominent hedge-fund manager who selected most of the mortgage bonds that underpinned the investment planned to bet against them. But investors had not been told that Goldman was planning to make money by selling housing-related investments "short," before their value declined. Indeed as the housing market began to fracture in 2007, top Goldman executives, including CEO Lloyd Blankfein, urged Goldman traders to sell the bank's housing-related investments. Goldman maintains that it never bets against its clients. But in January 2010, Blankfein did admit to the Financial Crisis Inquiry Commission that when Goldman sells a security to a customer and its value subsequently goes up, "we wish we hadn't sold it." And in July 2010, Goldman settled its conflict with the SEC, agreeing to pay a $550 million penalty, the largest ever against a Wall Street firm (although a drop in the bucket for Goldman), to settle what the *Wall Street Journal* described as "civil charges that it duped clients by selling mortgage securities that were secretly designed by a hedge-fund firm to cash in on the housing market's collapse." The case, said Wall Street historian Steve Fraser, confirmed the public's worst suspicions "about the total selfishness of these financial institutions. . . . This is way beyond recklessness. This is way beyond incompetence. This is cynical, selfish exploiting."

For decades, since the passage of the Glass-Steagall Act during the Great Depression, most U.S. banks were protected from some of the conflicts of interests that so warped the aims of Goldman Sachs. Glass-

Steagall was a law that enforced the norm of a banker's responsibility to his client. But the deregulation of banking in 1999 repealed the Glass-Steagall Act and permitted commercial banks to join the investment bank party. This furthered the disappearance of traditional banking norms as many large banks started to change what they did. "Why work for clients," they wondered, "when we can make more money just doing deals for ourselves?" This seems to have been the philosophy of IndyMac Bank.

IndyMac took advantage of the market for securitized mortgages promoted by Wall Street banks like Goldman Sachs, but even at its founding it never aimed at the kind of high purpose idealized by George Bailey. It started out as a mortgage company in 1985—Countrywide Mortgage Investment—whose main purpose was to collateralize mortgage loans and sell them on the market. Its parent company was Countrywide Financial, one of the biggest mortgage companies in the United States.

The loan IndyMac made to Ms. Manuel was not an aberration. Bankers at IndyMac routinely made risky and irresponsible loans to people who could not afford them, often on terms that were quite harmful to their clients. A number of loan officers resisted such practices, but it was hard to be a canny outlaw at IndyMac. The whole, explicit purpose of the enterprise was to collateralize mortgage loans and sell them on the market—not to put people into homes they could afford. Wesley Miller, an IndyMac underwriter in California from 2005 to 2007, says that when he rejected a loan application, the sales managers screamed at him. They then went over his head to a senior vice president and got it okayed. "There's a lot of pressure when you're doing a deal and you know it's wrong from the get-go—that the guy can't afford it. . . . And then they pressure you to approve it." The refrain from managers, Miller recalls, was simple: "Find a way to make this work."

Audrey Streater, a former underwriter and underwriting team leader for IndyMac in New Jersey, recounted: "I would reject a loan and the insanity would begin. It would go to upper management and the next thing you know it's going to closing. . . . I'm like, 'What the Sam Hill? There's nothing in there to support this loan.'" Until recent years, says Streater, "underwriter was spelled G-O-D, and our expertise and our knowledge was taken seriously." But then underwriting became window dressing—just a procedural annoyance that was tolerated because loans needed an underwriter's stamp of approval if they were going to be sold to investors. Many underwriters, she said, got worn down by the pressure to make loans or were stymied, afraid to make decisions because "somebody is going to yell at you." Some, she said, "were making decisions based on: 'I might as well do this because it's going to get approved anyway.'"

The culture inside the bank was not one of fiduciary care for the client, or service to the community. Granting loans with little documentation—just the borrower's stated income without supporting evidence such as tax documents or pay stubs—was policy at IndyMac, not the result of errant loan officials. These low- or no-documentation loans reflected a total lack of care about the borrowers' creditworthiness, or their well-being if they were forced to default. The pressure to get the loans out the door created an atmosphere where some bankers inflated the incomes of borrowers—often without their knowledge—in order to get the loans approved. Some misled clients with teaser rates, not making clear to them that the attractive initial monthly payments would soon balloon—as Ms. Manuel discovered. A former IndyMac fraud investigator said that these shoddily documented loans were known as "Disneyland loans" inside the bank—in honor of a mortgage issued to a cashier at Disneyland whose application claimed an income of $90,000 a year.

At the heart of good banking practice is the careful documentation of a borrower's income and assets—that's how a bank can tell whether a consumer can afford a loan. A bank needs to care about this if it is going to serve the borrower and the depositor. But during the housing and mortgage boom of 2003–2006, IndyMac, like many other banks, stopped caring. And they stopped caring because, for the bankers who ran IndyMac, the aim of the practice was no longer serving clients or the community but rather only making money. IndyMac bankers were not worried about losing money on bad loans because once they were repackaged and sold on Wall Street the consequences would be someone else's problem. When banks like IndyMac made their only goal the making of money, they lost their way as banks. They created a culture of irresponsibility and unreality. A Disneyland bank selling Disneyland loans. They encouraged the professionals who worked there to abandon their will to do the right thing and overrode or sanctioned those who tried to aim at it anyway.

PRACTICE MAKES PERFECT

If the pursuit of financial gain should not set the goals of a profession, then what should? What is the "soul" of medicine, or law, or teaching, or even banking? This question has been illuminated by Alasdair MacIntyre in his book *After Virtue*. MacIntyre, a contemporary Aristotelian, attempts in that book to reconstruct a moral philosophy, and central to that attempt is the concept of a *practice*. Among the characteristics of practices are these:

1. Each practice establishes a set of goals, or ends that are specific to it—Aristotle's telos. To be engaging in a practice is to be pursuing these goals. Promoting health and relieving suffering are specific to medicine. Fame and fortune are not. They may come to people who are engaged in the practice but they are not what a doctor aims at. They are external to the practice and not inextricably connected to engaging in the practice itself.

2. Practices establish their own standards of excellence. We would
    judge the excellence of a lawyer by things like her ability to
    counsel wisely, her perceptiveness about the nuances of the law,
    her ability to parse the significance of a precedent, or to "read"
    a judge and jury.

For example, the collection of activities referred to as "medical
science" is a practice. The goal of medical science is to discover gener-
alizations that describe and explain human physiology and pathology,
and identify tools for diagnosis and treatment. A medical scientist who
is a practitioner is pursuing these goals. But not all people who do what
looks like medical science are engaged in the "practice" of medical science. People who do research to achieve impressive publication records
are not engaged in the practice. The goals these scientists seek—fame,
fortune, status, promotion—are not specific to medical science. They
are not embedded in it. They are not, in MacIntyre's words, "internal"
or "intrinsic" to the practice. Fame and fortune are goals that are "external" to the practice, and research is just the means these scientists use
to achieve that fame and fortune. It is certainly true that people who are
pursuing such external goals may do good science, but they are not
themselves practitioners. The real danger to a practice like medical science is that more and more researchers will aim primarily at wealth and
status and not at understanding human physiology or the tools for treatment and diagnosis. Sometimes the external "payoffs" for doing good
science will yield good research, just like the payoffs for making bank
loans will sometimes yield good bank loans. But the more we depend
on the external payoffs, the greater the danger of getting bad results
when bad loans and bad science "pay."

The results for a practice like medical research, or banking, are potentially devastating. When medical scientists motivated by the wrong
goals are in the minority, the practice can continue as intended, with the

occasional misstep easily caught and corrected. But if everyone engaged in medical research were to start pursuing fame, wealth, and status, scientists would eventually have no more credibility in the public eye than any other businesspeople. And as their credibility was undermined, so would be the credibility of science in general. The practice of medical science would cease to exist. The core of the practice—the thread that keeps it going—lies in the actions of those whose goals are specific to the practice.

The same story can be told about law or medicine or teaching or any other profession. Each of them is a practice, largely defined by the pursuit of goals that are unique to it. Pursue justice, and see to the interests of clients by being a wise counselor or a zealous advocate. Promote health, diagnose and treat illness, ease suffering. Teach children the essential skills that will enable them to be productive adult citizens, and at the same time inspire them to teach themselves. Noble goals, all of them. But as doctors increasingly worry about earning a good living and keeping the practice afloat, as lawyers keep worrying about billable hours and making partner, and as teachers keep worrying about getting their students to score well on standardized tests, the goals of the practices—the souls of the professions—disintegrate.

The fact that some people are led into a practice in pursuit of goals that are external to the practice—money, fame, or what have you—need pose no threat to the integrity of the practice itself. So long as those goals do not penetrate the practice at all levels, those in pursuit of external goals will eventually drop out or be left behind or change their goals or be discredited by those in pursuit of a practice's proper goals. However, if external goals do penetrate the practice at all levels, it becomes vulnerable to corruption. Practices are always developing and changing, and the direction that development takes will be determined by participants in the practice. Good practices encourage wise practitioners who in turn will care for the future of the practice.

CONCLUSION

The demoralization of institutions like schools, health care organizations, law firms, and banks does more than discourage experienced practitioners from exercising practical wisdom. New practitioners entering a profession need a clear indication of what its proper goals are. They learn by recognizing good and bad examples of professional practice. They learn by watching their colleagues shake their heads at those who have lost their way. But what are the young teachers coming into Beck Elementary or doctors coming into the McAllen Texas hospitals or bankers going to work at banks like IndyMac going to learn?

The direction a profession takes is determined, in part, by its participants. If it becomes dominated by people with inappropriate aims, it may be corrupted to the point where it is unrecognizable. People will not possess the will—or the skill—to practice education, medicine, law, or anything else in the way we want to see it practiced. The "good doctor," the "good lawyer," and the "good teacher" will become first a dim memory, and then a romantic fantasy, en route to fading out of our collective consciousness altogether.

PART IV

Sources of Hope

INTRODUCTION

Sources of Hope

Detailed rules and procedures, however well intentioned, are undermining the skill that wisdom requires. Incentives, however well meaning, are undermining the will that wisdom requires. Canny outlaws, struggling to be wise in the face of significant obstacles, are not enough to stop the forces arrayed against practical wisdom.

Is there anything to be done? Is there a reason to be hopeful? In fact, there is a growing number of system changers—people who realize that wise practice needs to be encouraged in all practitioners—who are transforming both training and practice so that practical wisdom is nurtured, not suppressed.

And the motivation to develop practical wisdom can be quite powerful. As Aristotle thought, practical wisdom may be the key to happiness. Cultivating wisdom in ourselves enables us to sustain close and satisfying relations with others and to do work that is effective and significant. Wise practitioners improve not only the lives of the people they serve; they improve their own lives as well.

12.

System Changers

It's tough for a canny outlaw like Mrs. Dewey to continue to be a wise teacher. When the outside consultant told her just to focus on the bubble kids to get Beck Elementary's test scores up, she knew this was wrong. She told herself to ignore the test-centered approach, to continue to use her own judgment about which kids needed what kind of help and when. But as her school changed its aim from education to standardized-test-score performance, she was made to feel like a holdout, a throwback, as most of the faculty enjoyed pep talks, praise from the consultants and administrators, and reflected glory from the accolades the principal received. The motivations that sustained her and the other good teachers were questioned, discouraged, and derided all around her.

We all benefit from canny outlaws who have the moral will and skill to practice well, despite the formidable pressures assembled against them: the stress of time restrictions; the constraints of rigid rules and standardized scripts; the impediments of specialization and efficiency that drain them of empathy; the pressure of incentives that lure them to do the wrong thing. It can take courage and a streak of obstinacy to be a canny outlaw. And it not only takes wisdom to do the right thing. It also takes wisdom, including a certain shrewdness, to know how to carve out a space that enables you to practice well without threatening your job.

But being a canny outlaw is arduous, and sometimes precarious. Dr. Hilfiker was morally drained—exhausted—by his efforts to keep the monetarization of medicine from changing his character and diverting him from the aims of doctoring. Patrick Schiltz fled corporate law to escape the corrosive effects of money on legal practice. Judge Forer was overruled and given an ultimatum—conform or quit. Bankers like Wesley Miller and Audrey Streater were reprimanded for paying careful attention to the creditworthiness of their clients. Dr. Devra Marcus decided to quit her job rather than face the censure of colleagues for sacrificing the income of the group practice by referring a patient to a specialist.

Although we are grateful when we find them, canny outlaws are not enough. We cannot rely on people doing the right thing in spite of the institutional structures in which they work. What we want is institutions that encourage the skill and the will to do the right thing. Such institutions are within our grasp, and there are people working to create them. These system changers are building institutions that encourage practitioners to develop practical wisdom instead of draining it from them. They are trying to change the law, not evade it. They are like the legislators and statesmen—the lawmakers and institution builders— whom Aristotle wanted to encourage in ancient Athens. They, like the statesmen, need practical wisdom to fashion new institutions that encourage character and practical wisdom in citizens.

These system changers—or system builders—are not focused on serving individuals one on one as many practitioners are; they are not trying to balance competing principles or to interpret a rule or to figure out how to craft an action in a particular case. They need the wisdom to craft organizations that encourage others to learn to act wisely;

they need the wisdom to formulate new procedures, create new curricula, and teach teams of colleagues how to support one another. Their aim is to structure practices that give people wisdom-inducing instead of wisdom-draining experiences.

PUTTING THE JUDGMENT BACK INTO JUDGING

The two-decade campaign to use mandatory sentencing to squeeze the judgment out of judging was finally halted in 2005. It was the Supreme Court, led by Chief Justice William Rehnquist, that finally mounted the successful counterattack. The earlier opposition by judges and lawyers had not convinced Congress to reform the mandatory sentencing regimen it had put in place beginning in the early 1980s. In fact, efforts by some judges to challenge what had become mandated "guidelines" in their courtrooms had the opposite effect. The Justice Department and Congress clamped down further on judicial discretion by passing the 2003 Feeney Amendment. When the legislation was being debated in Congress, Justice Rehnquist took the highly unusual step of writing a letter arguing that the Feeney Amendment would "seriously impair the ability of courts to impose just and reasonable sentences." In a speech to the American Bar Association another Supreme Court justice, Anthony Kennedy, urged the ABA to tell Congress: "Please do not use our courts but then say the judge is incapable of judging. Please, Senators and Representatives, repeal federal mandatory minimums." The Judicial Conference of the United States (representing federal judges nationwide and headed by the chief justice), a group of seventy law professors, and a number of former U.S. attorneys strongly opposed the Feeney crackdown. All to no avail.

But the critics of judicial discretion had gone too far with the Feeney Amendment. In 2005, the Supreme Court finally turned against mandated sentencing. In *United States v. Booker* the Court undid the Feeney Amendment. In fact, it went even further. It declared mandatory guidelines unconstitutional and declared that, moving forward, the guidelines would be "advisory." Judges would be allowed to make the sentence fit the crime and to balance the aims of retribution, rehabilitation, and deterrence. The *Booker* decision removed the fear of judgment from judging and made it possible for judges to exercise practical wisdom again.

While the movement toward mandatory sentencing gained momentum throughout the 1980s and 1990s, another, less visible story was being written by state and local judges. In addition to those like Lois Forer who struggled to resist the strict mandatory minimums, there were others who were trying to transform the judicial system in ways that expanded the scope of judicial discretion. They created new courts where offenders could opt for alternative sentences instead of being charged with crimes that would trigger the mandatory minimums. These courts actually encouraged judges to exercise even greater practical wisdom.

On a typical Tuesday afternoon in 2008, Buffalo City Court Judge Robert Russell walked into a very different courtroom from the one Judge Lois Forer had presided over. The first thing he did was step down from his bench and walk into the gallery. It was filled with men and women accused of theft, drug offenses, and other nonviolent felonies. "Good afternoon," he said, smiling. He talked for a minute about what to expect. The expectations were very different from those in Judge Forer's courtroom, even though the crimes were very similar. This was a unique court, one that Judge Russell had created. All of the accused were veterans, most from the wars in Iraq and Afghanistan.

Gary Pettengill stepped before Judge Russell. "Hi, Gary," said the judge. "Nice to see you, and why not give me an update."

"My family and I moved into a new home," said Mr. Pettengill.

"That's good news," said the judge. "How do you like it?"

"It's pretty nice," said Pettengill. "Different neighborhood. Pretty quiet. A lot bigger, though, than before. More room for the kids to play inside."

And so began a long conversation that sounded like small talk. But it wasn't. Judge Russell was checking in on Gary Pettengill, looking for signs of stability that could keep him out of jail.

Gary Pettengill had wanted to make the army a career but was forced to take a medical discharge in 2006 after he severely injured his back in Iraq. He was then twenty-three, married, with a third kid on the way. He had started using marijuana to deal with nightmares from post-traumatic stress disorder (PTSD), and then he started selling it. He could get only part-time work with his bad back, and he didn't have enough money to put food on the table. Or buy diapers, he said. And "if you run out of formula, it's like $21 a can." He was busted in a drug sweep in February 2008. When he had first come to Russell's court, his family had been kicked out of their apartment, he was looking at losing his kids to the child welfare system because of the drugs, and he was at risk of doing serious prison time as a drug felon.

But Pettengill was given the option to go to the Veterans' Court instead of to the regular court. Instead of the normal trial and sentencing—and likely a tough prison sentence dictated by the state's mandatory sentencing laws—Pettengill had opted to accept the alternative sentencing offered by the Veterans' Court, with the understanding that noncompliance could land him back in the regular court, and in prison. The Veterans' Court mandated drug treatment. Working with the Veterans Administration, it helped Pettengill get part-time work, housing assistance for an apartment, and cash. He was assigned a volunteer mentor, also a former veteran. Judge Russell explained that "having a veteran who has gone through similar experiences being able to work with them, encourage them, assist them, we're finding some great rewards from those relationships." Pettengill had to stay off drugs and out of trouble or risk getting thrown back into the regular criminal justice system. How many chances does someone like Pettengill get? "There is not a scale or a chart of how many chances a person receives," says Judge Russell. "We understand that a person who is going through challenges, whether it's mental health or addiction, that it does take patience, and also takes a great amount of oversight. It takes a great amount of courage. It also takes a great amount, if need be, of sanctions, of consequences to motivate them to stay focused on what they need to stay focused with."

Judge Russell, like any good judge, aimed to balance retribution, deterrence, and rehabilitation when he sentenced Pettengill and other veterans. But he was particularly concerned with the rehabilitation and deterrence. He wanted to stop what many have called "revolving-door justice"—offenders with unsolved problems who end up coming right back into court after they are released from prison. He and his team of veterans' advocates and volunteers aim to make each run-in with the law the last for the veterans. They have been extraordinarily successful. By February 2010, there were 120 veterans enrolled in Judge Russell's program. Ninety percent of the participants successfully completed the program. The recidivism rate was zero.

Judge Russell is not simply a wise judge, interpreting the law and balancing general principles in light of particular circumstances. He saw a larger problem that wise judges could help resolve and he built an institution to encourage that kind of judging. Russell had had long experience witnessing the failure of the court system to deal with some of the social, medical, and psychological problems that got offenders into trouble in the first place. After earning his law degree at Howard University in 1979, he worked for twelve years as an assistant district attorney and assistant attorney general in Ohio and New York before becoming an associate judge in the Buffalo City Court in 1992. In his first years on the bench, he saw how the failure of the courts to deal with the problems of the addicted and mentally ill offenders overwhelmed the system. So, in 1995, with the help of Hank Pirowski, a Marine Vietnam

veteran and social worker, Judge Russell took the lead in establishing
Buffalo's first drug treatment court, and in 2003 Buffalo's first mental
health court. He had seen the success of such special courts in other
parts of the country. Mental illness and drug addiction were health problems that needed treatment; if these problems were not resolved, offenders would continue to resort to crime to support their habits. And
prison sentences were not going to solve this problem.

Then Judge Russell saw the large number of returning veterans
flooding Buffalo's courts with mental health and drug problems—three
hundred in 2007 alone. Pirowski, who heads Russell's staff, says that
many of these veterans are in trouble because they are dealing with the
aftermath of combat. Many are suffering from PTSD or substance
abuse problems. They get arrested for drunk driving, theft, drug possession, and drug dealing. "It starts out simply from a prescription abuse, to
illicit substances, to some type of crime activity to support that [drug]
activity, to being arrested, to going to jail," says Pirowski. He and Judge
Russell knew the problem would only get worse with four hundred
thousand vets nationwide coming home over the next few years. They
decided to build on the success of the drug court. In 2008, Judge Russell
took the initiative to create the first veterans' court in the country.

Judge Russell is the kind of wise statesman whom Aristotle would
have admired. Judge Russell figured out a way to create an institution
that encourages justice and relies on practical wisdom to mete it out. A
judge in a veterans' court does not need to be a canny outlaw. The very
structure of the veterans' court builds in wisdom-demanding tasks in
order to accomplish its aim of justice: the need to balance the competing
purposes of sentencing; the necessity to carefully examine the history,
context, and motives of offenders like Gary Pettengill; the need to empathize with offenders and imagine what they might be like if they received
help; and the need to balance this empathy with the sober detachment
necessary to craft and enforce alternative sentencing programs.

Judge Russell's Veterans' Court attracted national attention. By late

2009, twenty-two other cities had created their own veterans' courts and at least thirty-nine others were planned. Such veterans' courts are only the tip of a huge movement of judicial institution building. Judicial statesmen like Judge Russell began promoting such alternative "problem-solving" courts in 1989 when judges and local officials in Florida's Dade County realized that harsh mandatory minimum sentences were no way to handle the explosion of drug-related crimes. They opened the first drug treatment court offering offenders the choice between prison time and mandated substance abuse treatment. Since then, hundreds of drug courts have been created in the United States and these have become models for other problem-solving courts—teen courts, mental health courts, domestic violence courts. By 2007, nationwide, there were over thirty-two hundred problem-solving courts, about two-thirds of them drug courts. Such problem-solving courts, focusing on guided rehabilitation, have been, said the *New York Times*, "strikingly successful around the country in reducing crime, saving money and repairing lives." The judicial statesmen who built them were able to reinvigorate the importance of practical wisdom in the justice system at the very moment when mandatory sentencing regimens were elsewhere trying to squeeze it out.

THE ETHICAL LAWYER

Anthony Kronman has worried a lot about whether "ethical lawyer" is an oxymoron. In 1981, before he became dean of Yale Law School, he suggested to the editors of the *Yale Law Journal* that law might be a profession that was morally unworthy at its core. The reason was its commitment to advocacy as an ideal. Unlike "the truth-seeking enterprise of scholarship," Kronman said, advocacy "corrupts the soul by encouraging a studied indifference to the truth." But Kronman came to see that there was a better way to frame the problem. Yes, there is an inherent tension built into the practice of the law—the lawyer must defend his client, but the lawyer also has an equally important public obligation to seek justice and to act as an officer of the court. Loyalty to the client and loyalty to the public must always be balanced. Law professors and practicing lawyers who are concerned about the corrosion of practical wisdom are trying to build institutions that encourage lawyers to learn how to achieve this balance.

Nurturing Practical Wisdom in Law Students

The teaching method at the heart of a modern legal education is the case method. The cases studied are typically contested lower-court cases that have gone to appellate courts. Students are asked to consider what rule of law the appeals court judges used to determine their ruling, and, perhaps more important, they are asked to judge whether the reasoning and conclusions of the appeals court judges were sound. In the best classes, good law professors mentor and coach their students by forcing them to reenact the reasoning and the decisions of experienced judges in the classroom. Students are encouraged to think not just logically but analogically—to determine in what way this case is similar to or different from the precedent set in an earlier case. They are encouraged to pay attention to the context—*this* particular case—and not just general principles or rules. By reenacting the case, the participants are expected to simulate the kinds of thinking and argument that lawyers and judges engage in when they adjudicate.

The theory is that this kind of pedagogy encourages students to learn how to balance empathy and detachment appropriately because students have to enact both sides of the case. They are required to defend positions they do not agree with, or may even find morally offensive. They must strain to see the justice of whichever claim they have been given to defend, to sympathize with another perspective and not simply to tolerate it. But then students must move from being empathetic to being detached because they are also forced to play the role of judge, someone who does not have a bias toward one party or the other—someone who has a stake in the administration of justice.

The problem with this pedagogy, its critics say, is not the theory but the practice. A true Socratic dialogue may be a good way to promote reflective judgment, but far too often these classes are highly manipulative and authoritarian affairs "in which students compete to please the teacher with glib responses within rigid time constraints." And even when it is done well—even when the teacher is "a master artisan guiding a roomful of novices through the early stages of learning a craft"—there is still an important ingredient of practical wisdom missing—experience with the practical.

Professor William Sullivan, a director of the Carnegie Foundation's Preparation for the Professions Program until June 2010, has examined this dominant law school pedagogy and concluded that, even at its best, the overreliance on this method has a potentially damaging effect on the "moral apprenticeship" of lawyers. There is a message, Sullivan explained to us, in what the faculty focus on and what they leave out. And what the students are told to focus on, particularly in their all-consuming first year, are the procedural and formal aspects of legal reasoning. Not only is there no actual experience with clients, but the actors in the appeals court cases are reduced to legal categories like plaintiffs and defendants. The rich human narratives of these people are condensed into just those facts that the appeals court judges are considering. Furthermore, most faculty routinely ignore, or even rule out-of-bounds, ethical-social issues like compassion for the client and concern about substantive justice or equity. Sullivan found that the tacit messages many students learn are that it is "soft" to look at the human side and that legal thinking can justify anything.

Concern about this kind of demoralization of law and other professions led Sullivan to leave academia for the Carnegie Foundation. He thinks demoralization can be stemmed if professional schools build the right kind of programs, and he has brought together educators in engineering, theology, medical, nursing, and law schools to look at what's going wrong, to identify some "best practices" that get it right, and to bring research in the cognitive sciences to bear on how people learn not only technical skills but ethical skills and motivation. One successful program Sullivan's Carnegie Foundation group studied was the "legal clinic." They found that the kind of mentorship and hands-on experience that is built into such clinics promotes a technical and moral apprenticeship and encourages the students to develop wisdom that is quite practical.

Harvard law professor Robert Bordone runs just such a clinic. Bordone is the director of the Harvard Negotiation and Mediation Clinical Program. He is an expert on dispute resolution who has worked with corporate clients, public schools and universities, orchestras, hospitals, nonprofits, government agencies, and the International Criminal Court at The Hague, and is coeditor of *The Handbook of Dispute Resolution*. Bordone emphasized to us just how important practical wisdom is to being a good negotiator. It's impossible to anticipate every possible move in a negotiation. At any time, there can be unexpected outbursts: critical new facts can suddenly come to light, someone's "emotional hot button" can accidentally get pressed. Mediation is so dynamic and interactive that it can't be scripted. Negotiators, says Bordone, are like improvisational actors or jazz musicians. They need to "learn to be comfortable with the unexpected without learning prescriptive formulas." That means learning to listen carefully, to interpret words, actions, and emotions, and watching for body-language clues both onstage and in the audience.

Before students can get into Bordone's negotiation clinic, they need to take his class. He told us that one of the first things he has to do is *untrain* most of his law students. "They think negotiation is how to make a more persuasive argument. But it's not. It's about understanding the other. Perspective taking. How to help the clients you are working with know their own interests. The client may say: I want A, B, C, and D. But what are their actual underlying interests? It's rare that a client understands these. It's like fights over who is supposed to do the dishes. It's not about the dishes. It's about being unappreciated. It's about something else." To get at this something else, he tries to teach his academically sophisticated students how to do "active listening" and perspective taking. He and his assistants model what this looks like. He then divides the students into small teams, has each listen to a classmate argue for a contentious position, and then has them try to give a neutral summary. It turns out that it is remarkably hard for his bright Harvard law students to empathize with the speaker. The class then analyzes why. Bordone's method is "Tell. Show. Do. Review." And the students learn to improvise like actors.

The students who go on to take the negotiation clinic go much deeper, learning through practicing hands-on, actual negotiations. The center Bordone directs has little trouble finding clients who want help. One recent client was the Southern Coalition for Social Justice in North Carolina. The ownership of large blocks of land deeded to black families after the Civil War—some of it now quite valuable—was in frequent dispute. Over generations, the number of heirs had grown, and many had died without wills. The titles to the land were highly fractionated, and the Southern Coalition was worried. Not only were disputes over this land tearing families apart, but many low-income black families were at risk of losing their property.

Bordone assigned three of the clinic students to work out and implement a "consensus-based model" for resolving one such property dispute. With the guidance of Bordone and an assistant, the students first did a "stakeholders assessment." They contacted everyone in the family, Bordone explained. "Someone might say: 'No way am I going to give up this piece of land.' We ask why. We try to understand their reasons. We try to figure out: what are the different interests of each party and is it possible to bring them all to the table and build a consensus?" Next the students put together an assessment and developed a plan. Then they went down to North Carolina and brought together the whole family and met with them for a week. By the end of the process, the family had agreed to form a limited liability company and had decided that the company would do prawn farming.

Bordone's approach has all the hallmarks of the hands-on clinical practice Sullivan and his Carnegie Institute team found so valuable. Sullivan sees all professional practice—nursing, teaching, doctoring, engineering—as an exercise in practical wisdom. "Judgment in action," he calls it. Such judgment, he says, "is reasoning not from a set of rules but by analogy to model cases and precedent." But absent hands-on clinical experience, the judgment students can learn by sitting in a classroom—and looking only at model cases and precedents drawn from decisions of appeals court judges—is severely restricted. In a clinic, a student can develop this judgment by practicing how to support a client at the same time as he questions her. In actually assuming the role of a counselor, the student lawyer is put "in the role of cooperative problem solver with the client rather than the distanced expert who solves the client's problem." Discerning how to listen, resolving conflicts of interest or questions of confidentiality, balancing the inevitable tensions—between empathy and detachment, counseling and advocacy, duties to the client and duties to the public interest—all these issues are embedded in everyday clinical practice. And the student has the advantage of learning these skills with a mentor who can serve as a model and a coach.

We once knew, says Sullivan, that apprenticeship—modeling and coaching by mentors—was the way to prepare professionals. But that has been forgotten over the past century as professional education has moved into university classrooms and relied on more academic instruction. The expert practitioners and scholars he brought together at Carnegie point to recent findings in the learning sciences (cognitive psychology, linguistics, philosophy, evolutionary and neural biology, and artificial intelligence) that resurrect the central role of apprenticeship in initiating novices into the wisdom of practice. The habits of the practical mind are instilled "as the learner sees expert judgment in action and is then coached through similar activities." Sullivan likes to use the metaphor of "scaffolds" to underline how apprenticeships teach novice professionals expert judgment. Accomplished practitioners show students how things are done, sometimes breaking things down into discrete tasks or steps. Then the students practice themselves, and get coaching and criticism from their mentors—for example, Bordone's "Tell. Show. Do. Review." Rules and procedures are essential scaffolds for learning lawyering skills. They give the beginner a basic grasp of how to function in a variety of legal situations. But the particularities of each context will soon start to overwhelm efforts simply to apply rules. The expert mentor can model what to do. She can help the apprentice to focus on the goal and not just the formal rules, to see analogies that might help solve the problems, "to recognize new situations as similar to whole remembered patterns, and, finally, as an expert, to grasp what is important in a situation without proceeding through a long process of formal reasoning." Notably, this scaffolding is strikingly similar to the building of cognitive networks we discussed in chapter 6.

Sullivan and his colleagues are not simply urging more legal clinics. Hundreds of these have been created at law schools around the country. But they generally remain peripheral to legal education. Such practical training is optional, and the clinics are often taught by a separate faculty, one that typically is not tenured and has a lower academic status. Sullivan argues that the apprenticeship embodied by these clinics should be at the core of legal education. One model his colleagues analyzed was the law school at the City University of New York. It recruits students of far more limited means and far weaker academic backgrounds than Bordone's Harvard students, but it encourages a far more practical education. In addition to taking typical first-year law courses (criminal procedure, contracts, torts), the CUNY "first years" are also in small "lawyering" seminars that not only encourage close faculty mentoring but link legal theory to practice by assigning students to work on simulated cases. By the third year, all students are required to do real-world lawyering in a supervised field placement or in the school's on-site legal clinic.

This kind of education is not simply an apprenticeship in technical and moral skill. It is also an apprenticeship in moral will. As one clinical professor explained, "Clinics try to resensitize students after being desensitized in law school." Sullivan urges a restructuring of law programs so this desensitization doesn't happen in the first place. Clinical education changes the hypothetical questions typical in most legal education ("What might you do?") to questions that are more immediately involving and demanding: "What will you do?" or "What did you do?" Sullivan emphasizes that this "puts responsibility for clients and accountability for one's own actions [at] the center of clinical experiences." Such responsibility and accountability should be at the center of law school experience. They are what encourage moral will and moral skill.

AND AFTER LAW SCHOOL?

A law school graduate who wants to do good and to do well—to aim at the right things and earn a living—has a number of options. She could work at one of hundreds of nonprofits that deal with issues of environment, poverty, labor, health care, human rights, women's issues, and social justice. He could work in a legal clinic or as a public defender or in family law or perhaps start a small individual practice. She could work for an elected official or in a government agency. But what if this lawyer wanted to work for a corporate law firm? It's hard to find firms that encourage wise practices and minimize the demoralization that has become the norm. But it's not impossible. Chris Schultz helped shape and run such a firm.

Mahoney, Bourne, and Thiemes is not a social services or advocacy or public-interest law firm. The Buffalo firm's major clients are real estate developers, hospitals, a bank, and the Catholic archdiocese. But Schultz and his partners have intentionally created a firm that encourages practices far different from the prototypical corporate firm described by Patrick Schiltz.

Chris Schultz had been mentored by Brian Mahoney since he joined Mahoney's law firm right out of law school in the late 1960s. He was drawn in by Mahoney's commitment to social justice and the public interest, by his work with Catholic hospitals and charities and religious orders, and with liberal political campaigns. But when Mahoney died suddenly of a heart attack in 1972, and Schultz found himself catapulted into a management position, he realized that he had to change the legacy of Mahoney's rather loose and free-spirited business style, the lack of attention to the financial implications of his good works. Schultz quickly moved to put the firm on a more even financial keel, instituting procedures to better manage personnel, collect fees, create new billing processes, and control expenses. He looked to hire people who knew how to make money but who also shared his commitment to keep Mahoney's work going. He wanted a viable firm yet one in whose soul was a commitment to serve the public interest. "We knew we could make money," said Schultz, "and still do what Brian Mahoney did."

At a time when traditional pro bono work was being squeezed out of corporate firms by the pressures to work more billable hours, Schultz encouraged his lawyers to do more than pro bono. Serving the public, he argued, also meant working for low-paying community clients as part of the regular work of the firm. Arthur Laughlin, a partner, explained it as continuing the grand tradition that law was not a commodity to be bought and sold, but a form of public service. Schultz himself serves on boards of poverty organizations active in housing, neighborhood development, legal services, and care for the elderly. But he does more than model the behavior he encourages. He brings up public service at performance reviews, and firm policy encourages everyone to participate in some form of community service. And very important, he has made sure that the firm's compensation scheme doesn't discourage it.

Schultz set up a compensation system that aimed to minimize the monetarization of work. Schultz insisted that compensation would not be tied to billable hours or the revenues generated by a particular lawyer. He also maintained absolute secrecy about the number of hours each lawyer billed to avoid what he saw as the destructive internal competition over who bills the most or who is most valuable to the firm. Furthermore, the compensation differences among the highest- and lowest-paid lawyers are unusually low by law firm standards. All this encourages a dedication to work *and* service. The common pressure to abandon public-interest work to gain higher pay or status is not there. Schultz says, "I don't want anyone feeling that work for some Catholic Charities group is less valuable to the firm than real estate syndications." Laughlin explained that public service is "on an equal footing with, and sometimes even prevails over, economics." A senior associate who works largely in banking transactions explained that he feels much better to know that he is, in effect, subsidizing the firm's public-interest work.

The ethos of public service also spills over into the willingness of Mahoney's lawyers to do the tough work of wise counseling. Lawyers reported being more willing than most to restrain a client, convincing him, for example, to restructure a transaction to avoid an out-and-out sham. One of Mahoney's corporate clients suggested that public service at Mahoney informs its sophisticated thinking about service to their private clients. Public and private work together, he said, so that Mahoney's dedication to serving others is different from the ethos of "being an expert." Mahoney also encourages wise counseling by promoting long-term relationships with clients, which generates commitment and trust. Its lawyers are encouraged to know the client's organization and help the client figure out its long-term interests. One lawyer referred to the pleasure in dealing with "relationship clients." It allowed him to be a "full-blown counselor" who "brainstorms" with the client.

The lawyers at Mahoney describe an ethos of equal treatment and a collegial way of practice. "No one is looking at the hours," explained one partner. "Pride drives us to work hard." "The moment you worry or even begin to think about whether others should be making more or less than you," explained another, "you create tensions that aren't here now. The security, the respect, the fine clients, the fun that comes with association with this firm are part of the compensation." The effect of this organization and culture is to moralize work in another way—by building morale among lawyers and staff. They take pleasure in serving others and in the work relations they have with each other.

Schultz also takes great care—and pleasure—in developing the younger people in the firm. He is constantly giving them feedback, from pats on the back to criticism. His formal evaluations are carefully structured to address legal skills, progress toward partnership, and maturity with clients. He has periodic meetings with young lawyers in which he discusses his own mistakes and failures and how he dealt with them. He models his own process of learning through trial and error. And he wants to discourage the tendency he sees in large firms to talk only of successes, which then makes people feel terrible when the inevitable mistake or miscalculation occurs.

The firm Chris Schultz and his partners forged goes a long way toward encouraging young lawyers in the corporate world to aim at the right things and do so wisely. The firm's ability to survive and thrive is a testament to Schultz's wisdom as a lawyer-statesman. He knows what legal practice should aim at, he has the ability to balance the economic practicalities of running a for-profit firm with the ideals of legal practice, he has the skill to create structures that minimize the monetarization of legal practice, and he has the capability to educate lawyers with the passion and know-how to counsel wisely and to balance public interest and client demands. Schultz's success in building this kind of firm has only been possible because there were able and committed lawyers who were willing to work for a firm like Mahoney, who were willing to sacrifice the higher pay they could have gotten elsewhere in return for a supportive environment that encouraged work aimed at the right things. Schultz allowed such people to flourish, and they made possible a firm like the one he created.

As the profession of corporate law increasingly becomes the business of making money by practicing law, the competitive pressures to increase compensation, billable hours, size, and specialization will make wise lawyering harder to learn. Or even remember. But if lawyers like Schultz can succeed in building institutions that encourage lawyers to practice wisely, they will be keeping alive a model that others can emulate.

NURTURING THE WISDOM TO TEACH

The students at the K–8 school, in a town in Vermont we'll call Millerton (a pseudonym), had not been doing well on the statewide writing tests. When Joey Hawkins arrived to give writing workshops to the teachers, they were happy to see her. She was not an "outside consultant" coming to show them how to get test scores up by focusing on the bubble kids. She was one of them.

Ms. Hawkins was not trained to be a teacher of teachers. In 1983, she began teaching social studies (and a heavy dose of writing) to seventh- and eighth-graders at the Newton School in South Strafford, Vermont. She became a keen observer of how students learn to write—and what blocks the process. She was slowly drawn into teaching teachers as test-based educational reforms began to sweep across the country in the 1980s. In the late 1980s, Vermont began developing its own testing system. Ms. Hawkins, along with other teachers, worked with the Department of Education to build the new system. Dubbed the Vermont Portfolio Assessment Program, it started in 1991. Ms. Hawkins focused on her expertise: writing. Students at the fourth-, eighth-, and tenth-grade levels would be required to demonstrate their skills by submitting five kinds of writing in their "portfolios"—a reflective essay, a persuasive essay, a narrative, a response to an event or a film, and a report. This was not a standardized exam. It was not multiple choice. Assessment would not be a routinized affair carried out by computers or bureaucrats in the Department of Education. Instead, teams of teachers would be trained to read and evaluate student writing portfolios. How clear was the purpose of the essay? How well was it organized? How careful was its attention to detail? How good were the mechanics of writing? Ms. Hawkins and her colleagues developed model pieces of writing to serve as touchstones—standards—for those who assessed the portfolios. And these teachers created ways to train themselves and others to do the assessments.

It was a far cry from the Texas approach discussed in chapter 9. It was meant to be. Teachers participated in creating and tuning the standards. And the portfolio testing system had a far different impact on the students and teachers. The students had to meet the standards, but the teachers had to figure out how to get them there. There was no mandated, packaged, scripted curriculum. What *was* mandated were the portfolios in writing and in math. And "if your school does not do well," explained Hawkins, "we'll give you help." The high-stakes testing model from Texas was based on the assumption of bad faith—teachers are unwilling or unable to change, so rewards and punishments are needed to get them to change. The Vermont model, Hawkins told us, was based on the assumption of good faith—teachers want to get better, so we'll give them the assistance and training to do it.

Ms. Hawkins does not dismiss the importance of assessments. "The portfolios woke up a lot of teachers and made them take the standards more seriously. But they had to find their own way to meet them. Millerton had one of the four lowest writing test scores in Vermont. The state said: 'We're going to give you a lot of help and you are going to take it.' It was not standardization of the curriculum. But many needed help." After over a decade teaching under the new portfolio system, Joey Hawkins decided to cut back on her teaching of students and try her hand at teaching teachers. And that is how she found herself in Millerton's K–8 school.

Joey Hawkins observed that "the homes some of these kids came from were not very rich environments in terms of books and conversation. Teaching writing was like teaching a kid how to tie a shoelace. First you describe it. Then you show it. You 'scaffold' it; I'll make this loop, you make the next one."

The metaphor of scaffolding views teaching to be like building a building. The students need a frame—a structure to stand on as they construct one floor at a time. And the teacher needs to take them through the process again and again until they learn how to frame things themselves. Ms. Hawkins's approach to teaching the teachers is just the same.

When Ms. Hawkins met with the Millerton teachers, they wanted to work on teaching students how to analyze texts. She asked each one to pick a text and tell her the things they hoped the students would learn. She then came to each of their classes and did a demonstration of how she would teach the text the teachers had picked. In one class she read aloud a short article on castles. She had teams of students read it aloud to each other. She had each team answer questions like "How do castles keep people safe?" then report back to the class, then write the answers down, and then put the answers together to create a paper. Then Ms. Hawkins coached each teacher in designing her own lesson plan, had her try it out, and they discussed both what worked and what didn't. Then, together, all the teachers discussed what they had done. "You give them models. Then you tweak the model and have them apply it to new situations. It's like training wheels on a bike. And it's safe for them"—for the students and the teachers.

The teachers were initially skeptical of any outsider coming in, says Ms. Hawkins. But now she is welcomed, indeed invited, to many schools in the state. That's in part because she's a great teacher—ask almost any parent or former student in Strafford, or the University of Vermont panel that recognized her as one of the state's outstanding teachers in 2004. But it was the Vermont standards that got the schools to open their doors. Vermont insisted the schools meet them, and Ms. Hawkins was there to help.

We asked Joey Hawkins about the common defense of standardization. Don't teachers need to be held accountable to get them to improve? She winced. "Of course there need to be standards, but you can have standards without standardization." Better standards. Not ones whose only virtue is that they are quantifiable and easily measurable. "We've got tough standards in Vermont. We use the model papers, that teachers themselves developed, to teach teachers what good writing for their classes might look like. And then we help them figure out how to get their students there. Almost all the teachers want their students to make it, and they want to learn what it takes to teach them."

The public officials and teachers who built the Vermont portfolio system needed practical wisdom to construct it. They were wise enough to build an educational environment where expert teachers could help create the standards and assessments; where teachers could learn, through daily trial and error, the best "how-to" for meeting those standards and get mentoring and coaching if they needed it. It was not designed to be a teacher-proof system but a wisdom-encouraging system. Even today, with the introduction of standardized assessments in Vermont, the system encourages teachers to work within their own curriculum, collaborating and using their own best judgment, to help students meet standards. The portfolio system and the more recent standardized assessments were designed to develop good judgment in the same way that Lieutenant Colonel Leonard Wong was urging senior military leaders to encourage good judgment in their junior officers. Provide standards and basic guidelines "and then let the commander train."

"Overcome the desire to tell subordinates how to do it," Wong advised. "Refrain from detailing *how* a task is to be accomplished. . . . Demand *a* solution, not *the* solution." What Wong recognized about military training and what Joey Hawkins has learned about teaching is much like what Judge Forer learned about mandatory sentencing rules and Karl Weick observed about too many rules for wildfire fighters. Rules are set up to establish and maintain high standards of performance, and to allow the lessons learned by some to be shared by all. But if they are too strict or too detailed or too numerous, they can be immobilizing, counterproductive, and even destructive.

BECOMING A WISE DOCTOR

The call from Dr. Pieter Cohen was unexpected. Vanessa had been planning to meet him at four o'clock that afternoon for their weekly "walk and talk," an ambulatory tutorial and debriefing that had become something of a ritual with his third-year Harvard medical students training at Cambridge Health Alliance hospital in Cambridge, Massachusetts. But today, Dr. Cohen wanted Vanessa to visit a patient with him. He had just returned from vacation and checked his e-mail. The father of a family that he had long cared for was in the hospital—he had suddenly gone blind. Cohen immediately phoned the daughter (we'll call her Maria), who was at her father's bedside. She was distraught. Dr. Cohen checked the patient's record. It did not look good. Cohen wanted to get to the hospital quickly. Would Vanessa come along? "I'll fill you in on what happened when we meet up," he told her.

Third-year medical students would not normally be invited along on a visit like this. Physicians at most teaching hospitals barely know the third-year "clerks." Most third-year medical students do rotations at hospital inpatient wards as the junior member of a team that includes the "attending" physician, the chief resident, and some interns. They rotate every few months to complete their core clerkships (medicine, surgery, obstetrics-gynecology, pediatrics, neurology, psychiatry, radiology). They shadow their seniors, watch what is happening, and answer tough questions thrown their way from time to time. Most attendings would not think to call most Vanessas.

But only part of Vanessa's hands-on training is on the inpatient wards of the hospital. And Dr. Cohen does not see her as the low woman on the totem pole. Vanessa spends a full morning each week working with regular patients in Dr. Cohen's internal medicine clinic, and every other morning in one of the other core clinics—neurology, pediatrics, and so on. In each clinic she has a "preceptor"—a mentor—like Dr. Cohen. And from the very beginning of her third year she had been assigned certain patients to work with. She works with them every time they come into the clinic. In fact, anytime they visit any other clinic—or any time they come into the hospital—Vanessa is notified and she works with them. In the lingo of Dr. Barbara Ogur and Dr. David Hirsh, the two key builders of Harvard Medical School's Cambridge Integrated Clerkship (CIC) program, students have "longitudinal contact" with the faculty as well as the patients.

We met up with Dr. Ogur just before Vanessa and her eleven classmates arrived for "morning rounds" at seven a.m. The students sat with Dr.

Ogur around a small seminar table, a huge white board behind them. As one student, Anjana Sharma, presented what she called a medical mystery, another student volunteered to write a summary of the case on the white board. Anjana's patient—we'll call him John Edwards—is thirty-six. He came into the emergency room after suddenly collapsing at his residence in the local YMCA. He had type 2 diabetes, schizoaffective disorder, and hypotension (low blood pressure).

For the next twenty minutes, Anjana presented Edwards's history and physical condition (what he had eaten before his collapse, his blood sugar levels, his fluid intake), the medicines he was on, his temperature, his heart rate, his physical signs (huddled, shaking, awake, frightened). The students and Dr. Ogur worked together on a "differential diagnosis." Ari asked: "When he fell, was he feeling light-headed? Could he have had peripheral neuropathy in his lower extremities or other muscular problems? You mentioned back pain. Could that have led him to lose balance?" When the medicines Edwards was taking were listed on the board, one student interjected: "Could you go through what each of those is for? I'm really bad on my pharm. I need a way to get better." "That would be really helpful for me," said another. As the list of possible causes grew, the students tried to determine what they could rule out, given the various tests that were done, and what other tests they might try. Possibilities were raised, discussed, tested, and dismissed. The students clearly took this to be a collaborative enterprise. Ogur put her ideas on the table, too, but she did so as a member of the team. Ogur sometimes pushed or prodded: "Why would you order up this lab work—what would it show or rule out?" "Can you do more than just list the possibilities—try to make a case for and against each one. You need to be more like a lawyer here." As the time drew to a close, Ogur had the students generate a list of the things they needed to know more about. A half dozen volunteered to do some research and report back the next day.

Their easygoing teamwork and collaboration seem so natural.

Barbara Ogur is a superb teacher and an expert diagnostician. She is aiming to get her students to figure things out themselves. She knows when and how to challenge them, and when and how to be supportive. She knows what things they need to be perceptive about. But it's not just Ogur's teaching that makes this possible. It's the whole format of morning rounds that she and Hirsh created. The teamwork and back-and-forth problem solving were made possible because the program they built is based on a long-term relationship between faculty and students and the long-term, hands-on relationship students have with the patients. Anjana can make her presentation because it's about "her" patient. It's important for her to get it right because she feels a certain responsibility. And the students are committed to helping one another because they need to learn from one another in order to solve the real problems of their own patients.

Ogur emphasized that the long-term doctor-student relationship she and Hirsh built into the program is also important in encouraging this kind of collegial dialogue. "Teaching in the traditional setting is much more brief and fragmented. Often the attending physician comes in and either quizzes the students on what they know and don't know or else dispenses 'pearls' of wisdom." But in the CIC program, teaching is "a collaborative exploration where my experience can help guide them. They learn to challenge me and join me to push the knowledge forward. We've become comfortable enough to challenge each other and even expose our own ignorance and vulnerability." The students were very conscious of this. Michael Morse, a recent graduate of the program, told us that when a doctor made him feel like a colleague, "an equal who could problem-solve with him and listen to his problems," it was much easier to admit when he did not know something and ask for help. "I felt safe," he said, "like a *talmid haver*," a Talmudic term that means "a student who is a friend and colleague."

Rounds ended without Anjana telling her classmates the final outcome of the hospitalization. Curious, we asked her after class what had happened. No one figured it out, she said, but he was stable and was released after two days, and given an appointment to see his primary physician. But he didn't show. "I'm really worried. I've tried to call him a few times at his room at the Y but no answer." We asked if it was common to check up on a patient like this. "Well," she said, "I spent more time with him than any of the docs. And he knows me the best. And he trusts me. He may be really sick. Maybe not. Maybe it was just dehydration. But I would like to follow up, maybe go over to his residence and check up on him. But I'm hesitant to do it alone. I'm thinking it might be misinterpreted. I'm hoping after rounds tomorrow that if someone in the group gets interested, they will come over with me." At rounds the next day, conversation continued to focus on the John Edwards case. Suspicion grew that Anjana's patient might have been discharged with something serious, perhaps an infection that had not been identified. When Anjana asked if anyone would come with her on the house call, three students immediately volunteered.

Dave Hirsh and Barbara Ogur created the CIC program because they were deeply concerned about traditional medical school training. Third- and fourth-year students are normally given their first hands-on training in the inpatient wards of hospitals. It's a rushed, highly compressed enterprise with attending physicians and residents barely having enough time to visit and care for patients, let alone teach the students who are shadowing them. The students never get to know patients or follow up on their treatments after their short hospital stays. Hirsh and Ogur had another concern too—ethical erosion among medical students.

Hirsh's own observations—backed by considerable research— convinced him that students leave medical school with far less empathy and compassion than when they begin. "They come in being idealistic and patient centered," said Hirsh. "But they leave burnt out and cynical." Detachment and objectivity, Hirsh acknowledges, are essential.

"They need the science. That's critical. But if it's only the science they learn, it's a wash." Certain things are "core," said Hirsh. The students have to know how to put in an IV, but they also have to know how to honor patients. They need to know how to do a physical exam, but they also need to know how to help their fellow students learn. They need to know how to deliver a baby, but they also need to be able to imagine what it would feel like to deliver it. One of the purposes of the program was to reverse the ethical erosion. "You can't stem ethical erosion if you have standard block rotations (as in most third-year programs). In these programs, the only concern is how you show up for the chief resident physician in your ward, and for the attending physician in charge. These residents are not bad people. After med school, when I was doing my training as a resident, I was always tired, stressed out. To ask someone doing this kind of work, for this many hours, to coach, mentor, and model—they would have to do it after the fourteen hours of work they already put in. And even if a particular resident is fantastic, you're still working in an environment in which you are always seeing the residents and doctors rolling their eyes."

So Hirsh and Ogur set out to design a program to teach students the medical science, the clinical judgment, and the dedication and wisdom to stem ethical erosion.

The students' yearlong, one-on-one working relationship with their doctor-preceptor in outpatient clinics builds the close relations and allows the time for serious, ongoing mentoring. By doing morning rounds with their doctors and fellow students, doing real-time problem solving for real patients, students learn the ethical skills—commitment, respect, good listening—of working in a team. Doing "problem-based learning" with actual problems gives the students the clinical and ethical practice they need. Trial-and-error learning is built into the program. "You propose things that might be mistakes," explained Michael Morse, "and the experienced clinician catches you. You've made a mistake but you haven't hurt anyone because you had the mentorship before you implemented the plan. But if you've never had responsibility for a patient, you've never had the experience of almost making a mistake, and the learning that comes from figuring out why you almost got it wrong."

―――――――

When Michael Morse had been in the CIC program a year earlier, he had worked with Pieter Cohen in his clinic. He stressed how important the one-on-one mentoring was, and the hands-on responsibility Dr. Cohen gave him for patients whom Michael would see repeatedly over the course of a full year. He contrasted this experience with the more traditional teaching in the inpatient wards of hospitals.

Michael told us that the attending physicians or chief residents who taught him during hospital rounds were sometimes really good teachers, but often they were too busy to give much attention to a lowly third-year. "A student like me has to talk four times as long as a resident. The attendings don't have time to listen to our extended stories so they ask us an occasional question, which sometimes has the flavor of teaching and sometimes just pimping." "Pimping?" we asked. "That's where they ask you a tough question about the diagnosis or treatment," said Michael. "They're testing you but not because they want input in how to care for this patient. The patient is irrelevant. It's about the command and mastery of facts or medical knowledge that the trainer wants you to recall." The students learn lots of tricks to avoid being pimped "or to make it look like we know something." But what's most pernicious about this pimping, he explained, is that "you're motivated to get it right because you don't want to be embarrassed or ashamed, not because you want to care for the patient. It's the antithesis of patient-centered care . . . where everything you are doing is meant to care for the patient."

We asked Michael if ethics was part of his clinical training. Medical ethics, he said, "is a complex subject when you take the whole of it, but when you're doing your best to care for the patient, in partnership with the patient, and doing the research when you need to know more, and talking to your colleagues, and getting mentored by physicians to work better, you are probably acting as an ethical physician most of the time." He talked about a diabetic patient he had been working with. "You know that he is killing himself by eating a half-dozen doughnuts a day. So it is a pretty fundamental ethical question: how to engage a patient with this truth. If you say: 'If you keep eating these six doughnuts a day, and you look at this statistically, there is a fifty-fifty chance you will be dead in seven years. Whereas if you follow my suggestions and change your diet, you will live for fourteen years.' But just laying out the facts like this probably won't work, and you have an ethical obligation to explain the risks to the patient. But how?" asks Michael.

"Do you just check the box: I've warned the patient? That may reduce your risk of being sued. But the ethical obligation is to change their behavior to live a healthier life. And this is exceptionally difficult. Is he not getting it? Or is there a challenge in implementing these behaviors? It's tempting to give up. But sometimes it's not because a patient is unwilling to change, but because the conversation was not done well. It requires more skill in counseling than many physicians have."

What did Michael do in these cases? He brought the problem to Pieter Cohen or another doctor in the program. And they were open to helping him think it through. And he also brought the problem to his student colleagues at morning rounds. "I could be open in conversations with my peers. They knew it was a practical issue that I was facing, that I was meeting this patient in twenty minutes. And they could help me figure out the best way to counsel him."

———

Dr. Elizabeth Gaufberg, a professor of medicine and psychiatry in the CIC program, teaches Patient-Doctor III, a required course for third-year medical students. Its goal is that students develop the knowledge, skill, and attitudes integral to every doctor-patient relationship—things like "practicing in a mindful, self-reflective manner," "learning to tolerate pain, suffering, and death," "understanding decision making under uncertainty and the limits of evidence-based medicine in clinical practice," "understanding ethical dilemmas in clinic practice," "learning to give bad news."

The goal is that students *learn* these things, but Dr. Gaufberg was reluctant to describe what she did as *teaching* them. And she was not alone. We began to notice that many of the doctor-teachers in the program avoided using the word *teaching*, using various awkward circumlocutions: "provoking the students," for instance, or "causing judgment to be learned." We asked why. The students, they said, could be taught certain medical knowledge: best practices, the skills needed to do an exam or surgery. But they couldn't be taught to be perceptive. To care. To get inside the thoughts and feelings of their patients. To balance empathy and detachment. To work out a treatment program and encourage a patient to follow it. To deliver bad news. At least not if teaching meant telling or providing rules or "giving" knowledge to students.

"Students who are treating patients under me in my clinic," said Pieter Cohen, "at first come to me and ask what I would do in such and such a situation. I try not to answer, because if I do, then they will learn what I would do and when a situation like this comes up again, they might think to just do what I said to do in the first situation. So I come back at them and ask them what they would do. It may not be exactly what I would do, but it might be reasonable. I ask them: If we try that, do we have a way to measure if it will work? Is it a kind of treatment that the patient is likely to follow? If they're unsure, they go home and look up everything on the topic. And then bring this back to our discussions."

So when the doctors said they don't teach, they meant they don't just lecture and tell. They set up the CIC program to create situations where students would learn through practice with the help of mentors. But if Elizabeth Gaufberg wasn't "teaching," what did she actually do in class? Why, for example, was her first class held in the Sackler Museum to look at art?

When the students met Gaufberg at the museum, she gave them their first assignment. If you brought a depressed friend to the museum, what work would you show them? Or what would you show a friend who had difficulty empathizing? Each student chose a picture and explained to the class why they picked it. "I don't care what they pick," said Dr. Gaufberg, "as long as it gets them to be self-aware and more mindful." Mindful? "Self-reflective," she said. "One of the things I want them to learn in this course is to observe their emotional reactions to patients, colleagues, and illness, to the ways they communicate, to how they respond to personal vulnerability and failure or react under stress. They need to be mindful practitioners to have the kind of sensitive, confident, open relations with patients that they will need to be successful healers." She added: "The museum is also a great exercise to jump-start them at working with each other and talking to each other. It's not, 'Tell us about your CV.'"

Subsequent classes involve a range of issues the students will have to face as doctors: how to balance "patient rights" with "patient well-being"; how to meet the emotional needs of dying patients; how to identify and manage the "hidden curriculum"—the gap between what students are told is good practice and what they see modeled on the hospital floors; how to assume responsibility after a medical error; and how to deliver bad news. Liz Gaufberg has students read articles and research studies and examine what ethicists have to say. She uses case studies, stories, and poems to get the students to express their feelings and learn how to empathize. She shows them videos of doctors facing some of the dilemmas they will face. She brings in other doctors to role-play some of the issues. She has the students work with professional actors who are trained to be patients. She has them role-play themselves. But most important is the way these materials trigger student discussions about their own experiences with patients. And the thing that makes this possible, explained Gaufberg, is the way she and others constructed the CIC program. The students are actually *having* these experiences because they have their own patients.

How unusual is a medical school class like Liz Gaufberg's? Not too unusual anymore, she said. Many medical schools now have courses in humanistic medicine or patient-centered care. Dr. Rita Charon at Columbia University and Abraham Verghese at Stanford University head programs that use discussions of literature to teach students to be more empathetic and perceptive, and their ideas about teaching have spread to other schools. Allowing students to practice giving bad news to "patients" played by professional actors has become more common. But Gaufberg warns that her course wouldn't do much if it were just an "add on" to a regular medical school curriculum. What really makes the course work is the community context that is built into the CIC program. Because the students have ongoing relationships with their patients, these issues are real for them. "When we do the exercises or read the narratives or do the role playing, the issues aren't abstract or theoretical. They trigger discussions about issues the students are actually facing." Dave Hirsh was more blunt. "A course like Liz's isn't enough if you are in an environment where stressed-out residents are asking: 'How many hits did you get last night?' Every patient seems like more work. Another 'hit.' You have to see them as fast as possible. One course can't compete with all the other ethical messages. If you are abused all day, every day, and then ten minutes before your bedtime your parents say 'I love you,' this is not enough."

———

Delivering bad news was no longer role playing when Vanessa joined Pieter Cohen to visit the distraught family in the hospital. Marco (the name we'll give the father) was the patriarch of a close-knit Brazilian family who had come to Boston many years ago, supporting his wife and two daughters as a housepainter. Maria, the daughter—and now a nurse—had been the first to come to Dr. Cohen's clinic, but Cohen had long been treating the whole family. Marco had occasional problems with alcohol but when Dr. Cohen saw him six months ago he hadn't been drinking for over a year. Maria said he had started drinking heavily two weeks ago. In previous drinking bouts, the family cared for him and he usually stopped in a few days. Maria and her mother had again taken charge, taking away all the alcohol and the car keys. But this time Marco got out his paint thinner and drank that. He went into a coma, experienced acute kidney failure, and was rushed to the hospital. While he was in intensive care he lost his sight. When Dr. Cohen called Maria before heading for the hospital, she had blurted out that she wanted to arrange for her father to see a specialist at Mass. Eye and Ear. She said, "I know that doesn't make much sense, but I just need to have some hope."

Dr. Cohen and Vanessa headed for Marco's room, stopping the chief resident in the hall on the way in to borrow his tie. "I insist that my students look professional when they see a patient," he told us, "but I had rushed over so quickly I had forgotten to grab my tie." They found Marco sleeping, Maria sitting by his bedside. The family had been taking shifts to be there twenty-four hours a day. They and Maria went to a nearby family sitting room to talk quietly.

Cohen started by telling Maria how difficult this must be. He asked her to tell them what happened, hoping that just talking would be good for her. Vanessa remembers that Maria found it particularly hard to cope that day. Her father had been feeling hopeless. She said she was even more upset. Cohen was sitting next to her. He put his hand on her shoulder, let her cry for a bit, explain how she felt.

"I'm sorry I'm so upset," she said.

"Don't apologize," said Cohen. "This is difficult."

Cohen later explained to us the struggle he saw Maria having, her guilt, the burden of responsibility she was feeling. "She was feeling incredible pressure as the point person in all this. She was the nurse, the one who knew the system, the one who spoke English. She was feeling overwhelmed. So one thing I did was just acknowledge this."

When Maria asked whether her father might regain his vision, Cohen hedged. "I am not an expert here. . . . My understanding is that it would be very rare to regain vision in a case like this, but we will do research to see if there are other cases and we'll get back to you and help you with this. . . . Even though I am not a neurologist, I can help you make these connections and I will be following your father's case and make sure there is care."

Dr. Cohen, Maria, and Vanessa then went back to Marco's room. Cohen repeated to him what he had told Maria. How lucky he was to have family. That what his family was doing for him was incredible. With that kind of support he will be able to return to being an active member of the family. That was where the hope was. Cohen then shifted to something tangible Marco and his family could work on. "While we work this through, I'm concerned about your being bedridden. You need to start working with a physical therapist to get your strength back." Cohen asked Vanessa to connect them with a caseworker and to follow through on things the family needed.

Dr. Cohen and Vanessa went on a walk afterward to debrief. Vanessa said, "It was really good to reflect on what had happened. Like the use of silence. Pieter gave the daughter enough space to express her concerns. She led the conversation until the end." We asked Cohen about this. "We need to strategically stop our madness from time to time. Normally we only have twenty minutes to spend with every patient. If I heard every story a patient in the clinic wanted to tell me, I would be fired. I would be spending three hours with each patient. . . . But there are times you put everything down. Like a surprise diagnosis of cancer. Like suicide attempts. You just put everything down. If you do that, it gives the patient great confidence that you are there. It's time well spent, and good for the patient."

Dr. Cohen and Vanessa talked about hope and truth. "Most docs make the mistake of always giving hope," explained Dr. Cohen. "Try this new treatment . . . and most of the time we know it's unlikely to work but we don't want to tell the patient that there's no hope. I don't think this is a good idea, to hold out hope when there is none. But I explained to Vanessa that the daughter needs some hope now. So our job is how to keep that window open. That in this case it was good to keep options open. To tell Maria that we would leave no stone unturned . . . and that we would do some research and look to see if there was any treatment. The art is to recognize when there is no other treatment, and still offer hope in a non-false, non-damaging way."

"In situations like this, it's so important for patients to know that we are there for them," said Vanessa. "A patient is seeing all these new faces popping up all the time. And suddenly they see someone who knows who they are. It's reassuring to them. And it has a therapeutic value that I can't put my finger on. What will really make a difference at this time is Marco's care. You need to handle the medical stuff. The diagnosis. But being involved—in the hospital, in the rehab, in the treatment—is what's really important. And it's what will sustain me as a physician. Because that's why I want to be a doctor."

CAN BANKERS BE WISE?

Ron Grzywinski saw what discrimination looked like growing up in a white, blue-collar Chicago neighborhood, where racial tolerance, he says, wasn't the order of the day. When Grzywinski went into banking in Chicago's integrated Hyde Park neighborhood he saw the financial impact of that discrimination firsthand. In 1968, while serving as president of Hyde Park Bank, he remembers a turning point. Against the background of great racial and political turbulence in Chicago, he made a routine call on a customer in the inner city on Chicago's South Side. He witnessed "the absolutely outrageous interest rates" this local furniture store owner was charging customers for loans. "That was the moment that showed me I really ought to do something about this," he recalls.

Grzywinski hired three others—Mary Houghton, Milton Davis, and Jim Fletcher—to set up a division of the bank to offer an alternative. By 1973 the four had hatched an even more ambitious plan. They raised $800,000 and borrowed a quarter of a million dollars to buy Chicago's failing South Shore National Bank and turned it into a for-profit community development bank: ShoreBank. Their aim was to use traditional lending practices to restore inner-city neighborhoods. "Our inspiration arose from the melding of our experiences as bankers at Hyde Park Bank in our day jobs and in our night jobs trying to work for and support community-based organizations as volunteers," Grzywinski says. "So, the idea was to wed those two things into a self-sustaining, more comprehensive approach to community development."

ShoreBank has been doing that, and turning a profit, ever since. It recruited employees who believed in their mission. It has purchased and renovated fifty-five thousand units of affordable housing since it started doing business, 80 percent of them in low- and moderate-income neighborhoods. Despite the apparent risk of loans to people with marginal incomes, ShoreBank's loan losses in 2008 were less than 1 percent of outstanding loans.

ShoreBank writes conventional mortgages. It stayed away from the "adjustable, no-money-down, low teaser rate followed by high rate" mortgages that have wrecked the balance sheets of banks like IndyMac as their clients defaulted. Its bankers think that getting to know its customers is good business and the right thing to do. "Our philosophy," explain Grzywinski and Executive Vice President Ellen Seidman, "has much in common with all quality community banks—know and care about your customer, because both of you have a strong interest in the customer's success in repaying the first loan, growing net worth, and becoming more successful." In good times, ShoreBank's profit rate is lower than that of ordinary banks, because careful underwriting of smaller loans to clients who are good risks takes time and thus costs money.

The model Grzywinski created ties ShoreBank to the local community. The board members and employees come from the community. The bank holds most of the loans rather than selling them into capital markets. This gives the bank insight into what is happening in the neighborhoods and the incentive to help customers quickly when they run into problems. Contributing to the rebuilding of those communities is a significant part of why these bankers come to work every day. Shore-Bank talks about what it calls its "triple bottom line"—profitability, raising the value of homes in its community, and financing environmentally sustainable renovations. That's why it does things like make loans to people to weatherize their homes, loans that pay for themselves in lowered utility bills in three or four years.

ShoreBank experienced a period of difficulty when its competitors began offering subprime, predatory loans—the "no money down" and "low monthly payment" loans that then suddenly began to balloon dramatically. So customers took the better deals elsewhere, only to default as the interest rates on their loans exploded. Foreclosures in Chicago went up almost 35 percent, and housing prices dropped. The community development work of years threatened to be undone in a heartbeat. To stop the bleeding, ShoreBank has worked to refinance mortgages by making what it calls "rescue loans." By the middle of 2009, it had made $32 million worth of such loans, to over two hundred families. By mid-2010, as housing values dropped and borrowers fell increasingly behind on their payments, the national financial crisis put even this bank in difficult straits.

The bankers at ShoreBank are paid for what they do; the bank makes money. But the aim of making money does not overwhelm the aim of banking. And Grzywinski and the other bankers at ShoreBank don't do what they do *in spite of* the bank they work in. They do it *be-*

cause the bank they created aims at good banking and encourages them
to have the skill and will to do it well. "Essentially, we practice old-
fashioned banking," Grzywinski explained. "We stay focused on the
community and the consumers and what they need, and we try to figure
out ways to make a deal work."

Grzywinski and his colleagues are banker-statesmen. They created
the first community development bank in the country. It eventually
expanded its operations to Cleveland, Detroit, and the Pacific North-
west. It became a model for others to follow. When President Bill Clinton created the community development financial institutions (CDFI)
legislation, he cited ShoreBank as the model. By 2009 there were fifty
CDFI banks, 150 credit unions, and six hundred nonprofit loan funds.
Today such CDFIs, as well as many other small community banks, are
all trying to balance the making of money with service to clients and
the community. These banks encourage bankers to aim at the right
thing, not because of external incentives like bonuses or merit pay, but
because it is the right thing. This is what good banking is all about.

LEARNING WHAT CAN'T BE TAUGHT

The doctors in Cambridge have it right. "We're not teaching good judgment to the medical students. We're causing it to be learned." Practical
wisdom is not something that can be taught, at least in the narrow sense
of listening to classroom lectures, reading books, and doing exams or
papers. And it can't be learned as an isolated "subject" or even as a general
skill that we can go around "applying." Practical wisdom is embedded
in the actual practices of being a lawyer or a teacher or a doctor or a
banker or a military officer or a violence counselor or a custodian like
Luke. It can't be learned outside of those practices. Moral skill and will,
like technical skill, are learned by practicing the craft. That, of course, is
why wisdom is associated with experience. But it's not just any experi-

ence. Experience must be structured in ways that "cause wisdom to be learned." That is what wise system changers do.

The system changers know that novices learn best with mentors who work alongside them while they practice. These experienced practitioners help steer the way by showing them how it's done, by telling them stories of their own experiences, by providing basic rules and procedures that serve as "scaffolds" or training wheels, by coaching them step-by-step through their first experiences, and by serving as a safety net. These mentors know that their students will develop wisdom by running up against the limits of rules as they try to apply them.

Something else the system changers know is that practitioners need to learn how to learn from experience when mentors are not by their side to coach them—what Pieter Cohen encourages by giving increasing responsibility for patient care to his medical students. This kind of self-evaluation and reflection demands more than skill. It takes courage and honesty to confront mistakes.

The system changers also know that creating wisdom-encouraging experiences demands more than having a few good mentors. They have built institutions with the culture and organization to encourage wisdom in everyday practice. They have created communities of practitioners who not only nurture moral skill but help inspire moral will, the commitment to do right by those the practitioners serve. Preaching commitment is not enough. It must be embodied in the interaction among practitioners, students, patients, and clients. Law students are more likely to develop compassion and concern for justice working in walk-in legal clinics for indigent urban clients than they are from a legal ethics class. The bankers in community development banks are encouraged by their colleagues to promote the financial well-being of their clients and their community. The novice doctors at the Cambridge Health Alliance work in a patient-centered environment where they are given the responsibility and the time to know and care about their patients. Their patients teach them empathy and commitment, and their teacher-mentors model patient care.

The system changers know that rules and incentives are a necessary part of the institutions they build. But they also know that they are but initial scaffolds, or sometimes last resorts. The first resort is to create institutions that pursue the right goals and encourage their practitioners to do the same, precisely because they are right.

This statesmanship is not utopian. It is within our grasp. Many novices still go into their work because they are dedicated to doing the right thing—dedicated to pursuing the ideals, and the ideal execution, of their chosen professions. It is their training and the structure of their workplaces that erode this commitment. Building institutions that pay attention to creating communities of learners with a commitment to do right by those they serve is what will cause wisdom to be developed.

13.

Wisdom and Happiness

We have seen that we don't have to accept the rules and incentives that drain the wisdom out of our lives. But the trial and error it takes to develop practical wisdom is often tough and frustrating. Why would anyone bother? Why take on the burden and risk of being canny outlaws, like the Houston schoolteachers who resisted the pressures to conform to scripted curricula? Or why take on the even harder task of transforming institutions to encourage the exercise of wisdom, like Ron Grzywinski at ShoreBank, or Dave Hirsh and Barbara Ogur at the Cambridge Health Alliance, instead of just adding another layer of rules and incentives?

One reason is a sense of duty. Many people feel an obligation to serve others and do work that benefits society generally. But when we talked to people like Dave Hirsh, Barbara Ogur, and Joey Hawkins, what we found was not so much duty as joy. Yes, wisdom improves the lives of the patients, clients, and students we serve as doctors, lawyers, and teachers. But it also improves our own lives. The wiser we are in what we do, the happier we are.

Aristotle understood this when he argued for the importance of practical wisdom. The purpose of life, he insisted, was human flourishing—what we translate as happiness. But you couldn't flourish unless you had the will and skill to make everyday ethical choices. Practical wisdom was what provided that skill and will. With practical wisdom, we flourish; without it, we languish.

What Aristotle meant in connecting wisdom to happiness is not immediately obvious. We know, because we didn't get it at first when our teachers tried to explain it to us. And we see the same look of puzzlement when we try to communicate the idea to our students.

The breakthrough we had in explaining the wisdom-happiness connection to our students came when we had students talk about friendship and love. They all agreed that it was crucial to them that they have meaningful and close social relationships—that loving others and being loved were essential to being happy. The students brought stories to class about episodes from their own friendships. As they presented them, it soon became apparent that what they wanted in friends, and what their friends wanted in them, were honesty, kindness, commitment, patience, empathy, perceptiveness, and courage. It also became clear how difficult it is to cultivate and display these virtues. Knowing how to be honest, or how to balance honesty with kindness, takes judgment. Perceptiveness and empathy are hard-earned skills. Having a friend and being a friend depends on dozens of everyday ethical choices, each of which, in turn, depends on practical wisdom. And the hard knocks of learning—the crises, the fights, the broken friendships, the trial and error—are usually painful. But the students seemed to keep picking themselves up off the floor and trying again and again to become wiser, because they wanted the goods of friendship. Being a good friend made others happy, but it also made them happy. And they couldn't have this happiness unless they developed the practical wisdom to "do friendship" well.

This same kind of wisdom-happiness connection is easily understandable to anyone who is raising a child. Having a family is a way we can flourish and achieve happiness. But nothing is more challenging than raising a child. There are so many tough choices that need to be made, every hour of every day, it is difficult to know where to begin cataloging them: when to comfort a baby and when to let him cry; when and how to say no; when and how to teach kids to help around the house; when to reason with kids and when to just put your foot down; how to balance protecting your children with the need to let go and watch them struggle as they become independent.

We heard child psychologist Wendy Mogel speak in a school gymnasium in suburban Philadelphia about the challenge of negotiating the independence of your children. The standing-room-only audience was not there to be entertained (though Mogel was very entertaining) but to hear some of the advice she had to offer about child rearing. The advice they heard was that most of them were too protective and too controlling for their children's good. When we talked with Mogel, we asked what had led her to this conclusion. Her practice, she said, was constantly filling up with parents seeking help to solve their kids' problems. But their concerns didn't belong in any standard psychiatric diagnostic category. Their kids suffered no psychopathology. In her book *The Blessing of a Skinned Knee*, Mogel reflected on a pattern common to many of the "problems" she heard. First, the parents wanted their kids' lives to be perfect, spared any hurt or disappointment. And second, the parents didn't trust their own judgment about how to make perfect lives. Mogel concluded that a central issue for parents was the problem they had in letting go. They were so intent on assuring their kids' safety and success that the children never had a chance to make mistakes and learn from them. The parents wanted to keep their kids' lives error-free. Mogel came to see that her psychological training offered almost nothing to meet the concerns of these parents. She turned, instead, to a traditional source of wisdom from her own Jewish heritage, the Talmud.

As she spoke that night, Mogel's examples had parents laughing and wincing at the same time, as they heard their own overcontrolling mis-steps reflected in her stories about others—like the parents who watched their kids at overnight camp on live video cams. When they saw lit-tle Suzie walking alone behind a group of chatting peers, they called the director to do something about the ostracism. "The Talmud," says Mogel, "sums up the Jewish perspective on child rearing in a single sentence: 'A father is obligated to teach his son how to swim.'" The parents Mogel saw were so desperate to protect their kids from every misfortune and misadventure that they weren't teaching their kids how to swim. "Real protection," argues Mogel, "means teaching children to manage risks on their own, not shielding them from every hazard." She continues: "By giving them a chance to survive some danger and letting them make some reckless or thoughtless choices, we teach them how to withstand the bumps and knocks of life."

But if being too controlling is a problem, simply letting go is not the solution. Letting your daughter date anyone she wants and come home whenever she feels like it, or letting your child ride his bike into any neighborhood he chooses, or letting drug or alcohol use go unchecked, might teach your child in the school of hard knocks, but the risk is too great. The knocks may be too hard. It takes moral know-how to find the balance, to teach your child to be independent, just as it takes practi-cal know-how to know when and how to let go of the child you're teaching to swim. You don't just throw him in the deep water and hope for the best. You might let him play in shallow water and then carry him into slightly deeper water and hold him while he learns to float. You might demonstrate what you are saying. You might put flotation devices on him, holding him but watching carefully for a sign that it's okay to let go. You mentor your child by scaffolding, modeling, and coaching. And it's not just the wisdom to know when to let go: teaching children how to swim means helping them have the confidence (cour-age, patience, discipline, fortitude) to persist, and the judgment to know what water to go into, how far to go, and when to get out.

The wisdom to balance "protecting our kids" with "letting them learn by skinning their knees" is developed in many ways—from the guidance of people like Mogel, by listening to advice from friends and family, by remembering our own growing-up experiences, and above all from reflecting on our own falls and bruises as we try to teach our children. In fact, our children often serve as our "mentors" because they let us know when our trials are errors. As psychologist Bonnie Ohye says of the wisest mothers she knows: "They laugh and tell me their children 'grew them up.'" "Pleasure" would not be the first word that comes to mind to describe how we felt as we were being taught, through trial and error, by our children. But we wanted to learn how to be good parents and how to help our children grow up, so we struggled to find the practical wisdom to make parenting work. We needed to learn to judge our success not in the moment but in the arc of the whole of child rearing. It was there that we found the happiness and the pleasure, which is probably what Aristotle meant when he said: "For one swallow does not make spring, nor one fine day; and similarly one day or a brief period of happiness does not make a man supremely blessed and happy."

WHAT MAKES PEOPLE HAPPY

Recent research into what happiness is and what makes people happy sheds some contemporary light on the connection Aristotle claimed between wisdom and happiness. Students of the "science of happiness" try to measure happiness, identify its components, determine its causes, and specify its consequences. This work doesn't tell us what *should* make people happy. It aims to tell us what *does* make people happy.

Ed Diener is perhaps the world's leading researcher on happiness. His recent book, written in collaboration with his son, Robert Biswas-Diener, confirms some things we might expect. The major determinants of happiness (or "well-being," as it is sometimes called) include material wealth (though much less than most people think, especially when their standard of living is above subsistence), physical health, freedom, political democracy, and physical, material, and psychological security. None of these determinants of happiness seems to have much to do with practical wisdom. But two other factors, each of them extremely important, do. Well-being depends critically on being part of a network of close connections to others. And well-being is enhanced when we are engaged in our work and find meaning in it.

The work of Martin Seligman, a distinguished psychologist at the University of Pennsylvania, points in the same direction. Seligman launched a whole new discipline—dubbed "positive" psychology—in the 1990s, when he was president of the American Psychological Association. We've talked to Seligman often about his work. He had long been concerned that psychologists focused too exclusively on curing the problems of their patients (he himself was an expert on depression) and spent too little time investigating those things that would positively promote their well-being. He kick-started positive psychology with his book *Authentic Happiness*.

The word *authentic* is there to distinguish what Seligman is talking about from what many of us sometimes casually take happiness to be— feeling good. Feeling good—experiencing positive emotion—is certainly important. But just as important are engagement and meaning. Engagement is about throwing yourself into the activities of your life. And meaning is about connecting what you do to the lives of others—knowing that what you do makes the lives of others better. Authentic happiness, says Seligman, is a combination of engagement, meaning, and positive emotion. Seligman collected a massive amount of data from research on people all over the world. He found that people who considered themselves happy had certain character strengths and virtues. He further found that in each individual, some of these strengths were more prominent than others. Seligman concluded that promoting a person's particular strengths—he dubbed these a person's "signature strengths"— promoted authentic happiness.

The twenty-four character strengths Seligman identified include things like curiosity, open-mindedness, perspective, kindness and generosity, loyalty, duty, fairness, leadership, self-control, caution, humility, bravery, perseverance, honesty, gratitude, optimism, and zest. He organized these strengths into six virtues: courage, humanity and love, justice, temperance, transcendence, and wisdom and knowledge. Aristotle would have recognized many of these strengths as the kind of "excellences" or virtues he considered necessary for *eudaimonia*, a flourishing or happy life.

Like Aristotle, we consider wisdom to be the "master virtue." Without moral skill, many of the other character strengths and virtues that Seligman identifies as essential to happiness would not do the job. Without such know-how, these strengths would be more like unruly children, leading to well-meaning actions that leave disaster in their wake—recklessness, not courage; indecisiveness, not patience; blind loyalty, not commitment; cruel confrontation, not helpful honesty. Practical wisdom is the maestro. It's what conducts the whole symphony.

Seligman suggests that "authentic happiness" may only be achievable *indirectly*, as a by-product of living an engaged and meaningful life. And the two spheres of life Seligman singles out as most likely to provide such positive emotion, engagement, and meaning are the same two Ed Diener's research turned up: close social relations with others and participation in meaningful work.

It's not surprising that close social relations make us happy, and we've seen that they depend on practical wisdom. But what about work? Throughout this book we've examined how essential practical wisdom is to doing certain kinds of work well, but what is the wisdom-happiness connection here? It turns out that the characteristics of work that most demand the exercise of practical wisdom are the same characteristics that make work engaging, meaningful, and potentially satisfying.

WORK, WISDOM, AND HAPPINESS

Without work all life goes rotten. But when work is soulless, life stifles and dies.

— ALBERT CAMUS

Remember Luke, the hospital custodian who cleaned a patient's room a second time because the patient's father hadn't seen Luke do it the first time? Luke gets great satisfaction from his work. Not from emptying trash cans. Not from washing floors. And not from restocking supplies. Luke's satisfaction comes from the interactions he has with patients and their families.

What enables Luke to do this? First, Luke's job is organized so that he has broad discretion when it comes to social interactions with the patients. He has the flexibility to craft his job in important ways. Second, the way Luke has crafted it allows him to play an important role in easing suffering and providing comfort. He makes the lives of patients and their families better. The meaning this gives Luke's work is an important source of satisfaction. Third, the challenge of getting these social interactions right is engaging, and meeting that challenge is another source of satisfaction, and happiness. And that's where practical wisdom comes in. Meeting the challenge to do meaningful work demands all the features of moral skill we've described: the improvisation, empathy, good listening, perceptiveness to know when to stay in the background and when to come forward, when to joke and when to comfort. Having the wisdom to do this work well makes Luke's day. Having these moral skills is not simply something Luke *ought* to have; it's something he *wants* to have.

At first glance it might seem that engagement alone would be enough to make work satisfying. We tend to admire, even envy, people who are engaged and passionate about their work—people who can get so caught up in the tasks at hand that they lose track of time and stop being distracted by concerns about what other people may think of them, or by the errands they have to run on the way home from the office. But Peter Warr, a professor of work psychology, has pointed out that to be happy with their work, people need more than this kind of engagement and passion. They also need variety in what they do, discretion in how they do it, and a belief in the purpose of the enterprise. It is nice if work is exciting. Think of the adrenaline rush of the cardiac surgeon who saves a life or the lawyer who wins a trial. But you can derive meaning from your work without excitement, and excitement without meaning will not produce the well-being that people get from good work done well.

The work of psychologist Amy Wrzesniewski and her colleagues (who did the research on Luke) confirms the conclusions of Warr and Seligman about the importance of meaningful, engaging, discretion-encouraging work as a source of satisfaction. She calls work that has such characteristics a "calling" and distinguishes it from work that is a "job" or a "career." Wrzesniewski and her team have spent over two decades studying these aspects of work. People who see their work as a "job" enjoy little discretion and experience minimal engagement or meaning. People with jobs see work as a necessity of life, they work for pay, they would switch jobs if given the chance to earn more money, they can't wait to retire, and they would not encourage their friends or children to follow in their footsteps. People who see their work as a "career" enjoy more discretion and are more engaged, but find little meaning in their work. They enjoy what they do, but they see the heart of their work as following a trajectory that leads to promotion, higher salary, and better work.

It is people who see their work as a "calling" who find it most satisfying. For them, work is one of the most important parts of life, they are pleased to be doing it, it is a vital part of their identity, they believe their work makes the world a better place, and they would encourage their friends and children to do this kind of work. People whose work is a calling have great discretion at work. And having the wisdom to use the discretion well—to meet the challenges necessary to do the meaningful work—is crucial to the high level of satisfaction they get.

What, then, determines how people think about their work? The kind of work one does is a major factor. Doctors and educators like Dave Hirsh and Barbara Ogur work in professions with a great deal of discretion, whose purpose is to serve and educate others. Their kind of work encourages them to develop the practical wisdom they need to do the work well (including their work helping their students to develop such wisdom), and they find this work fulfilling and satisfying, despite the many frustrations.

But Wrzesniewski came up with a surprising finding when she studied administrative assistants working at a college. Ostensibly they all did the same things every day. But when she surveyed them, she found that some thought their work was a job, some thought it was a career, and some thought it was a calling. Why? To some degree, the differences are explained by the attitudes these people brought to their work—who *they* were, not what the work was. But to a large degree, Wrzesniewski found that their attitude toward work depended on how their seemingly similar work was organized and integrated into the mission of the larger units of which they were a part. If the workers had a sense of organizational purpose, and it was a purpose they could be proud to contribute to, if they had a sense of partnership, and if they had a fair degree of discretion and control, they were more likely to view what they did as a calling.

Wrzesniewski's findings about discretion at work are particularly interesting in light of the connections we've seen throughout this book between discretion and wisdom. Discretion is critical if practitioners are going to exercise the kind of judgment they need to read the particular situations of those they serve and to act appropriately. Furthermore, a degree of discretion is what allows people (through trial and error, and often with the help of mentors) to develop the practical wisdom that enables them to use that discretion to do good work. Wrzes- niewski's research now adds an additional piece: discretion is also im- portant if people are going to consider their work a calling and find it satisfying. There is a virtuous circle here. We are happiest when our work is meaningful and gives us the discretion to use our judgment. The discretion allows us to develop the wisdom to exercise the judg- ment we need to do that work well. We're motivated to develop the judgment to do that work well because it enables us to serve others. And it makes us happy to do so.

Promoting that virtuous circle helps ameliorate the vicious circle we've been worried about. The more people's behavior at work is con- trolled by rules and incentives, and the less opportunity they have to exercise—and develop—practical wisdom, the worse their work will be. Now we see that it is also likely to be less engaging and meaning- ful, and, therefore, less satisfying, which may discourage people from learning how to do it better. Contrast Luke's work with that of Donna Moffett, the New York teacher whom we met in chapter 9. Moffett works at a job that begs for empathetic, perceptive, flexible, and im- provisational human interaction. But she has a script to follow. And Moffett is chided by her official mentor when she deviates from the script. The rigid rules and procedures that governed Moffett's workday turn what could and should be a calling into little more than a job. Mof- fett left a successful career as a legal secretary and took a huge pay cut because she was "called" to teach New York inner-city kids. Script fol- lowing was not what she envisioned her job to be, and she was exasper- ated by the constraints imposed on her from above. In the throes of her first year in the classroom, she still remembers why she changed careers, and still feels satisfaction and joy as her students make progress. But will it last? We saw her own reflections: "I don't think the call for help [by the New York City public schools in an appeal to talented people to become teachers in midlife] was to have people come into these schools and say, 'Open your book to page blah-de-blah.'" Take discretion, engagement, and meaning out of work and people get less satisfaction from doing it. As they get less satisfaction from doing it, they do it less well. As they do it less well, their supervisors take even more discretion away. Putting in motion this vicious circle risks having school systems full of teachers who routinely do formula-based teaching, at the insistence of supervisors who believe that the teachers can't be trusted to work out their lessons on their own. And we may have hospital supervisors who respond to budget deficits by cutting staff, increasing the custodians' workload, and so closely monitoring custodian-patient interactions that they drive out the motivation to care and the skill to do it well—a phenomenon that is not unfamiliar to many nurses and doctors too. And once this has happened, supervisors may, seemingly quite reasonably, justify the rules limiting such interactions by pointing to the unwillingness or inability of staff to care in this way for patients.

Staff members like Luke are a precious resource. Wrzesniewski's interviews with hospital custodians revealed, again and again, that their greatest source of satisfaction came from their interactions with patients. That is when they felt the most useful, the most important, the most skilled. Not all custodians were like Luke, but the ones who were thought their jobs required a great deal of skill and experience. Not to mop floors, but to interact humanely and effectively with patients. What a gift for the patients, the hospital, and the custodians themselves—people who want to serve the caring mission of a hospital, who are willing to learn how to do it well, and who take great satisfaction and pride in their work. "Making a patient smile can make my day," one custodian explained to Wrzesniewski.

Carlotta, a colleague of Luke's, told Wrzesniewski about her custodial work in a unit of the hospital where people recovered from various brain injuries and were often unconscious for extended periods of time. Carlotta took it upon herself to change the pictures on the walls in these patients' rooms as a subtle means of cheering them up, even though, in her words, she was "not very clear they noticed, but you never know."

As Carlotta described it: "Sometimes I'll change the pictures on the wall, like every week, 'cause our patients stay for months and months and months . . . so, they know they're getting that much closer to being home." Carlotta was clear about the joy this kind of move brought her:

> I enjoy entertaining the patients. That's what I enjoy the most. And that is not really part of my job description. But I like putting on a show for them per se. Dancing if there is a certain song on. I get to dance and if a talk show is on, I get to talk about that talk show or whatever, that's what I enjoy the most. I enjoy making the patients laugh.

But Carlotta not only takes joy in knowing when and how to make a patient laugh. She also knows when care involves a strong hand and a brave heart, and this too makes her work a source of happiness. Carlotta explained:

> One of our patients was in distress and he was a quad [quadriplegic], and I just happened to be there when he was stressing out, and so I pushed the button [for staff assistance] and I told them to get in here . . . they were drawing his blood in one arm and trying to stick an IV in the other and he wasn't into needles . . . so, I stayed with him while the nurses did what they had to do because he was sliding out of his wheelchair, he was getting ready to pass out, you know, and so the nurse wanted to take his blood pressure and he wouldn't let her because he was kind of upset with them, and I explained to him, I said, "Well, listen, I'm going to give you five minutes to kind of calm down, but they have to take your blood pressure to make sure everything else is going all right, and I will stay in here with you." So, that's what I did, I stayed there with him and let him calm down and I told the nurse, "Come on in and take his blood pressure." . . . From that point on I think we were buddies for life . . . I just happened to be in the right place at the right time.

Luke and Carlotta were not actively encouraged to craft their work into callings. Meaningful and engaged work emerged, along with the practical wisdom to do it, because they wanted to craft their jobs into callings, and—and this is key—because it was not forbidden.

Protecting good work, and the practical wisdom to do it, means recognizing the many places it flourishes unattended and finding ways to protect it from the time pressures, the rules, and the external incentives that threaten to push it out. Nurturing practical wisdom in those areas where work and wisdom are under assault demands even more. In our schools, hospitals, law firms, banks, and armed forces, it is important to actively promote the conditions that encourage wisdom—the kind of work that people like Joey Hawkins, Chris Schultz, Ron Grzywinski, Dave Hirsh, Barbara Ogur, Judge Robert Russell, and Robert Bordone have tried to do.

Being a good friend, a good parent, a good colleague, or a good community member; being a good teacher, a good doctor, or a good lawyer—these are things we do both for the sake of others and for the sake of ourselves. We can't do any of these things well without practical wisdom. That's why it's worth struggling to be wise. That's why it's important to resist those rules and incentives that eviscerate discretion and threaten wisdom. That's why we need to reform those institutions that are driving wisdom out.

Wisdom is not the mysterious gift of a handful of sages, but a capacity that we all have and need. Aristotle was right: to flourish, to achieve *eudaimonia*, demands *phronesis*, practical wisdom. Practical wisdom creates its own circle, a virtuous circle. Having the know-how to do right by others makes us happy; it gives us the know-how to do right by ourselves.

ACKNOWLEDGMENTS

We have been teaching a course on practical wisdom together or separately for nearly a decade, and over that time we have learned an incalculable amount from our students. They have taught us how to connect what could be fairly abstract ideas with everyday experience. There are several hundred of them, and we have learned from them all, but there are a few whom we would particularly like to thank. Emily Zackin helped us at the founding of the project, offering sage advice as she worked with us over the course of two years to find and prepare materials. We also benefited greatly from the research assistance and insights of Rebecca Brubaker and Renee Witlen.

We learned much from discussions or interviews with many people. We want to give particular thanks to David Bor, Robert Bordone, Pieter Cohen, Molly Cooke, Jerrold Coombs, Laurel Eckhouse, Keith Fifield, Mark Fifield, Timothy Floyd, Jane Gaskell, Elizabeth Gaufberg, Nancy Gertner, Joey Hawkins, David Hirsh, David Irby, Mark Jones, James Kurth, William Leo-Grande, Jenny Lunstead, Roger Masters, Wendy Mogel, Michael Morse, Barbara Ogur, Vanessa Redditt, Jack Sammons, Rich Schuldenfrei, Martin Seligman, Anjana Sharma, Jill Sharpe, Peter Sharpe, and William Sullivan.

We are particularly grateful to those who took the time to provide careful and often critical comments on earlier drafts of chapters: Joe Bernheim, Eva Bertram, Morris Blachman, Max Cameron, Bruce Cate, Gary Dell, Charlie DePuy, Raph Fine, Jonathan Haidt, Jay McClelland, James Murphy, Dan Reisberg, Valerie Ross, Irwin Sharpe, Eran Thomson, Ramsey Thorpe, and Erica Turner.

We appreciate the perceptive, encouraging, and persistently firm hand of our editor, Sean McDonald, who helped us craft the final draft of this book, and of editor Jake Morrissey, who saw the project through to completion, without a hitch, after Sean's departure. Our agent, Tina Bennett, helped us through several rough spots with great insight, encouragement, empathy, and judgment. Tina exemplifies practical wisdom.

Special thanks go to Chris Anderson and the other organizers and attendees at the 2009 TED (Technology, Entertainment, Design) conference in Long Beach, California. The enthusiastic audience response to Barry's talk there helped galvanize us for the final push. We are also grateful for continual institutional support we received from Swarthmore College and from the Department of Government at Dartmouth College.

Finally, we would never have finished this book without the unflagging support of our wives, Myrna Schwartz and Madeleine Thomson. They kept us on track by reading early drafts and criticizing them. And more important, they kept us inspired by assuring us that what we had to say was important enough for us to keep plugging away.

NOTES

Chapter 1. Introduction: The Need for Wisdom

Our discussion of Aristotle, and all quotations, are taken from Martin Oswald's translation of *Nicomachean Ethics: Aristotle*. (1962). New York: Library of Liberal Arts.

Page 5. *and for what purpose:* Aristotle, *Nicomachean Ethics*, book 4, ch. 5 (1125b–1126a).

Page 6. *This is what took practical wisdom:* A more detailed philosophical discussion of practical wisdom in Aristotle can be found in Zagzebski, L. T. (1996). *Virtues of the Mind*. New York: Cambridge University Press.

Chapter 2. What Wisdom Is: The Janitor and the Judge

Page 13. *"I kind of knew the situation":* The study of Luke and other hospital custodians was done by Amy Wrzesniewski and her collaborators. See Wrzesniewski, A., Dutton, J. E., and Debebe, G. (2009). Caring in constrained contexts. Unpublished manuscript; Wrzesniewski, A., and Dutton, J. E. (2001). Crafting a job: Revisioning employees as active crafters of their work. *Academy of Management Review*, *26*, 179–201; Wrzesniewski, A., Dutton, J. E., and Debebe, G. (2003). Interpersonal sensemaking and the meaning of work. *Research in Organizational Behavior*, *25*, 93–135. See also Wrzesniewski, A., McCauley, C., Rozin, P., and Schwartz, B. (1997). Jobs, careers, and callings: People's relations to their work. *Journal of Research in Personality*, *31*, 21–33.

Page 17. *"Michael's case appeared routine"*: This and other quotations from Lois Forer come from Forer, L. G. (1992). Justice by numbers. *Washington Monthly*, *24*, Issue 4, 12–18.

Page 22. *"and in navigation"*: Aristotle, *Nicomachean Ethics*, book 2, ch. 2 [1104a].

Page 22. *"of particular facts"*: Ibid., book 6, ch. 11 [1143a–1143b].

Page 22. *in the moment:* For a striking account of this process in psychotherapy, see Fowers, B. J. (2005). *Virtue and Psychology: Pursuing Excellence in Ordinary Practices*. Washington, DC: American Psychological Association, especially pp. 118–120 and 139–141.

Page 22. *"in light of what could be"*: This quotation is from John Dewey's *Human Nature and Conduct: An Introduction to Social Psychology*. New York: Prometheus (original work published 1922). It is cited in Narvaez, D. (2010). Moral complexity: The fatal attraction of truthiness and the importance of mature moral functioning. *Perspectives on Psychological Science*, *5*, 163–181.

Page 24. *"mark of virtue"*: Aristotle, *Nicomachean Ethics*, book 2, ch. 6 [1106b].

Page 24. *"articulated by it"*: See Nussbaum, M. (1990). *Love's Knowledge*. New York: Oxford University Press, p. 95.

Page 25. *key characteristics of practical wisdom:* Terms like "practical wisdom" are difficult to define because any definition will be either too precise to capture this expansive concept or too vague to be of much use. Nonetheless, there are three contemporary approaches to defining practical wisdom that we have found useful: "Choosing and acting well in the pursuit of what is good in our daily lives" (Fowers, B. J. [2005], p. 117); "More than the other virtues, phronesis [practical wisdom] endows its possessor with the deliberative capacity to reason well with respect to the means to be used to attain the good of the activity in which we have been engaged" (Pelligrino, E. D., and Thomasma, D. C. [1993]. *The Virtues in Medical Practice*. New York: Oxford University Press, p. 90); "A chain of reasoning whose first premises concern the human good, whose intermediate steps specify what the virtues require, if the human good is to be achieved, and whose

conclusion is the action that is good and best for us to perform here and now"
(MacIntyre, A. [1981]. *After Virtue: A Study in Moral Theory*. Notre Dame, IN:
University of Notre Dame Press, p. 159).

Chapter 3. Balancing Acts: Why Wisdom Is Practical

Page 27. *Massachusetts Constitution of 1780:* This quotation is famously cited by
Supreme Court Justice John Marshall in the landmark *Marbury v. Madison* case
in 1803.

Page 28. *"just and fitting rule":* This and the subsequent quotation of Benjamin
Cardozo are from Cardozo, B. (1921). *The Nature of the Judicial Process*. New
Haven, CT: Yale University Press, p. 143.

Page 28. *penalty was the same:* See Finkel, N. (1998). *Commonsense Justice*. Cambridge, MA: Harvard University Press, pp. 80, 85.

Page 29. *proof of blameworthiness:* So did ancient biblical law. The Hebrews were
commanded by God to establish cities of refuge to protect from hot-blooded
revenge those who have killed unintentionally and without hate: "as when a
man goes to the woods with his neighbor to cut timber, and his hand swings a
stroke with the ax to cut down the tree, and the head slips from the handle and
strikes his neighbor so that he dies; he shall flee to one of these cities and live"
(Deuteronomy 19:5). We thank Roger Masters for pointing this out to us.

Page 31. *scene of the accident:* Simon, W. (2000). Lawyer advice and client autonomy.
In D. L. Rhode (ed.). *Ethics in Practice* (pp. 165–176). New York: Oxford University Press, p. 166.

Page 34. *what they want:* Rose, M. (2004). *The Mind at Work: Valuing the Intelligence
of the American Worker*. New York: Viking, p. 43.

Page 34. *"for a lover's benefit":* Kronman, A. T. (1993). *The Lost Lawyer*. Cambridge,
MA: Harvard University Press, p. 128.

Page 38. *quietly and comfortably:* See Lowenstein, J. (1997). *The Midnight Meal and
Other Essays About Doctors, Patients, and Medicine*. New Haven, CT: Yale University Press, pp. 76–80.

Page 39. *"state of inaction":* Pelligrino, E. D., and Thomasma, D. C. (1993). *The
Virtues in Medical Practice*. New York: Oxford University Press, p. 81.

Page 40. *not enough detachment:* Groopman, J. (2007). *How Doctors Think*. Boston:
Houghton Mifflin, pp. 48–54.

Page 40. *"good at doing so"*: Kronman (1993), p. 72.

Page 41. *fiercest and fastest*: Weick, K. E. (2001). Tool retention and fatalities in wildland fire settings: Conceptualizing the naturalistic. In G. Klein and E. Salas (eds.), *Naturalistic Decision Making* (pp. 321–336). Hillsdale, NJ: Erlbaum. See also Maclean, N. (1992). *Young Men and Fire*. Chicago: University of Chicago Press, p. 100.

Page 42. *improvisation was shut down:* Weick (2001), p. 333.

Page 42. *"with the horn"*: Maggin, D. C. (1966). *Stan Getz: A Life in Jazz*. New York: Morrow, p. 21.

Page 42. *"the embellishments themselves"*: Weick (2001), p. 331.

Chapter 4. Born to Be Wise

Page 51. *judge wisely in practical matters:* Aristotle, however, had a much more constrained view of who could be a citizen than we do today, and also required more of citizens. Like America's founding fathers and many of its nineteenth-century statesmen, he argued that women, and what he called "natural slaves," did not have the capacity for citizenship. For a useful discussion of Aristotle's view of slavery and why it does not condemn his political theory as a whole, see Sandel, M. J. (2009), *Justice: What's the Right Thing to Do?* New York: Farrar, Straus & Giroux, pp. 200–203.

Page 54. *philosopher Ludwig Wittgenstein*: Ludwig Wittgenstein (1973). *Philosophical Investigations*. New York: Prentice Hall.

Page 54. *psychological research:* See Rosch, E. (1975). Cognitive representations of semantic categories. *Journal of Experimental Psychology: General, 104,* 192–233; Rosch, E. (1978). Principles of categorization. In E. Rosch and B. B. Lloyd (eds.), *Cognition and Categorization* (pp. 189–221). Hillsdale, NJ: Erlbaum. There is much subtlety and complexity to the organization of categories. For a readable summary, see Reisberg, D. (2007). *Cognition: Exploring the Science of the Mind* (3rd ed.), ch. 9. New York: W. W. Norton.

Page 56. *into common classes:* Weinreb, L. L. (2005). *Legal Reason: The Use of Analogy in Legal Argument*. Cambridge, England, and New York: Cambridge University Press.

Page 57. *"in case of a fire"*: Barsalou, L. (1983). Ad hoc categories. *Memory and Cognition, 11,* 211–227.

Page 61. *judgments we make:* Kahneman, D., and Tversky, A. (1984). Choices, values, and frames. *American Psychologist, 39,* 341–350; Kahneman, D. (2003). A perspective on judgment and choice. *American Psychologist, 58,* 697–720.

Page 62. *"Community Game":* Liberman, V., Samuels, S. M., and Ross, L. (2004). The name of the game: Predictive power of reputations versus situational labels in determining prisoner's dilemma game moves. *Personality and Social Psychology Bulletin, 30,* 1175–1185; Kay, A. C., and Ross, L. (2003). The perceptual push: The interplay of implicit cues and explicit situational construals on behavioral intentions in the Prisoner's Dilemma. *Journal of Experimental Social Psychology, 39,* 634–643.

Page 63. *Is 150 lives a lot or a little:* Slovic, P., Finucane, M., Peters, E., and MacGregor, D. C. (2002). The affect heuristic. In T. Gilovich, D. Griffin, and D. Kahneman (eds.), *Heuristics and Biases: The Psychology of Intuitive Judgment* (pp. 397–420). New York: Cambridge University Press.

Page 64. *pound of beef:* Pollan, M. (2002). Power steer. *New York Times Magazine,* March 31.

Page 66. *quiet Sunday morning:* Covey, S. (1989). *Seven Habits of Highly Effective People.* New York: Simon & Schuster, pp. 30–31.

Page 67. *"in order to live":* Didion, J. (1979). *The White Album.* New York: Simon & Schuster, p. 11.

Chapter 5. Thinking with Feeling: The Value of Empathy

Page 69. *"reasonings of its members":* Rousseau, J.-J. (1964). *The First and Second Discourses.* (R. D. Masters, ed.) New York: St. Martin's Press, pp. 131–133.

Page 71. *empathy in children:* Hoffman, M. L. (1981). Is altruism part of human nature? *Journal of Personality and Social Psychology, 40,* 121–137; Hoffman, M. L. (2000). *Empathy and Moral Development: Implications for Caring and Justice.* Cambridge: Cambridge University Press; Eisenberg, N. (1986). *Altruistic Emotion, Cognition, and Behavior.* Hillsdale, NJ: Erlbaum. For a summary of recent evidence about empathy and even rudimentary moral judgment in infants and toddlers, see Bloom, P. (2010, May 9). The moral life of babies. *New York Times Magazine.*

Page 71. *psychologist Alison Gopnik:* Gopnik, A. (2009). *A Philosophical Baby: What Children's Minds Tell Us About Truth, Love and the Meaning of Life.* New York: Farrar, Straus & Giroux.

Page 72. *what the right kind of experience is:* Hoffman, M. L. (2000); Eisenberg, N. (1986).

Page 73. *Mark did was wrong:* Haidt, J. (2001). The emotional dog and its rational tail. *Psychological Review, 108,* 814–834 (quotation on p. 814). See also Haidt, J. (2007). The new synthesis in moral psychology. *Science, 316,* 998–1002; Haidt, J., and Joseph, C. (2008). The moral mind: How five sets of innate intuitions guide the development of many culture-specific virtues, and perhaps even modules. In P. Carruthers, S. Laurence, and S. Stich (eds.), *The Innate Mind. Vol. 3: Foundations and the Future* (pp. 367–392). New York: Oxford University Press. For a critical discussion of this line of research and argument about morality, see Narvaez, D. (2010). Moral complexity: The fatal attraction of truthiness and the importance of mature moral functioning. *Perspectives on Psychological Science, 5,* 163–181.

Page 74. *"searching for the truth":* Haidt (2001), p. 814.

Page 75. *a moral signal:* Pizarro, D. (2000). Nothing more than feelings? The role of emotion in moral judgment. *Journal for the Theory of Social Behavior, 30,* 355–375.

Page 75. *reactions to suffering:* Slovic, P. (2007). "If I look at the mass, I will never act": Psychic numbing and genocide. *Judgment and Decision Making, 2,* 79–95.

Page 76. *captures the problem facetiously:* Dillard, A. (1999). *For the Time Being.* New York: Alfred A. Knopf.

Page 76. *"Nothing to it":* Ibid., p. 47.

Page 76. *"dots in blue water":* Ibid., p. 131.

Page 76. *"Save the Panda":* Hsee, C. K., and Rottenstreich, Y. (2004). Music, pandas, and muggers: On the affective psychology of value. *Journal of Personality and Social Psychology, 133,* 23–30.

Page 77. *"feel for another":* Kingsolver, B. (1996). *High Tide in Tucson.* New York: HarperPerennial, pp. 231–232.

Page 77. *neurologist Antonio Damasio:* Damasio, A. (1994). *Descartes' Error.* New York: G. P. Putnam's Sons; See also Damasio, A. (1999). *The Feeling of What Happens.* New York: Harcourt Brace; Anderson, S. W., Bechara, A., Damasio, H., Tranel, D., and Damasio, A. R. (1999). Impairment of social and moral behavior related to early damage in human prefrontal cortex. *Nature Neuroscience, 2,* 1032–1037.

Page 78. *"incessant and repetitious questioning":* Damasio (1994), p. 45.

Page 78. *"parents, all of us"*: Ibid., p. 38.

Page 79. *passed the man by:* Darley, J., and Batson, C. D. (1973). From Jerusalem to Jericho: A study of situational and dispositional variables in helping behavior. *Journal of Personality and Social Psychology, 27,* 100–108.

Page 79. *research on* emotional intelligence: Mayer, J. D., and Salovey, P. (1997). What is emotional intelligence? In P. Salovey and D. Sluyter (eds.), *Emotional Development and Emotional Intelligence: Educational Implications* (pp. 3–31). New York: Basic Books; Salovey, P., and Mayer, J.D. (1990). Emotional intelligence. *Imagination, Cognition, and Personality, 9,* 185–211; Goleman, D. (1995). *Emotional Intelligence.* New York: Bantam.

Chapter 6. Learning from Experience: The Machinery of Wisdom

Page 82. *pattern recognition:* See Reisberg, D. (2007). *Cognition: Exploring the Science of the Mind.* New York: W. W. Norton.

Page 83. *in his book* Blink: Gladwell, M. (2005). *Blink.* New York: Little, Brown.

Page 85. *priority of the particular:* The importance of "the priority of the particular" or "the priority of perception" in Aristotle's conception of practical wisdom (as opposed to general rules as being sufficient for correct choice) is developed in Nussbaum, M. (1990). *Love's Knowledge: Essays on Philosophy and Literature.* New York: Oxford University Press, pp. 37–40.

Page 86. *Jonathan Schooler and Timothy Wilson:* Wilson, T. D., and Schooler, J. W. (1991). Thinking too much: Introspection can reduce the quality of preferences and decisions. *Journal of Personality and Social Psychology, 60,* 181–192; Schooler, J. W., Ohlsson, S., and Brooks, K. (1993). Thoughts beyond words: When language overshadows insight. *Journal of Experimental Psychology: General, 122,* 166–183.

Page 86. *Wilson and several colleagues:* Wilson, T. D., and Kraft, D. (1993). Why do I love thee? Effects of repeated introspections about a dating relationship on attitudes toward the relationship. *Personality and Social Psychology Bulletin, 19,* 409–428; Wilson, T. D., Hodges, S. D., and LaFleur, S. J. (1995). Effects of introspecting about reasons: Inferring attitudes from accessible thoughts. *Journal of Personality and Social Psychology, 69,* 16–28.

Page 86. *Neuropsychologist Elkhonon Goldberg:* Goldberg, E. (2005). *The Wisdom Paradox.* New York: Gotham Books.

Page 87. *"almost unfairly easy insight"*: Ibid., pp. 8–9.

Page 88. *cognitive scientist Paul Churchland:* Churchland, P. M. (1988). *Matter and Consciousness*. Cambridge, MA: MIT Press. See also Churchland, P. M. (1996). The neural representation of the social world. In L. May, M. Friedman, and A. Clark (eds.), *Minds and Morals* (pp. 91–108). Cambridge, MA: MIT Press; Churchland, P. (1989). *A Neurocomputational Perspective: The Nature of Mind and the Structure of Science*. Cambridge, MA: MIT Press; Churchland, P. (1995). *The Engine of Reason, the Seat of the Soul: A Philosophical Journey into the Brain*. Cambridge, MA: Bradford Books/MIT Press.

Page 90. *as accurately as radiologists do:* See Mitchell, T. (1997). *Machine Learning*. New York: McGraw-Hill; Pettitt, R. A., Redden, E. S., Turner, D. D., and Carstens, C. B. (2009, March). Recognition of combatants-improvised explosive devices (ROC-IED) training effectiveness evaluation. Army Research Laboratory TR-4744; Sharp, W. J. (2010, 18 February). IED trainer helps prepare warfighters for Afghanistan. (www.army.mil/news/2010/02/18/34640-ied-trainer-helps-prepare-warfighters-for-afghanistan/); Kulkarni, S., and Haidar, I. (2009). Forecasting model for crude oil price using artificial neural networks and commodity futures prices. *International Journal of Computer Science and Information Security, 2*.

Page 90. *in an e-commerce setting:* Honarvar, A. R., and Ghasem-Aghaee, N. (2009, December 15–19). An artificial neural network approach for creating an ethical artificial agent. *CIRA 2009*, 290–295.

Page 92. *parallel distributed processing (PDP):* The landmark work on PDP networks is Rumelhart, D. E., and McClelland, J. L. (eds.) (1986). *Parallel Distributed Processing,* Vols. 1 and 2. Cambridge, MA: MIT Press.

Page 99. *to be empathetic:* Cottrell, G. W., and Metcalfe, J. (1991). Empath: Face, gender, and emotional recognition using holons. In R. Lippman, J. Moody, and D. Touretzky (eds.), *Advances in Neural Information Processing Systems 3* (pp. 564–571). San Mateo, CA: Morgan Kaufman.

Page 99. *called "moral networks":* Flanagan, O. (1998). Ethics naturalized: Ethics as human ecology. In L. May, M. Friedman, and A. Clark (eds.), *Mind and Morals* (pp. 19–44). Cambridge, MA: MIT Press; Churchland (1996).

Page 99. *"moral sensitivities and sensibilities":* Flanagan (1998), p. 25.

Page 100. *"expects them to react":* Ibid., p. 28 (emphasis in original).

Page 101. *"long and painful social experience":* Churchland (1989), p. 302.

Page 101. *"mastering the relevant intricacies":* Ibid., p. 300.

Page 103. *changes to the networks:* We thank Gary Dell for alerting us to this point.

Page 106. *"serious menace to society":* Churchland, (1996), pp. 105–107.

Chapter 7. Ruling Out Wisdom: When Judges Stop Judging and Doctors Stop Prescribing

Page 114. *Faced with this prospect, he disappeared:* All the quotations from Judge Forer are from Forer, L. G. (1992). Justice by numbers. *Washington Monthly, 24,* Issue 4.

Page 115. *crimes like narcotics possession:* Stith, K. (2008). The arc of the pendulum: Judges, prosecutors, and the exercise of discretion. *Yale Law Journal, 118,* 1429.

Page 115. *took early partial retirement:* The sentencing guidelines increased the likelihood that district court judges would take senior service (a 25 percent workload) three years earlier than they otherwise would. See Boylan, R. T. (2004). Do the sentencing guidelines influence the retirement decisions of federal judges? *Journal of Legal Studies, 33,* 234.

Page 116. *"to be experts in proportionality":* Interview with Judge Nancy Gertner, September 16, 2009. For an elaboration of some of these arguments, see Gertner, N. (2007). From omnipotence to impotence: American judges and sentencing. *Ohio State Journal of Criminal Law, 4,* 523–539.

Page 116. *"wind the key":* Kozinski, A. (2002). Carthage must be destroyed. *Federal Sentencing Reporter, 12,* 67.

Page 117. *"all-important area of sentencing":* The Honorable Patricia M. Wald, Chief Judge, United States Court of Appeals for the District of Columbia Circuit (Retired), on behalf of the American Bar Association before the Inter-American Commission on Human Rights, Washington, DC (2006, March 3), p. 7.

Page 117. *"abject fear of judging":* Stith (2008), p. 1495. For a detailed history of the impact and causes of mandatory sentencing, see Stith, K., and Cabranes, J. A. (1998). *Fear of Judging: Sentencing Guidelines in the Federal Courts.* Chicago: University of Chicago Press.

Page 117. *many judges and lawyers:* Ibid., pp. 195–196.

Page 117. *constitutionality of the guidelines: United States v. Mistretta,* 488 U.S. 361 [1989].

Page 117. *restrictions on doing so:* By the late 1990s, this resistance showed up in gradual increases in the number of "downward departures" from the guidelines. See Stith (2008), pp. 1461–1465.

Page 117. *representing more than 400,000 lawyers:* The ABA's 1994 Standards for Criminal Justice on Sentencing argued that legislatures should not prescribe such mandatory minimums and that the sentence imposed should instead take into account "the gravity of the offense, the culpability of the offender, the offender's criminal history, and the personal characteristics of an individual offender." Surveys documented the widespread opposition of judges. In 1993 a study conducted for the *ABA Journal* found that 45 percent of federal judges thought the sentencing guidelines should be scraped. [DeBenedictis, D. J. (1993). The verdict is in: Throw out mandatory minimum sentences, judges tell *ABA Journal* poll. *American Bar Association Journal*, October, p. 79.] In 1996, the Federal Judicial Center found that about 80 percent of federal district judges and circuit judges thought Congress should allow them greater discretion in sentencing, and 86 percent believed that the guidelines had given federal prosecutors too much power. [Johnson, F., Treadway, M., and Gilbert, S. A. (1997). The U.S. sentencing guidelines: Results of the Federal Judicial Center's 1996 survey. Washington, DC: Federal Judicial Center.] Even some members of the Supreme Court began to shift their positions by the late 1990s. [Stith (2008), p. 1476.]

Page 117. *judges with the guidelines:* Stith (2008), pp. 1465–1470.

Page 119. *In January 2003:* Ignatieff, M. (2003). The burden. *New York Times Magazine,* January 5.

Page 119. *In August 2007:* Ignatieff, M. (2007). Getting Iraq wrong. *New York Times Magazine,* August 5.

Page 121. *Carl Schneider . . . recounts:* Schneider, C. (1998). *The Practice of Autonomy.* New York: Oxford University Press, pp. 16–17.

Page 123. *W. M. Strull:* Strull, W. M., Lo, B., and Charles, G. (1984). Do patients want to participate in medical decision making? *Journal of the American Medical Association*, 252, 2990–2994.

Page 123. *want to decide:* Schneider (1998), p. 41.

Page 123. *difficult medical decisions:* Hoffman, J. (2005). Awash in information, patients face a lonely, uncertain road. *New York Times*, August 14.

Page 124. *"I nodded numbly":* Tauber, A. I. (1999). *Confessions of a Medicine Man: An Essay in Popular Philosophy.* Cambridge, MA: MIT Press, pp. 63–64.

Page 124. *"decisions made for them":* Mandell, H., and Spiro, H., eds. (1987). *When Doctors Get Sick.* New York: Plenum Medical, pp. 455–456.

Page 126. *National Academy of Sciences:* Berwick, D. M. (2009). What "patient-centered" should mean: Confessions of an extremist. *Health Affairs, 28,* 555–565.

Page 127. *term "patient centered":* For some of the most important early work on patient-centered care, see Brown, S. M., Weston, J. B., McWhinney, I. R., McWilliam, C. L., and Freeman, T. R. (1995). *Patient-Centered Medicine: Transforming the Clinical Method.* Thousand Oaks, CA: Sage.

Page 127. *medical school deans:* See the Ad Hoc Committee of Deans (2004). *Educating Doctors to Provide High Quality Medical Care: A Vision for Medical Education in the United States.* Washington, DC: Association of American Medical Colleges.

Page 127. *planning and decision making:* See *A Resource Guide for Hospital Senior Leaders, Medical Staff and Governing Boards,* prepared by the American Hospital Association and the Institute for Family-Centered Care (www.aha.org).

Page 128. *more patient centered:* Ponte, P. R., Conlin, G., et al. (2003). Making patient-centered care come alive. *Journal of Nursing Administration, 33,* 82–90.

Chapter 8: Eroding the Empathy to Be Wise

Page 130. *"teach the opposite":* Lowenstein, J. (1997). *The Midnight Meal and Other Essays About Doctors, Patients, and Medicine.* New Haven, CT: Yale University Press. Citations here and below are from "Can you teach compassion?" (pp. 12–19).

Page 131. *refer derogatorily to patients:* Feudtner, C., Christakis, D. A., and Christakis, N. A. (1994). Do clinical clerks suffer ethical erosion? Students' perceptions of their ethical environment and personal development. *Academic Medicine, 69,* 670–679.

Page 131. *Robert J. Lifton's work:* Lifton, R. J. (1968). *Death in Life: Survivors of Hiroshima.* New York: Random House.

Page 131. *work with patients:* For the details of this research and a review of similar findings in other research, see Hojat, M., et al. (2009). The devil is in the third year: A longitudinal study of erosion of empathy in medical school. *Academic Medicine, 84,* 1182–1191.

Page 131. *that follows medical school:* Feudtner, C., Christakis, D. A., and Christakis, N. A. (1994).

Page 131. *Pennsylvania medical students:* Hojat et al. (2009), p. 1189.

Page 131. *"actually apply to us"*: Spoken by a fourth-year student at Wake Forest University School of Medicine, as quoted in Crandall, S. J., and Marion, G. S. (2009). Identifying attitudes towards empathy: An essential feature of professionalism. *Academic Medicine, 84*, 1174–1176.

Page 132. *"hidden curriculum"*: Hafferty, F. W. (1998). Beyond curriculum reform: Confronting medicine's hidden curriculum. *Academic Medicine, 73*, 405. See also Pellegrino, E. D. (1999). The commodification of medical and health care: The moral consequences of a paradigm shift from a professional to a market ethic. *Journal of Medicine and Philosophy, 24*, 243–266.

Page 132. *"considered myself an empathetic person"*: Hojat et al. (2009), p. 1189.

Page 132. *"return on equity"*: Hafferty (1998), p. 405. See also Pellegrino, E. D. (1999), 243–266.

Page 132. *a canny outlaw:* This term is sometimes used to describe canny and honorable folklore outlaws like Robin Hood, but we first saw the term *canny outlaw* used to describe wise and courageous professionals in the work of David Kearns, former CEO and chairman of Xerox Corporation and deputy secretary of education from 1991 to 1993 under George H. W. Bush. His canny outlaws were "the best and the brightest teachers" who survived in overly bureaucratized schools. See Kearns, D. T., and Doyle, D. P. (1988). *Winning the Brain Race: A Bold Plan to Make Our Schools More Competitive*. San Francisco: ICS Press.

Page 134. *diagnostician and teacher:* Barbour, A. (1995). *Caring for Patients: A Critique of the Medical Model*. Stanford, CA: Stanford University Press. All quotations from Barbour are taken from this book.

Page 138. *minutes at best:* Weed, J. (2009, June 6). If all doctors had more time to listen. *New York Times*.

Page 139. *from the ear to the eye:* Spiro, H. (2009). The practice of empathy. *Academic Medicine, 84*, 1177–1179.

Page 141. *empathy and listening skills:* Kaiser Permanente, for example, has used workshops to train staff doctors in skills like eliciting the patient's concerns, asking for the patient's ideas, determining the patient's specific request or goal, and demonstrating empathy by being open to the patient's emotions, by making empathetic statements, and by conveying empathy nonverbally (pause, touch, facial expression). Lando, L. (2005, September 21). Teaching doctors how to interview. *Wall Street Journal*.

Page 143. *intervening early in conflicts like this:* Kotlowitz, A. (2008, May 4). Blocking the transmission of violence. *New York Times*.

Page 145. *into joining them:* See an evaluation of CeaseFire-Chicago by Skogan, W. G., Hartnett, S. M., Bump, N., and Dubois, J., with the assistance of Hollon, R., and Morris, D. www.northwestern.edu/ipr/publications/ceasefire.html, pp. 4–29 to 4–32.

Page 145. *"condone criminal activity":* Kotlowitz (2008), p. 58.

Page 147. *lawyers as counselors:* The depiction of lawyers as simply zealous advocates has a long tradition too. In 1821, for example, Lord Brougham in England was praising lawyers who aimed to save their client "by all means and expedients, and at all hazards and costs to other persons." This, he said, "is his first and only duty; and in performing this duty he must not regard the alarm, the torments, the destruction which he may bring upon others." Lord Brougham (1821). *Trial of Queen Caroline.* (J. Nightingale, ed.), p. 8.

Page 149. *this market competition:* For a fuller discussion of this transformation, see Kronman, A. T. (1993). *The Lost Lawyer.* Cambridge, MA: Harvard University Press, ch. 5. And see Galanter, M., and Palay, T. M. (1991). *Tournament of Lawyers: The Transformation of the Big Law Firm.* Chicago: University of Chicago Press, pp. 46–50.

Page 149. *long-term interests:* Kronman (1993), pp. 288–289.

Page 149. *coming up in the firm:* Kirkland, K. (2005). Ethics in large law firms: The principles of pragmatism. *Pierce Law Faculty Scholarship Series,* Paper 5. (http://lsr.nellco.org/piercelaw_facseries/5/).

Page 150. *"promotion-to-partner tournament":* This is a term popularized by Galanter and Palay in Galanter, M., and Palay, T. M. (1991).

Page 150. *"looking up and looking around":* The quotations in this paragraph and the next are from Kirkland (2005).

Page 150. *"survival and advantage":* Kirkland here quotes Jackall, R. (1983, September–October). Moral mazes: Bureaucracy and managerial work. *Harvard Business Review,* 61.

Page 151. *"officers of the court":* For a more detailed discussion of these issues, see Gordon, R. (2000). Why lawyers can't just be hired guns. In D. Rhode (ed.), *Ethics in Practice* (pp. 42–55). New York: Oxford University Press, ch. 3.

Page 152. *"before the law's":* Kronman (1993), pp. 144–145.

Page 152. *had with their clients:* For a discussion of how this relationship has changed, see ibid., pp. 283–291.

Page 152. *when counseling them:* Nelson, R. L. (1988). *Partners with Power: The Social Transformation of the Large Law Firm.* Berkeley: University of California Press.

Page 153. *"They settled the strike in a day"*: Interview with Ralph Fine, April 3, 2008.

Page 153. *subservience to client interests:* Nelson (1988), pp. 11–12, 227–228.

Page 153. *interests with public ones:* Suchman, M. C. (1998). Working without a net: The sociology of legal ethics in corporate litigation. *Fordham Law Review, 67,* 837–857.

Page 153. *used-car salesmen:* See, for example, the Gallup Poll (2006). The most honest and ethical professions. December 8–10.

Page 153. *St. Louis that:* Remarks at the dedication of Anheuser-Busch Hall, Washington University School of Law, St. Louis, Missouri (1997, September 26).

Chapter 9. Right by Rote: Overstandardization and the Rise of the Canny Outlaw

Page 155. *Journalist Dan Baum:* Baum, D. (2005, January 17). Battle lessons: What the generals don't know. *The New Yorker.*

Page 156. *had the opposite results:* Wong, L. (2002). Stifled innovation? Developing tomorrow's leaders today. *Strategic Studies Institute Monograph*, April. All Wong quotations are from this monograph.

Page 158. *"reflective practice":* Schön, D. (1983). *The Reflective Practitioner: How Professionals Think in Action.* New York: Basic Books.

Page 159. *drew to a close:* Ball, D. L., and Wilson, S. M. (1996). Integrity in teaching: Recognizing the fusion of the moral and intellectual. *American Educational Research Journal, 33,* 155–192.

Page 162. *as opposed to memorizing:* Dewey, J. (1983; originally published 1929). *Experience and Education.* New York: Peter Smith Publisher. See also Hiebert, J., et al. (1996). Problem solving as a basis for reform in curriculum and instruction: The case of mathematics. *Educational Researcher, 25,* 13–21.

Page 163. *has dubbed it:* Hirsch, E. D. (1987). *Cultural Literacy.* Boston: Houghton Mifflin; Hirsch, E. D. (1996). *The Schools We Need: And Why We Don't Have Them.* New York: Random House.

Page 163. *an even number:* Green, E. (2010, March 7). Can good teaching be learned? *New York Times Magazine.*

Page 164. *"not going to wing it":* Ms. Moffett is described in Goodnough, A. (2001, May 23). Teaching by the book, no asides allowed. *New York Times.*

Page 166. *approved "praise words":* McNeil, L. (2000). *The Contradictions of School Reform: The Educational Costs of Standardized Testing.* New York: Routledge.

Page 166. *question with a question:* Darling-Hammond, L. (1997). *The Right to Learn.* New York: Jossey-Bass, pp. 74–75.

Page 167. *Franklin Bobbitt observed:* The Bobbitt quotation, from 1913, is cited in Darling-Hammond (1997), p. 45.

Page 167. *and student learning:* Cohen, D. K., and Ball, D. L. (1999). *Capacity and Building Capacity for Instruction.* Lansing: Michigan State University Press; see also Kilpatrick, J., Swafford, J., and Findell, B. (eds.) (2001). *Adding It Up: Helping Children Learn Mathematics.* Washington, DC: National Academy Press.

Page 167. *with these materials:* Apple, M. W. (1995) *Education and Power.* New York: Routledge, p. 144.

Page 168. *"take your bath":* Steinberg, J. (1999, November 26). Teachers in Chicago school follow script from day 001. *New York Times.*

Page 169. *"sequence of activities":* Darling-Hammond (1997), p. 79.

Page 169. *innovation, not standardization:* This discussion derives from McNeil (2000).

Page 172. *read and write:* Joseph, R. (2005, April). No one curriculum is enough: Effective California teachers tailor literacy instruction to student needs despite federal, state, and local mandates to follow scripts. Paper presented at First International Congress of Qualitative Inquiry (www.iiqi.org/C4QI/httpdocs/qi2005/papers/joseph.pdf).

Page 173. *school's literacy coordinator:* Jaeger, E. (2006). Silencing teachers in an era of scripted reading. *Rethinking Schools* (www.rethinkingschools.org/archive/20_03/sile203.shtml), 20.

Page 173. *"students and teachers":* http://coe.arizona.edu/tls/goodman_award.

Page 174. *next round of tests:* Knopp, S. (2009). Los Angeles teachers say NO to more testing. *Rethinking Schools* (www.rethinkingschools.org/archive/23_04/boyc234.shtml); and Blume, H. (2009, January 28). L.A. teacher's union calls for boycott of testing. *Los Angeles Times* (http://articles.latimes.com/2009/jan/28/local/me-lausd28/3).

Page 174. *year-round schedules:* A year at Locke, benchmark exams not only improve student performance, they help make instructors accountable (2009, May 10). *Los Angeles Times* (http://articles.latimes.com/2009/may/10/opinion/ed-assess10).

Page 176. *were required to do:* Tye, B. B., and O'Brien, L. (2002, September). Why are experienced teachers leaving the profession? *Phi Delta Kappan, 84,* 24–32.

Chapter 10. The War on Will

Page 177. *third-generation immigrants:* The Beck school case is drawn from Booher-Jennings, J. (2005). Below the bubble: "Educational triage" and the Texas Accountability System. *American Educational Research Journal, 42,* 231–268; and Booher-Jennings, J. (2007). Rationing education in an era of accountability. *Phi Delta Kappan, 87,* 756–761.

Page 180. *she could start another:* For experimental support of the point made by this anecdote, see Lepper, M. R., Greene, D., and Nisbett, R. E. (1973). Undermining children's intrinsic interest with extrinsic rewards: A test of the "overjustification" hypothesis. *Journal of Personality and Social Psychology, 28,* 129–137.

Page 183. *"to third-party payers":* Rodwin, M. A. (1993). *Medicine, Money, and Morals: Physicians' Conflicts of Interest.* New York: Oxford University Press, p. 14.

Page 183. *Cardiologist Sandeep Jauhar:* Jauhar, S. (2008, September 9). The pitfalls of linking doctors' pay to performance. *New York Times.*

Page 183. *coronary bypass surgery:* See Kenney, C. (2008). *How the New Quality Movement Is Transforming Medicine.* New York: Public Affairs Books.

Page 185. *the educational process:* See Dweck, C. S. (2006). *Mindset: The New Psychology of Success.* New York: Random House; Dweck, C. S., and Leggett, E. L. (1988). A social-cognitive approach to motivation and personality. *Psychological Review, 95,* 256–273.

Page 187. *"rewards to everybody".* Ripley, A. (2010, April 19). Should kids be bribed to do well in school? *Time;* Medina, J. (2010, April 8). Cash offers not enough to improve student test scores. *New York Times.*

Page 188. *called "incomplete contracts":* See Bowles, S. (2008). Policies designed for self-interested citizens may undermine "the moral sentiments": Evidence from economic experiments. *Science, 320,* 1605–1609.

Page 188. *paralyzed production:* See Schwartz, B. (2000; originally published 1994). *The Costs of Living: How Market Freedom Erodes the Best Things in Life.* Philadelphia: XLibris.

Page 189. *"on trust":* Hirsch, F. (1976). *Social Limits to Growth.* Cambridge, MA: Harvard University Press.

Page 190. *meet that obligation:* The day care case was studied by Gneezy, U., and Rustichini, A. (2000). A fine is a price. *Journal of Legal Studies, 29,* 1–17.

Page 192. *a waste dump in their community:* Frey, B. S., and Oberholzer-Gee, F. (1997). The cost of price incentives: An empirical analysis of motivation crowding out. *American Economic Review, 87,* 746–755.

Page 193. *waiting for the experimenter to return:* See Deci, E. (1975). *Intrinsic Motivation*. New York: Plenum; Kohn, A. (1993). *Punished by Rewards*. Boston: Houghton Mifflin. Other research that confirms such findings includes: Lepper, M. R., and Greene, D. (eds.) (1978). *The Hidden Costs of Reward*. Hillsdale, NJ: Erlbaum; Schwartz, B. (1982). Reinforcement-induced behavioral stereotypy: How not to teach people to discover rules. *Journal of Experimental Psychology: General, 111*, 23–59; Schwartz, B. (1990). The creation and destruction of value. *American Psychologist, 45*, 7–15; Vohs, K. D., Mead, N. L., and Goode, M. R. (2006). The psychological consequences of money. *Science, 314*, 1154–1156.

Page 194. *nursery school children:* Lepper, Greene, and Nisbett (1973).

Page 194. *a similar point:* Heyman, J., and Ariely, D. (2004). Effort for payment: A tale of two markets. *Psychological Science, 15*, 787–793. See also Gneezy, U., and Rustichini, A. (2000). Pay enough or not at all. *Quarterly Journal of Economics, 115*, 791–810.

Chapter 11. Demoralizing Institutions

Page 197. *"a healer of the sick?":* Socrates' question to Thrasymachus. Plato, *The Republic*, Book I, p. 341.

Page 198. *doing the right thing:* One compelling demonstration of why it is easier to be moral in a moral world is the book by economist Fred Hirsch titled *Social Limits to Growth* (Cambridge, MA: Harvard University Press, 1976). See also Schwartz, B. (2000; originally published 1994). *The Costs of Living: How Market Freedom Erodes the Best Things in Life*. Philadelphia: XLibris.

Page 200. *"physician as servant":* Hilfiker, D. (1997). *Healing the Wounds: A Physician Looks at His Work*. Omaha, NE: Creighton University Press, especially chs. 13 and 14. All quotations and discussion of Hilfiker in this chapter derive from this book.

Page 203. *charged for their services:* See, for example, Paul Starr's Pulitzer Prize–winning book *The Social Transformation of American Medicine*. New York: Basic Books, 1982.

Page 203. *"quality of medical care":* Cited in Rodwin, M. A. (1993). *Medicine, Money, and Morals: Physicians' Conflicts of Interest*. New York: Oxford University Press, p. 270.

Page 203. *prescriptions they wrote:* See Schwartz (2000).

Page 203. *drug manufacturers:* Relman, A. (2009, June). The health reform we need and are not getting. *New York Review of Books.*

Page 203. *"services is injured":* Starr (1982), p. 217.

Page 203. *dismissal from the profession:* Stone, D. (1998). The doctor as businessman: The changing politics of a cultural icon. In M. A. Peterson (ed.), *Healthy Markets: The New Competition in Medical Care* (pp. 161–182). Durham, NC: Duke University Press, p. 168.

Page 205. *"best for the patients":* Rodwin (1993), p. 145.

Page 206. *medical facilities:* Ibid., p. 17.

Page 206. *"refer a patient for a scan":* Jauhar, S. (2008, September 9). *New York Times.*

Page 206. *and a business:* Relman (2009).

Page 206. *still incredibly expensive:* These are inflation-adjusted figures from Schwartz (2000).

Page 207. *in a positive light:* Singer, N. (2009, August 5). Medical papers by ghostwriters pushed therapy. *New York Times*; Wilson, D., and Singer, N. (2009, September 11). Ghostwriting widespread in medical journals. *New York Times.*

Page 208. *The Commonwealth Fund:* McCarthy, D., Mueller, K., and Wreen, J. (2009, August). *Mayo Clinic: Multidisciplinary Teamwork, Physician-Led Governance, and Patient-Centered Culture Drive World-Class Health Care.* Commonwealth Fund Publication, *27*, 1306.

Page 208. *was very different:* Gawande, A. (2009, June 1). The cost conundrum. *The New Yorker*, pp. 36–44.

Page 210. *Sandeep Jauhar says:* Jauhar, S. (2009, July 7). A doctor by choice, a businessman by necessity. *New York Times.* See also Jauhar, S. (2008, September 9).

Page 211. *"more effective care":* Hartzband, P., and Groopman, J. (2009). Money and the changing culture of medicine. *New England Journal of Medicine, 360,* 101–103. See also Bach, P. B. (2008, July 24). Paying doctors to ignore patients. *New York Times*; Berenson, A., and Abelson, R. (2008, June 29). Weighing costs of a look inside the heart. *New York Times.*

Page 211. *Mayo model:* Harris, G. (2009, July 24). Hospital savings: Salaries for doctors, not fees. *New York Times*; Steffy, L. (2009, September 18). A different way of paying doctors. *Houston Chronicle.* Bassett Medical Care, for example, has a 180-bed hospital and 260 doctors—all on salary. They take home the same amount of money no matter how many tests or procedures are performed. Medical costs there are lower than 90 percent of the hospitals in New York and the quality of care ranks among the top 10 percent in the nation. And many of the doctors there are deeply committed to its mission to care for patients.

Page 212. *"about myself changed"*: Schiltz, P. J. (1999). On being a happy, healthy, and ethical member of an unhappy, unhealthy, and unethical profession. *Vanderbilt Law Review*, 52, 871–918, p. 938.

Page 212. *"the primary purpose"*: Pound, R. (1953). *The Law from Antiquity to Modern Times*. St. Paul: West, p. 5.

Page 212. *less to seniority:* Kronman (1993), pp. 295–296.

Page 213. *"favorite baseball players"*: Schiltz, P. J. (1999), p. 914.

Page 213. *"goal of law practice"*: American Bar Association (1986). *". . . In the Spirit of Public Service. A Blueprint for the Rekindling of Lawyer Professionalism*, p. 15.

Page 213. *"water from a firehose"*: O'Connor, S. D. (1997, September 26). Remarks at the dedication of Anheuser-Busch Hall, Washington University School of Law, St. Louis, Missouri.

Page 213. *"with making money"*: This quotation and those that follow (unless otherwise noted) are from Schiltz (1999), pp. 912–918.

Page 214. *"promotion-to-partner tournament"*: We referred to this in chapter 8. See Galanter, M., and Palay, T. M. (1991). *Tournament of Lawyers: The Transformation of the Big Law Firm*. Chicago: University of Chicago Press.

Page 216. *"on his time records"*: Trotter, M. (1997). *Profit and the Practice of Law: What's Happened to the Legal Profession?* Athens, GA, and London: University of Georgia Press, pp. 186–187.

Page 216. *"I'm giving up"*: See Devoe, S. E., and Pfeffer, J. (2007). When time is money: The effect of hourly payment on the evaluation of time. *Organizational Behavior and Human Decision Processes*, 104, 1–13.

Page 216. *can look to:* Kronman (1993), pp. 298–299.

Page 216. *"the public interest"*: Nelson, R. (1988). *Partners with Power: Social Transformation of the Large Law Firm*. Berkeley: University of California Press, p. xi.

Page 217. *dissatisfaction, and suicide:* See Sheldon, K. M., and Krieger, L. S. (2007). Understanding the negative effects of legal education on law students: A longitudinal test of self-determination theory. *Personality and Social Psychology Review*, 33, 883–897; Sheldon, K. M., and Krieger, L. S. (2004). Does legal education have undermining effects on law students? Evaluating changes in motivation, values, and well-being. *Behavioral Sciences and the Law*, 22, 261–286. Sheldon and Krieger review evidence that lawyers have the highest incidence of major depressive disorder among 104 occupational groups, that they manifest clinical levels of depression, anxiety, phobia, and interpersonal sensitivity five to fifteen times more commonly than the general population, that substance abuse is more frequent than in the population at large, and that the suicide rate is exceptionally high as well.

Page 217. *"game at times"*: Schiltz (1999), p. 938.

Page 217. *at IndyMac Bank:* Manuel's case is drawn from Hudson, M. (2008). *Indy-Mac: What Went Wrong? How an "Alt-A" Leader Fueled Its Growth with Unsound and Abusive Mortgage Lending.* Center for Responsible Lending Report (www.responsiblelending.org).

Page 219. *"how we operate?"*: Barack Obama, December 18, 2008, press conference.

Page 220. *"bonds in Christendom"*: Cited in Surowiecki, J. (2008, October 20). The trust crunch. *The New Yorker.*

Page 221. *"say, mortgage securities"*: References are from Lowenstein, R. (2010, March 21). Who needs Wall Street? *New York Times Magazine.*

Page 222. *housing-related investments:* Story, L., and Morgenson, G. (2010, April 18). For Goldman, a winning bet carries a price. *New York Times.*

Page 222. *"wish we hadn't sold it"*: Lowenstein, R. (2010, March 21).

Page 222. *"housing market's collapse"*: Craig, S., and Scannell, K. (2010, July 16). $550 million deal ends showdown that shook street. *Wall Street Journal.*

Page 222. *"cynical, selfish exploiting"*: Wall Street historian and author Steve Fraser, interviewed in Story and Morgenson (2010).

Page 223. *investment bank party:* The Glass-Steagall Act of 1933 forbade commercial banks from becoming investment banks. It barred banks that took deposits from underwriting securities because of the dangers to depositors and the banking system. Such investments tempted bankers to take too much risk with depositors' money in the hopes of big gains—a policy that had hurt investors in the Great Depression. Glass-Steagall forbade banks from making speculative investments with depositors' money. For a good account of the decades of political pressure that led first to the weakening, and finally to the repeal, of the Glass-Steagall Act, see the *Frontline* chronology at www.pbs.org/wgbh/pages/frontline/shows/wallstreet/weill/demise.html.

Page 223. *"to make this work"*: Interview with Wesley Miller in Hudson (2008), p. 9.

Page 223. *Audrey Streater:* Interview with Audrey Streater in Hudson (2008), pp. 3, 8, and 9.

Page 224. *errant loan officials:* Cited in Hudson (2008), p. 3.

Page 224. *Ms. Manuel discovered:* Hudson (2008), pp. 11–15.

Page 224. *$90,000 a year:* Cited in Hudson (2008), p. 3.

Page 225. *book* After Virtue: MacIntyre, A. (1981). *After Virtue: A Study in Moral Theory*. Notre Dame, IN: University of Notre Dame Press, p. 159.

Chapter 12. System Changers

Page 235. *"repeal federal mandatory minimums":* Address by Anthony M. Kennedy, Associate Justice, Supreme Court of the United States, at the American Bar Association Annual Meeting (2003, August 9).

Page 235. *Feeney crackdown:* Cited in Stith (2008). The arc of the pendulum: Judges, prosecutors, and the exercise of discretion. *Yale Law Journal, 117*, 1467, n. 182.

Page 236. *practical wisdom again:* It may be some time before some judges regain the experience to wisely exercise discretion in criminal sentencing. As Judge Gertner pointed out, the majority of judges were denied that experience for over two decades. Furthermore, the guidelines are still in place, framing judicial decision making and serving as an anchor to define a reasonable decision. But judges like Gertner have some hope. She told us that judges still know what judgment is and practice it in all the work they do outside of criminal sentencing—reviewing punitive damage awards, setting civil monetary penalties, ruling in tort and contract cases. See Gertner, N. (2007). From omnipotence to impotence: American judges and sentencing. *Ohio State Journal of Criminal Law, 4*, 523–539.

Page 236. *what to expect:* Thompson, C. (2008, July 7). Special court for veterans addresses more than crime: Treatment for mental health issues included. Associated Press.

Page 236. *stepped before Judge Russell:* The Pettengill story is from Lewis, L. (2008, April 29). Court aims to help vets with legal troubles. *Morning Edition*, National Public Radio.

Page 237. *"from those relationships":* Russell, interviewed by Cheryl Corley on *Tell Me More*, National Public Radio (2010, June 18).

Page 238. *"stay focused with":* Ibid.

Page 238. *rate was zero:* Lithwick, D. (2010, February 22). A separate peace: Why veterans deserve special courts. *Newsweek*.

Page 239. *next few years:* Lewis (2008).

Page 240. *others were planned:* Vets get aid with legal problems: Special courts work
with VA, bar association (2009, November 24). *USA Today*.

Page 240. *them drug courts:* Huddleston, C. W., III, Marlowe, D. B., and Casebott,
R. (2008). *Painting the Current Picture: A National Report Card on Drug Courts
and Other Problem-Solving Court Programs in the United States*. Washington, DC:
Bureau of Justice Assistance, U.S. Department of Justice. Although there had
been earlier models for such courts—the first "juvenile court," for example, was
created in 1899—the surge in contemporary problem-solving courts began in
1989. A quick sampling of the variety and operations of these problem-solving
courts can be found in a special issue of *The Judge's Journal*, Winter 2002.

Page 240. *New York Times:* A court for veterans. Editorial (2008, June 4). *New York
Times*. For research supporting such conclusions see Huddleston et al. (2008),
p. 6.

Page 240. *"indifference to the truth":* Kronman, A. T. (1993). *The Lost Lawyer*. Cambridge, MA: Harvard University Press, p. vii.

Page 241. *when they adjudicate:* Weinreb, L. L. (2005). *Legal Reason: The Use of
Analogy in Legal Argument*. Cambridge and New York: Cambridge University
Press.

Page 242. *administration of justice:* Kronman (1993), pp. 114–119.

Page 242. *"rigid time constraints":* Gordon, R. W., and Simon, W. H. (1992). The re-
demption of professionalism? In R. L. Nelson, D. M. Trubek, and R. L. Solomon
(eds.), *Lawyers' Ideals/Lawyers' Practices* (pp. 224–243). Ithaca, NY, and London:
Cornell University Press, p. 237.

Page 242. *with the practical:* Sullivan, W. M., Colby, A., Wegner, J. W., Bond, L.,
and Shulman, L. S. (2007). *Educating Lawyers: Preparation for the Profession of
Law*. New York: Jossey-Bass, pp. 62–63.

Page 242. *can justify anything:* Sullivan (2007), pp. 56–59, 140–142.

Page 243. *in the audience:* Interview, September 15, 2009. This vision is elaborated
in Balachandra, L., Bordone, R. C., Menkel-Meadow, C., Ringstrom, P., and
Sarath, E. (2005). Improvisation and negotiation: Expecting the unexpected.
Negotiation Journal, 21, 415–423.

Page 245. *"solves the client's problem":* Sullivan (2007), p. 102.

Page 246. *from their mentors:* Sullivan et al. (2007), pp. 95–99.

Page 246. *"formal reasoning":* Ibid., pp. 116–117. We discussed the importance of
such pattern recognition in chapter 6.

Page 247. *"clinical experiences"*: Ibid., p. 121. Another excellent source on teaching good practice to lawyers, and the importance of legal clinics, is Stuckey, W. M., et al. (2007). *Best Practices for Legal Education*. Clinical Legal Association.

Page 248. *run such a firm*: The following case is drawn from Kelly, M. (1994). *Lives of Lawyers: Journeys in the Organization of Practice*. Ann Arbor: University of Michigan Press; and from Kelly, M. (2007). *Lives of Lawyers Revisited: Transformation and Resilience on the Organizations of Practice*. Ann Arbor: University of Michigan Press.

Page 249. *law firm standards:* Kelly notes that "the ratio of Mahoney's highest-compensated to its lowest-compensated partners is less than two to one, and the ratio of highest-compensated partner to lowest-compensated associate is about four to one. These ratios would be considered preposterous in large firms, where rainmakers (the lawyers who attract sizable clients) and senior people in the firms claim very substantial shares of the profits of the enterprise" (Kelly [2007], p. 77).

Page 251. *When Joey Hawkins:* Interviews with Hawkins, August 2 and 23, 2006.

Page 252. *writing and in math:* For a discussion of the math portfolios, see Fiske, E. B. (1991). *Smart Schools, Smart Kids*. New York: Simon & Schuster, pp. 132–138.

Page 255. *the introduction of standardized assessments in Vermont:* Beginning in 2005, Vermont added a standardized literacy assessment to the portfolio system. This assessment, known as the NECAP (New England Common Assessment, developed and used by Vermont, New Hampshire, Rhode Island, and Maine) adheres to many of the standards in the portfolio system. It minimizes the use of fill-in-the-bubble questions and regularly requires students in grades three through eleven to demonstrate writing and thinking competence (to "construct meaning" educators like Hawkins would say) in reading, math, writing, and science. Because of this, teachers in all content areas in Vermont schools are increasingly looking for ways to help teach their students to write clearly and thoughtfully within their own curricula—the opposite of a lockstep, scripted approach.

Page 255. *"not the solution":* Wong, L. (2002, April). Stifled innovation? Developing tomorrow's leaders today. *Strategic Studies Institute Monograph*, p. 31.

Page 256. *he told her:* The interviews with faculty and students discussed in this section of the chapter were done during an extended visit to the Cambridge Integrated Clerkship program at the Cambridge Health Alliance in Cambridge, Massachusetts, in September 2009.

Page 259. *concerned about traditional medical school training:* For an excellent recent overview of the problems in current medical training and some of the alternatives being tried, see the Carnegie Foundation's study of medical education: Cooke, M., Irby, D. M, and O'Brien, B. C. (2010). *Educating Physicians: A Call for Reform of Medical School and Residency.* San Francisco: Jossey-Bass.

Page 261. *"Pimping?":* For more detail on "pimping" and the tricks medical students learn in order to defend themselves, see Detsky, A. S. (2009). The art of pimping. *Journal of the American Medical Association, 301,* 1379–1381.

Page 268. *"do something about this":* Johnson, C. (2004). *ShoreBank: A Self-Sustaining Institution.* Weatherhead School of Management, Case Western Reserve University.

Page 269. *"approach to community development":* Johnson, C. (2004).

Page 269. *"becoming more successful":* Seidman, E., and Grzywinski, R. (2009). *A Bank as Courageous Investor.* innovations/World Economic Forum special edition, Davos–Klosters.

Page 271. *"make a deal work":* Johnson, C. (2004).

Page 271. *ShoreBank as the model:* Johnson (2004).

Page 271. *nonprofit loan funds:* Seidman and Grzywinski (2009).

Chapter 13. Wisdom and Happiness

Page 276. *psychologist Wendy Mogel:* The Mogel lecture was at the Agnes Irwin School in Villanova, Pennsylvania, February 8, 2007. We interviewed Mogel in late 2006.

Page 277. *"'how to swim'":* Mogel, W. (2001). *The Blessing of a Skinned Knee.* New York: Simon & Schuster, p. 90.

Page 277. *"every hazard":* Ibid., p. 95.

Page 277. *"knocks of life":* Ibid., pp. 92–93.

Page 278. *mothers she knows:* Ohye, B. (2001). *Mothering from the Heart.* New York: Penguin.

Page 278. *"'grew them up'":* Ibid., p. 131.

Page 278. *"supremely blessed and happy":* Aristotle, *Nicomachean Ethics,* book 1, ch. 5 (1098a).

Page 278. *researcher on happiness:* Diener, E., and Biswas-Diener, R. (2008). *Happiness: Unlocking the Mysteries of Psychological Wealth.* New York: Blackwell.

Page 279. *of Martin Seligman:* Seligman, M. E. P. (2002). *Authentic Happiness.* New York: Free Press. See also Peterson, C., and Seligman, M. E. P. (2004). *Character Strengths and Virtues.* New York: Oxford University Press; Lyubomirsky, S. (2007). *The How of Happiness.* New York: Penguin Press; Fredrickson, B. L. (2009). *Positivity.* New York: Crown.

Page 280. *the whole symphony:* For a fuller discussion of the relationship between Aristotle and positive psychology, see Schwartz, B., and Sharpe, K. (2006). Practical wisdom: Aristotle meets positive psychology. *Journal of Happiness Studies,* 7, 377–395.

Page 281. *"life stifles and dies":* A. Camus, cited in O'Toole, J. (1973). *Work in America.* Cambridge, MA: MIT Press, p. 186.

Page 282. *engagement and passion:* Warr, P. (2009). *The Joy of Work? Jobs, Happiness, and You.* New York: Routledge.

Page 282. *source of satisfaction:* See Wrzesniewski, A., and Dutton, J. E. (2001). Crafting a job: Revisioning employees as active crafters of their work. *Academy of Management Review,* 26, 179–201; Wrzesniewski, A., Dutton, J. E., and Debebe, G. (2003). Interpersonal sensemaking and the meaning of work. *Research in Organizational Behavior,* 25, 93–135; Wrzesniewski, A., Dutton, J. E., and Debebe, G. (2009). Caring in constrained contexts. Unpublished manuscript. See also Wrzesniewski, A., McCauley, C., Rozin, P., and Schwartz, B. (1997). Jobs, careers, and callings: People's relations to their work. *Journal of Research in Personality,* 31, 21–33.

Page 283. *administrative assistants working at a college:* Wrzesniewski, A., McCauley, C., Rozin, P., and Schwartz, B. (1997).

Page 285. *"but you never know":* The Carlotta quotations are from Wrzesniewski, A., Dutton, J. E., and Debebe, G. (2009).

INDEX

Adams, John, 27
advance directives, 125
advocacy, 240–41
After Virtue (MacIntyre), 225–26
allied with emotion, 70–74
American Bar Association (ABA), 117, 153,
    213, 235
The American Lawyer, 212–13
American Medical Association (AMA),
    202–3, 206
apprenticeship, 245–47
Ariely, Dan, 194
Aristotle, 278, 287
    balancing acts and, 6–7
    deliberation and discernment of, 19,
        21–22
    emotions and, 24
    ethics and, 51
    masons of Lesbos and, 28–29
    Nichomachean Ethics, 5–6, 44
    particular facts and, 22
    phronemoi and, 12

practical wisdom and, 5–12, 85, 105,
    234, 275
telos and, 7, 16
wisdom-happiness connection, 278
army soldiers, 156–59
Atlanta Legal Aid Society, 218
Authentic Happiness (Seligman), 279–80

balancing acts, 6–7, 29–30, 163
    asking and telling, 30–36
    Brad's story, 39–40
    Dr. Lowenstein's story, 36–38
    empathy with detachment, 39–41
    honesty with care and kindness, 36–39
    lawyers and, 151–54
    Miriam's story, 38–39
    Mrs. Jones's story, 30–34
    Rules Talk and Wisdom Talk,
        43–45
    why wisdom is practical, 27–45
    wisdom as moral jazz, 41–43
Ball, Deborah, 159–63

bankers, 9, 11
good, 219–21
housing bubble and, 217–25
wise, 268–71
banking crisis, 218
banks, 3, 217–25
Barbour, Dr. Allen, 133–41
Bassett Medical Care (Cooperstown,
New York), 211
Batson, C.D., 78–79
Baum, Dan, 155
Beck Elementary School (Texas), 177, 233
Ben Taub General Hospital (Houston, Texas),
211
Berlin, Isaiah, 120
Berwick, Dr. Donald, 126–27
billable-hours (law firms), 213–16, 248
Biswas-Diener, Robert, 278–79
Blankfein, Lloyd, 222
The Blessing of a Skinned Knee (Mogel), 276
Blink (Gladwell), 83
Bobbitt, Franklin, 167
bond-rating agencies, 3
Bordone, Robert, 243–45
born to be wise, 51, 68
categories, 52–58
framing, 61–63
with narratives, 66–67
moral skill components, 51–52
similarity, 58–61
brain injury patients, 77–78
"bubble kids," 177–79
Buchanan, Calvin, 146

Cambridge Health Alliance, 256–60, 271–72
Cambridge Integrated Clerkship (CIC),
256–68
Camus, Albert, 281
canny outlaws, 10, 140, 171–75, 196–97,
233–34, 274, 302
teachers as, 169–76
Cardozo, Benjamin, 28
*Caring for Patients: A Critique of the Medical
Model* (Barbour), 134
case method, 241–42
cash rewards in schools program (NYC), 187
categories
change in, 57–58
formal, 52–53
fuzzy, 52–53

gray, 57
natural, 54–57, 81
of networks, 95–96
similarity of, 58–61
CeaseFire, 143–47
Chapman University (California), 175
Charon, Dr. Rita, 265
Chicago, Illinois, 142–47
children
empathy development in, 71–72
initiation into moral community, 105–6
moral networks of, 99–101
performance vs. mastery goals of, 185–86
raising, 276–78
Churchland, Paul, 88–90, 99–101, 105–6
City University of New York, 246–47
Clark, General Wesley, 159
Cleveland Clinic, 211
client interests, 30–36
Clinton, Bill, 271
cognitive networks, 88–91
architecture and operation of, 92–98, 93–94
pattern recognition and, 88–91
Cohen, Dr. Pieter, 255–56, 261–63, 265–68,
272
college professors, 198
commercial banks, 223
Commission on Professionalism (ABA), 213
community development banking, 269–71
community development financial institutions
(CDFI), 271
complexity, 43, 82
computer network, 90
connectionism, 92
consensus-based model, 244
context, 51–52, 65
counselors, 24, 65, 142–47, 153
marginalizing lawyers as, 147–51
Covey, Stephen, 66–67, 69–71
Crossing the Quality Chasm (IOM), 127
curriculum, 165–69

Dade County, Florida, 240
Damasio, Antonio, 77–78
Dana-Farber Cancer Institute (Boston),
127–28
Darley, J. M., 78–79
Darling-Hammond, Linda, 169
Dartmouth Medical School, 208–9
Davis, John W., 154

deliberation, 19–21, 40, 104
demoralizing institutions, 197–99, 228
   banks, 217–25
   medical practices, 199–211
   law firms, 211–17
demoralizing practices, 225–27
derivatives (financial), 222
detachment, 39–41, 142
Dewey, John, 22, 162
Didion, Joan, 67
Diener, Ed, 278–80
Dillard, Annie, 76
discernment, 19, 22–24
discretion, 283–85
disease model, 140–41
doctors, 3–4, 6–7, 9, 12, 37, 69, 188
   empathic, 137–38
   paternalistic, 121–24
   patient autonomy and, 121–28
   patient-centered, 124–28
   performance incentives, 182–84
   practice of, 133–41
   specialization by, 139, 233
   training, 69, 129–33
   wise, 255–68
Doctors Hospital (McAllen, Texas), 208–9
Dweck, Carol, 185–86

educational reforms, 166–69
Eisenberg, Nancy, 71–72
Ekman, Paul, 83
emotion, 23–24, 26, 69
   allied with reason, 70–72
   facial expression of, 83
   moral evaluation and, 72–74
   motivation and, 75–79
emotional intelligence, 79–80
empathy, 23, 39–41, 80
   erosion in medical practice, 133–41
   erosion in professional training, 129–33
   moral evaluation and, 72–74
   motivation and, 75–79
   as reason allied with emotion, 70–72
End of Wall Street, The (Lowenstein),
   221–22
English common law, 28
ethics, 5–8, 30–32, 43–44, 51, 118, 122–24, 132,
   203, 261
Ethics: Beyond the Rules (ABA), 153
Ethics Talk, 44

experience, 8, 21, 26, 42, 44, 49, 52, 59, 61, 65,
   68, 81–106, 111, 116, 147, 149, 158,
   164–65, 175–176, 235, 242, 245,
   247, 261, 271–72
   categorizing, 52–58
experiential learning
   cognitive networks, 88–91
      architecture and operation of, 92–98,
      93–94
   moral networks and moral skill, 98–106
   rules and, 85–87
   pattern recognition, 82–85
external goals, 226–27
externalities, 64

fairness, 161–62
Federal Deposit Insurance Corporation
   (FDIC), 218
Federalist No.51, 27
Federal Sentencing Guidelines, 115
Feeney Amendment, 117, 235–36
financial crisis, 11–12
Financial Crisis Inquiry Commission, 222
financial incentives, 180–81, 184, 198–99
Fine, Ralph, 152–53
fines for lateness, 190–92
firefighter survival guidelines, 41–42
Flanagan, Owen, 99–100
Florida Performance Measurement System,
   166
Forer, Lois, 17–19, 29, 58, 67, 70, 113–15, 234,
   236
framing, 61
   choosing right frames, 64
   context and, 65
   marketing context, 62–63
   medicine and, 122, 132, 140
   with narratives, 66–67
   political context, 63
Fraser, Steve, 222
Frey, Bruno, 192–93

Gaufberg, Dr. Elizabeth, 262–65
Gawande, Dr. Atul, 208–9
Gertner, Nancy, 116
Getz, Stan, 42
Gladwell, Malcolm, 83
Glass-Steagall Act, 222–23
Goldberg, Elkhonon, 86–87
Goldman Sachs, 221–23

Goleman, Daniel, 80
good banker, 219–21
Good Samaritan parable, 78–79, 139
Gopnik, Alison, 71
Gottman, John, 83
graded relationship, 53
Great Depression, 222
greed, 197–99
Green Dot Public Schools (Los Angeles), 174
Groopman, Dr. Jerome, 210–11
Grzywinski, Ron, 268–71, 274
guided rehabilitation, 235–40

Hafferty, Dr. Frederic, 132
Haidt, Jonathan, 73–74
hairdressers, 35
Hartzband, Dr. Pamela, 210–11
Harvard Medical School, 256
Harvard Negotiation and Mediation Clinical
    Program, 243–45
Hawkins, Joey, 251–55, 274
health care
    commercialization of, 199–211
    costs, 208–9
    incentives in, 182–84
    See also doctors; medical profession
Health Maintenance Organizations (HMOs),
    204–6
Heraclitus, 84
Heyman, James, 194
high-stakes tests, 167
Hilfiker, Dr. David, 199–202, 211, 213, 234
Hippocrates, 37
Hirsch, E. D., 162–63
Hirsch, Fred, 189
Hirsh, Dr. David, 256–60, 265, 274, 283
Hoddenbach, Zale, 143–44
Hoffman, Martin, 71–72
Hojat, Dr. Mohammadreza, 131–32
honesty, 36–39
housing bubble, 218
Hsee, Christopher, 76
Hughes, Lieutenant Colonel Chris,
    155–56
Hussein, Saddam, 119–20
Hyde Park Bank (Chicago), 268–69

ideological thinking, 120–21
IEDs (improvised explosive devices), 90
Ignatieff, Michael, 118–20

incentives, 4–5, 9, 11–12, 110, 233–34, 287
    doctor performance, 182–84
    incomplete contracts, 188–90
    motivational competition, 190–96
    performance vs. mastery, 184–87
    problems with, 180–81, 184, 198–99
    reading prizes, 179–80
incest, 73–74
incomplete contracts, 188–90
individualized sentencing, 114
IndyMac Bank, 217–18, 221, 223–25
innovation, 157
Institute of Medicine, 126–27
institutions, 3, 8–9, 110, 120, 234
    building institutions, 8, 234, 241, 251, 273
    demoralizing, 197–228
intuition, 26, 42, 73–74
Iraq, 90, 118–20
Iraq War, 155
It's a Wonderful Life (movie), 219

James, William, 82
Jauhar, Dr. Sandeep, 183, 206, 210
Joseph, Rebecca, 172
judges
    mandatory minimum sentencing and,
        114–17
    putting judgment back into judging,
        235–40
    See also individual judges: Forer, Lois;
        Gertner, Nancy; Kennedy, Anthony;
        and Russell, Robert
Judicial Conference of the United States, 235
judicial discretion, 113–17
Justice Department, U.S., 117

Kant, Immanuel, 120–21
Kennedy, Anthony, 235
kindness, 36–39
Kingsolver, Barbara, 77
Kirkland, Kimberly, 149–51
Kotlowitz, Alex, 143–46
Kroesen, General Frederick, 159
Kronman, Anthony, 34–35, 40, 152, 216,
    240–41
Kurds, 119

language, 52
    medical, 132
"laptop docs," 139

Laughlin, Arthur, 248–49
law students, 241–47
lawyers, 30–35, 69–70, 84, 188
  demoralizing, 211–17
  ethical, 240–41
  marginalizing
    as counselors, 147–51
    as public servants, 151–54
  post law school options, 247–51
  training, 241–47
legal clinic, 243–47
legal profession, 211–17
legal system, 3, 118
lies vs. truth, 59–61
Lifton, Robert Jay, 131
living will, 125
Lowenstein, Dr. Jerome, 36–38, 58–59, 129–33
Lowenstein, Roger, 221–22

MacIntyre, Alasdair, 225–26
Madison, James, 27
magnet schools, 169–71
Mahoney, Bourne and Thiemes, 248
Mahoney, Brian, 248–51
malpractice insurance, 206
malpractice suits, 125
mandatory minimum sentencing, 114–17,
    235–36
Manuel, Elouise, 217–18, 223–24
Marcus, Dr. Devra, 205, 234
marital discord detectors, 83
Massachusetts, 182
Massachusetts Constitution (1780), 27
mastery goals, 185–86
mathematical knowledge, 161
Mayer, John D., 79
Mayo, William J., 208
Mayo Clinic, 208–9, 211
McAllen, Texas, 208–9
McClelland, James, 92
McNeil, Linda, 169–71
mediation, 243
medical ethics, 122, 261–62
medical profession
  commercialization of, 199–211
  golden age of, 124
  incentives in, 182–84
  patient autonomy and, 124–28
medical science, 226
medical training, 69, 129–33

mentoring, 245–46, 272, 277
metaphor, 21, 132
Mike's Hard Lemonade case, 109–10
Miller, Wesley, 223, 234
Mind at Work, The (Rose), 35
mine detector, 88–90
Mistretta decision, 117
Moffett, Donna, 164–65, 284
Mogel, Wendy, 276–78
moral ambiguity, 104, 104
moral community, 105–6
moral evaluation, 72–74
moral imagination, 22–23
moral networks, 98
  children and, 99–102
    initiation into, 105–6
moral perception, 21–24, 84
moral skill, 8, 271, 281
  components of, 51–52
moral will, 247, 271
Morgan, J. P., 220
Morse, Dr. Michael, 258, 260–62
motivational competition, 190–96

narratives, 66–67
negotiation clinic, 243–44
Nelson, Robert, 152–53, 216
Netflix, 97–98
networks
  architecture and operation of, 92–98,
      93–94
  categories of, 95–96
  computer, 90
  schematic of, 92, 93
  trained, 91
neurons, 96–97
New York Board of Education, 165–69
New Yorker, The, 208
New York Times, 119, 123, 240
New York Times Magazine, 119
Nichomachean Ethics (Aristotle), 5–6, 44
No Child Left Behind Act, 167, 170
Northwestern University (Chicago),
    143, 145

Obama, Barack, 209, 218–19
Oberholzer-Gee, Felix, 192–93
O'Connor, Sandra Day, 153–54, 213
Ogur, Dr. Barbara, 256–60, 274, 283
Ohye, Bonnie, 278

Open Court (California literacy curriculum),
    172–74
overstandardization
    in the military, 155–59
    teachers as canny outlaws, 169–76, 233–34
    in teaching, 159–69
overtreatment (medical), 209

parallel distributed processing (PDP), 92
    theories of, 93–94
parental letting-go, 276
parenting, 276–78
Partners with Power (Nelson), 216
patient autonomy, 121–28
Patient Protection and Affordable Care Act,
    182
pattern recognition, 82–85
    cognitive networks and, 88–91
    moral networks and moral skill, 102–6
    rapid, 93
    rules and, 85–87
Pellegrino, Edmund, 39
Pennsylvania Supreme Court, 113
performance goals, 185–86
Perot, H. Ross, 170
Perry, Michael, 218
Pettengill, Gary, 236–39
Pfizer Inc., 207
phronemoi, 12
Pirowski, Hank, 238–39
Plato, 5
poker player tells, 83
political policy, 118–21
Pollan, Michael, 64
positive psychology, 279
practical wisdom, 5–12, 27, 51
    balancing acts, 27–45
    born to be wise, 51–68
    custodian Luke, 13–17
    demoralizing institutions, 197–228
    empathy and, 69–80
        erosion in training and practice,
            129–41
    Judge Lois Forer, 17–19
    key characteristics of, 25–26
    learning from practice, 271–73
    machinery of, 81–106
    marginalizing good counsel, 142–47
    marginalizing lawyer as counselor,
        147–51

marginalizing public service, 151–54
overstandardization, 155–76
system changers, 233–73
training in, 110
    army soldiers, 156–59
    bankers, 268–71
    doctors, 69, 129–33
    law students, 241–47
    teachers, 159–69
war on will, 177–96
practices, 225–27
predatory loans, 270
Preparation for the Professions Program
        (Carnegie Foundation), 242–43,
        245–47
principles, 118
    patient autonomy, 121–28
    political policy, 118–21
Principles of Medical Ethics (AMA), 203
"prisoner's dilemma" game, 62
pro bono work, 248
professionals
    temptations of greed/profit, 197–99
    training, 69, 129–33
    See also bankers; doctors; judges; lawyers;
        teachers
profit, 197–99
proportionality of penalty to crime, 114, 116
prototypes, 54
psychic numbing, 131
public service, 151–54, 249

reason, 73
reflective deliberation, 104
reflective practice, 158
Rehnquist, William, 235
risk-sharing agreements, 205
Rochester, Minnesota, 208–9
Rogers, Will, 88
Rosch, Eleanor, 54
Rose, Mike, 35
Rottenstreich, Yuval, 76
Rousseau, Jean-Jacques, 69
rules, 4–6, 9–12, 287
    overreliance on, 27, 42, 103, 110
    pattern recognition and, 85–87
    rigid, 118, 233
Rules Talk, 43–45, 69, 79, 129
Rumelhart, David, 92
Russell, Robert, 236–40

Salovey, Peter, 79
"Save the Panda," 76
Saxon code, 28
scaffolding, 253, 272–73
Schiltz, Patrick, 211–15, 217, 234, 248
Schneider, Carl, 121–23
Schon, Donald, 158
Schooler, Jonathan, 86
schools, 3
    curriculum, 165–69
    incentives in, 179–81
    performance vs. mastery in, 184–87
    teacher training, 159–69
    test-centered approach in, 233
Schultz, Chris, 248–51
scientific management, 166
Securities and Exchange Commission (SEC),
    222
Seidman, Ellen, 269
self-reflection, 25, 119, 133
self-understanding, 67
Seligman, Martin, 279–80
Sentencing Reform Act, 115
Sharma, Dr. Anjana, 257–59
Shinseki, General Eric, 156
ShoreBank (Chicago), 269–71
similarity, 58–61, 81
Simon, Scott, 110
Simon, William, 30–35, 65, 188
al-Sistani, Ali, 155
Slovic, Paul, 75–77
Slutkin, Dr. Gary, 144–45
Socrates, 197
soldier training, 156–59
Southern Coalition for Social Justice
    (North Carolina), 244
Spiro, Dr. Howard, 139–40
standardization, 159–69, 254
Stanford Diagnostic Clinic, 133, 140
statesmanship, 273
Stith, Kate, 117
Stone, Deborah, 203
storytelling, 21
Streater, Audrey, 223–24, 234
Strull, W. M., 123
subprime loans, 270
suffering, 75–77
Sullivan, William, 242–43, 245–47
Supreme Court, U.S., 117, 235–36
surgical report cards (NY State), 183

Swarthmore, Pennsylvania, 179–80
Switzerland, 192–93
system changers, 10–11, 233–35
    ethical lawyer, 240–41
    law school graduates, 247–51
    learning from practice, 271–73
    putting judgment back into judging,
        235–40
    wise banker, 268–71
    wise doctor, 255–68
    wise law students, 241–47
    wise teacher, 251–55

Talmud, 276–77
Tauber, Dr. Alfred, 123–24
Taylor, Frederick Winslow, 166
teachers, 4, 11–12, 84
    as canny outlaws, 169–76, 233–34
    nurturing wisdom to teach, 251–55
    training, 159–69
teaching hospitals, 207
telling, 30–36
telos, 7, 9, 16, 184, 225
test-centered approach, 233
Texas Accountability System, 177
Texas Career Ladder program,
    165–66
Tocqueville, Alexis de, 151
Torres, Martin, 142–44
training
    army soldiers, 156–59
    bankers, 268–71
    doctors, 129–33
    law students, 241–47
    teachers, 159–69
trial-and-error learning, 89, 164,
    260, 275
Trotter, Michael, 215–16
truth vs. lies, 59–61

underwriting, 223–24
United States v. Booker, 236
United Teachers of Los Angeles, 174
University of Arizona College of Education,
    173–74

Verghese, Dr. Abraham, 265
Vermont Portfolio Assessment Program,
    252–55
Veterans' Court, 237–40

Wald, Patricia, 116–17
Wall Street Journal, 222
war on will
   "bubble kids," 177–79
   incentives
      doctor performance, 182–84
      incomplete contracts, 188–90
      performance vs. mastery,
         184–87
      reading prizes, 179–81
   motivational competition, 190–96
Warr, Peter, 282
Weick, Karl, 41–42, 157
White, Mark, 170
white lie, 60
Wilson, Timothy, 86
wisdom
   balancing acts, 27–45
   born to be wise, 51–68
   empathy and, 69–80
   experience and, 8
   happiness and, 274–87
   machinery of, 81–106
   as moral jazz, 41–43
   need for, 3–12

war on, 109–11
   judicial discretion, 113–17
   patient autonomy, 121–28
   policy making, 118–21
what it is, 13–26
   custodian Luke, 13–17
   Judge Lois Forer, 17–19
   See also practical wisdom
wisdom-happiness connection, 274–78
   research on, 278–80
   work and, 281–87
Wisdom Paradox, The (Goldberg), 86–87
Wisdom Talk, 44-45
wise banker, 268–71
wise custodian Luke, 13–25, 281, 285
wise doctor, 255–68
wise laws, 27
Wittgenstein, Ludwig, 54–56
Wong, Lieutenant Colonel Leonard, 156–59,
      171, 255
work and happiness, 281–87
Wrzesniewski, Amy, 282–87
Wyeth Pharmaceuticals. *See* Pfizer Inc.

Yale Law Journal, 240

Barry Schwartz is the Dorwin Cartwright Professor of Social Theory and Social Action at Swarthmore College, specializing in psychology and economics. The author of the bestselling *The Paradox of Choice*, he is a frequent lecturer at business conferences around the world. He lives in Philadelphia with his family.

Kenneth Sharpe is the William R. Kenan, Jr., Professor of Political Science at Swarthmore College, specializing in political philosophy, public policy, and U.S. foreign policy. He lives in Swarthmore, Pennsylvania.